PRIDE PARADES

3
E
P

MW01004832

X116699638

BOL

Pride Parades

How a Parade Changed the World

Katherine McFarland Bruce

NEW YORK UNIVERSITY PRESS

New York

NEW YORK UNIVERSITY PRESS
New York
www.nyupress.org

References to Internet websites (URLs) were accurate at the time of writing. Neither the author nor New York University Press is responsible for URLs that may have expired or changed since the manuscript was prepared.

Library of Congress Cataloging-in-Publication Data
Names: Bruce, Katherine McFarland, author.
Title: Pride parades : how a parade changed the world / Katherine McFarland Bruce.
Description: New York : New York University Press, 2016. | Includes bibliographical references and index.
Identifiers: LCCN 2016015941 | ISBN 9781479803613 (cl : alk. paper) | ISBN 9781479869541 (pb : alk. paper)
Subjects: LCSH: Gay pride parades—United States—History. | Gay liberation movement—United States—History. | Gays—United States—History. | Multiculturalism—United States—History.
Classification: LCC HQ76.965.G38 B78 2016 | DDC 306.76/60973—dc23
LC record available at https://lccn.loc.gov/2016015941

New York University Press books are printed on acid-free paper, and their binding materials are chosen for strength and durability. We strive to use environmentally responsible suppliers and materials to the greatest extent possible in publishing our books.

Manufactured in the United States of America

10 9 8 7 6 5 4 3 2 1

Also available as an ebook

To the brave women and men who organized and marched in the first parades at a time when doing so could have cost them everything.

CONTENTS

ACKNOWLEDGMENTS

I owe a debt of gratitude to many people who helped me write this book. They listened to me talk (sometimes ad nauseum) about Pride, offered invaluable advice, edited what I found difficult to articulate, told me when I was on the wrong track, and, perhaps most importantly, believed in me and cheered me on. First and foremost I thank my mentor, Andrew J. Perrin, for doing all of the above and more to support this project. He has read and improved many drafts and spent many hours offering guidance and encouragement on this project. If I could, I would appoint him Grand Marshal of my Pride parade.

My editor, Ilene Kalish, saw the potential of this book at our first meeting in 2012. "Everybody loves a parade," she said, as we proceeded to plan all the great photographs and personalities I would share in telling the story of Pride. I am grateful for her encouragement, critical feedback, and advice as I revised this manuscript into a book.

Several portions of this book were presented in some form at the University of North Carolina's Culture and Politics Workshop, now in its tenth year. I am grateful to Andrew Perrin, Kenneth Andrews, and Charles Kurzman for starting this workshop, as well as to the many who participated. As the saying goes, the hardest steel is forged in the hottest fires and this workshop provided the sharp, critical feedback that, I hope, has made this book strong.

I owe thanks to many more people who moved this project forward. Verta Taylor, Tina Fetner, Mary Bernstein, Elizabeth Armstrong, Amy Stone, Amin Ghaziani, and Steven Valocchi provided a wealth of knowledge about the LGBT movement in America and were kind enough to share it with me and offer feedback on drafts. Lauren Joseph is one of the few scholars who also researches Pride parades and her insight on this project has been invaluable. Thanks also to Catherine Harnois, Robin Simon, Christin Munsch, Hana Brown, Catherine Corrigal-Brown, Margarita Mooney, Neal Caren, Holning Lau, Charles Kurzman, and Kenneth Andrews for offering insightful comments on early drafts. Heather Branstetter, Joseph Lee, Libby Sharrow, Megan Carroll, and Derrick Matthews have all offered me advice from their areas of expertise, be they queer women's rhetoric or LGBT health disparities. Thank you also to my research assistants Kelly Wolfe and Leigh Edmonson who worked long hours, sometimes for free. Kelly spent many hours coding, transcribing, and generally keeping me organized. Leigh worked with me at the beginning of this project and put together the database of U.S. Pride parades. Thank you to the UNC Sociology Department staff—Ben Haven, Anitra Jones, Pam Stokes, and Sally Wilcox—for their helpfulness and for putting up with my buzzing around the office, always needing supplies or help with the fax machine.

Thank you to my research participants, who took time out of their days to talk to me about Pride. Thanks especially to Ralph, the participant in New York in 2010, who had also marched forty years earlier in the city's inaugural Pride march. After learning of my project, Ralph contacted others who had marched with him in 1970, which led to me ultimately being able to interview ten of these pioneers. I am dedicating this book to these early activists who took the bold step to declare themselves publicly, beginning this long parade toward equality.

This book is also the product of the support of many family and friends. My parents, Mac and Carolyn McFarland, have been there all along the way (and then some), celebrating every step forward, from defending this project as a dissertation proposal to securing the book contract. My granny, Ruth McFarland, provided the financial support that allowed me to travel to each parade—even though she remains mystified by my chosen profession—and reads every article I publish and invariably tells me it was brilliant. In addition to being an all-around great friend, Ian Conlon has been a valuable sounding board as he has always been willing to talk with me about all things sociological. Samantha Snow, Jessica Brandes, and Maureen Earley gave me feedback on final drafts of this book to make sure that it is still readable to "normal" people, not just academics. Thanks for keeping me real, guys. Shout outs also go to Erin Branch, Shawn Shifflett, Anne Eshleman Conlon, Dendy Lofton, Gregory Boyer, Nick and Kate Bavin, Alyson Culin, Abbe Golding, Megan Wooley Ousdahl, Ashley Chaifetz, Emily Kotecki, Bree Kalb, Megan and Trevor McCorkindale, and Andy and Joan McFarland for being great people and for at least feigning interest when they found me talking about Pride yet again. To my niece and nephews, I hope you will one day read this book and be amazed at how far we have come. Thank you to my aunt and uncle Sara and Bill McFarland, in whose Montana cabin I apply the finishing touches to this manuscript while gazing at the clearest full rainbow I have ever seen. I am convinced it is a sign of some sort.

Last but, as the saying goes, certainly not least, I thank my wife, Hillary Waugh Bruce. Hillary fills my life with light and love. She articulates this project much better than I do, after listening to me ramble on about Pride parades, cultural contestation, collective effervescence, and all the rest, while only rarely betraying her exhaustion with the subject. Time with Hillary has been my reward for a hard day's work and my motivation to continue. Hillary is truly my partner in all things.

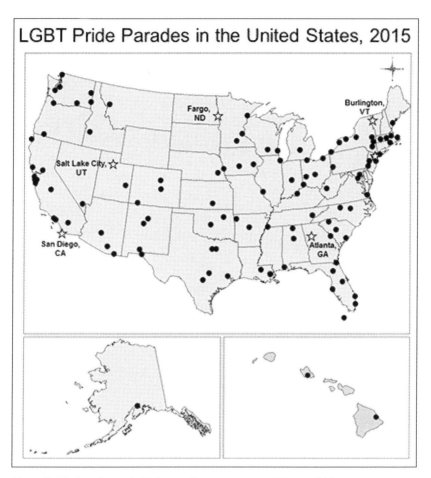

Map of Pride Parades in the U.S., 2015. Image courtesy of Shawn Shifflett.

Introduction

Changing the World with Pride

At the corner of Peachtree and Tenth, a small group of Christian evangelicals armed with a loudspeaker and large signs protested the 2010 Atlanta Pride parade. One person held a sign emblazoned with the words: "THE WAGES OF SIN IS DEATH," while another proclaimed into the loudspeaker that, "Homosexuals must repent!" In front of them, joyous contingents representing lesbian, gay, bisexual, and transgender (LGBT)-friendly churches, school gay-straight alliances, recreation leagues, and local and national businesses—cheered, danced, and waved rainbow flags as they marched along the route. In terms of exposure, the evangelical counter-protesters could not have picked a better spot. Neither could the crowd of Pride spectators. This was where the parade route turned the corner, moving from the commercial Peachtree Street with wide sidewalks and large shops into the densely built Midtown neighborhood along Tenth Street. Counter-protesters chose a spot where many could hear their message, while spectators gathered for the open space and good views afforded by the wide corner as the parade turned. The two groups did not enjoy one another's company and showed it with occasional heated exchanges.

From my vantage point on the steps of an office tower opposite the counter-protesters, I watched as the parade's official marching band approached the turn. They were playing their version of "Poker Face," the most recent Lady Gaga hit. By 2010, with her vocal support of LGBT political issues and catchy dance tunes, Lady Gaga had become an icon of the LGBT community. That summer her music was ubiquitous at Pride parades. With the marching band drawing near, counter-protesters continued their condemnations over the loudspeaker. When they completed the turn and were directly in front of the protest group, Atlanta's Pride Band halted, turned to face the loudspeaker, and belted out the song's chorus. The evangelical protesters were briefly drowned out by Lady Gaga, a marching band decked in rainbows, and a few hundred cheering spectators.

I imagine that members of Atlanta's Pride Band were given the same advice as me when, four years earlier, I was preparing to march with the LA Gay and Lesbian Center in the Los Angeles Pride parade. "There will be people saying vile things about us," our group's organizer said. "They're allowed to protest just the same as we are, but don't let them draw you into their anger. Answer them by being your fabulous selves." At Pride, being fabulous *is* protest. As counter-protesters loudly condemn the open expression of queer sexuality, participants defy them by turning up the volume.

Conflict between Pride participants and evangelical counter-protesters is a small window into the broader cultural challenge issued by Pride parades across the country. Nearly a half-century since the first Pride marchers stepped off in New York, Los Angeles, and Chicago, America—and much of the Western world—has reached a crucial point in this long journey towards full social inclusion of queer sexuality and gender. On the one hand, LGBT Americans enjoy unprecedented political rights and cultural visibility, prompting many to argue that we have turned a corner and entered a new era of equality.[1] As of this writing, same-sex marriage is legal throughout the United States after a landmark (though narrowly decided) Supreme Court case in June 2015. LGBT characters now regularly appear in mainstream television and movies in ways that largely avoid the narrow stereotyping of the past. Particularly in urban and more liberal areas of the country, many LGBT people are able to live fully open lives with partners and children that are accepted by their families, neighbors, and coworkers.[2] LGBT people across the country encounter a tolerance today that the first Pride marchers could scarcely imagine possible.

On the other hand, the persistent discrimination, denigration, and exclusion of queer people that continues to occur signals that queer sexuality and gender are still widely understood as inferior to heterosexuality. In its harshest form, family and community rejection leads to alarming rates of homelessness and suicide among LGBT youth across the country.[3] Debates in the public sphere include prominent mainstream voices condemning queerness as immoral and even dangerous, while polls continue to reveal that a significant minority (nearly 40%) of Americans believe that homosexuality is morally wrong.[4] More subtly, even as a majority of Americans support legal rights such as same-sex marriage, they are less accepting of informal public displays of affection between same-sex couples.[5] Thus, while LGBT people have made tremendous strides towards inclusion in American society, legally and culturally they are not yet fully equal to their heterosexual neighbors.

Queer theorists and feminists use the concept of heteronormativity to describe the cultural basis for LGBT inequality. Heteronormative culture makes heterosexuality the standard for romantic coupling in public spaces. Weddings, proms, and even the generic idea of "family" posit a man/woman couple as the norm and thus make same-sex pairs deviant.[6] Heteronormativity imposes a strict gender binary on individuals such that there are two opposite and complementary genders that naturally experience sexual desire for the other.[7] LGBT people deviate from the heteronormative standard in two ways: through sexual orientation (desire for the same sex) and gender transgression (identification with and/or display of qualities incongruous with one's corresponding male/female body).[8] While heteronormativity underpins some laws, certainly those regarding marriage, the concept is not driven by the state.[9] This cultural concept existed prior to modern laws that codified definitions of family and marriage and continues to resonate even as laws excluding LGBT families dissipate. Instead, heteronormativity is rooted into culture and often expressed through the writing and enforcement of laws.

Heteronormativity in contemporary America coexists with an ethos of tolerance for difference. This means that while many Americans welcome openly queer people into their neighborhoods, friendship circles, and families, this acceptance comes more *in spite* of their sexuality and gender, not *because* of it. LGBT people still feel consistent pressure to downplay their difference, particularly by following traditional gender norms.[10] Though explicit homophobia no longer permeates American culture, heterosexuality still reigns as normal and desirable, rendering queer sexuality and gender inferior. Queer theorists argue that as long as heteronormative culture remains dominant, queerness can be at best tolerated, but not celebrated or normalized.[11]

Against this cultural backdrop, Pride parades are loud, colorful, and joyful celebrations of LGBT identity. Like Atlanta's Pride Band, marchers and spectators confront a negative and silencing culture by facing condemnations head on, turning up the volume, and refusing to stop the celebration. Similarly, just as spectators cheered on the band, Pride participants show public support for LGBT people by joining in and drowning out negativity. Pride participants challenge the heteronormativity in American culture by celebrating and supporting LGBT people with myriad displays. At the Pride parade in Fargo, North Dakota, an eighty-year-old woman named Ruth marched with her fellow Episcopalians to show that Christianity leads some to accept homosexuality rather than condemn it. In Burlington, Vermont, Ginger celebrated Pride by attending in full drag, saying that the day was unique because the rest of the year she feels she must wear "civilian clothes"—masculine attire that corresponds with her male body—while on city streets.[12] In these ways, Ruth, Ginger, and millions of other Pride participants challenge culture by enacting a new vision of what LGBT acceptance can look like. On one day in many cities, they bring to fruition the motto of gay rights pioneer Frank Kameny: "Gay Is Good!"[13]

Lady Gaga, marching bands, and drag queens do not fit with many people's image of protest. Nor do they fit into a typical sociologist's catalogue of protest activity. When most people, academics included, think of a protest, their heads fill with images of indignant young activists holding signs, chanting slogans, and marching together in a block towards a civic site of power—like city hall or the county courthouse. Indeed, throughout Pride's history, many LGBT advocates have questioned the wisdom of such a festive tactic to effect social change, preferring instead a traditional solemn protest against the state. In particular, scholars of social movements most often conceptualize protest as a collective action to gain political power for a marginalized group, or are interested in how the movements might change government laws or policies. Considerable work has shown how activists pursue cultural change alongside state-focused protest, expanding our understanding of what activists do while keeping a definition of protest as oriented toward the state. Some scholars explicitly say that to be considered a protest, an action *must* target the state, while others promote this definition implicitly through an empirical focus on state-directed protest actions.[14] While many critique this view and argue that groups may protest cultural ideas, attitudes, and norms of behavior, fewer have shown what this looks like in the real world.[15] I hope to change that.

In this book, I tell the story of Pride parades from their origin in New York City, Los Angeles, and Chicago in 1970 to their vibrant contemporary life in diverse cities across the country. I reconcile how these festive affairs do the serious work of protest by challenging cultural meanings as marchers and spectators publicly revel in the joy of being themselves. I consider the ways in which these parades can, at times, become too festive, too commercial, or project an unhelpful image of LGBT people. After travelling to six Pride parades and talking to participants in places as disparate as Fargo, North Dakota and New York City, I describe how the form of these challenges are unique to each location. At the same time, their common history and shared symbols unite parades into a coherent national, even global, phenomenon.

What Is Pride Anyway?

LGBT Pride parades, or simply "Pride," are staged annually in cities all over the world. Every year, over six million people either march or watch a Pride parade in 116 cities in the U.S., and many more take part in parades in Canada, Europe, Latin America, and elsewhere.[16] A few thousand people staged the first Pride events on June 28, 1970 in New York City, Los Angeles, and Chicago to commemorate the 1969 Stonewall riots, which occurred when patrons of a New York City gay bar, the Stonewall Inn, reacted violently to a routine police raid. Many activists then and now interpret the riot as a monumental act of defiance that inaugurated a new era of gay and lesbian (later adding bisexual and transgender) activism.[17] On the anniversary of Stonewall, activists held Pride parades to carry forward this era of joyous and unashamed public declaration of gay and lesbian identity. Like today's parades, Pride events in 1970 were more festive and colorful than traditional protest marches and focused more on achieving broad cultural change than enacting specific government laws.

Today, the stated purpose of Pride for many of its planning committees is much the same as it was in 1970: to promote the visibility and validate the existence of gay, lesbian, bisexual, and transgender people.[18] Parade participants do this by transforming public streets into sites of resistance to heteronormativity.[19] In a study of two large parades in the United Kingdom, geographer Kath Browne described Pride as a "party with politics" in which participants defy heterosexual norms by showing same-sex affection and playing with conventions of gender presentation.[20] Similarly, marketing researchers Stephen M. Kates and Russell W. Belk found that Toronto Pride participants celebrated their queer identities by buying goods such as rainbow flags that visibly marked them as LGBT.[21] Though Pride parades are often popularly thought of as uncomplicated spectacles, these studies show that there is more going on. In this book, I extend their insights into the ways that these events resist and challenge heteronormativity.

Pride today happens in many surprising—and unsurprising—places. Twenty-two of the most populated twenty-five cities in the U.S. host Pride parades, the two largest of which draw nearly one million people to the streets of New York City and San Francisco. But Pride parades also occur in places like St. George, Utah; Spartanburg, South Carolina; and Mankato, Minnesota. Likewise, they come in all sizes, from one million marchers and spectators covering two miles of New York City in five hours to a convergence of 350 people along seven blocks in Fargo, North Dakota that lasts just under twenty minutes. California tops out with the most Pride parades of any state—thirteen—but there is at least one parade in forty-three states, and one parade in the District of Columbia. All seven states without a parade host Pride festivals with informational booths and entertainment, usually on public grounds. In Wyoming, participants get creative with "Rendezvous," a five-day campout in a national forest. Pride parades across the country reflect and respond to the local cultures.

Pride parades are not the only game in town when it comes to promoting visibility and acceptance for LGBT people. Across the country, LGBT employee groups, gay-straight alliances at schools and universities, and LGBT community centers work to support LGBT people and educate the public about queer sexuality and gender. Nationally, groups such as the Gay and Lesbian Alliance Against Defamation (GLAAD) and the Gay, Lesbian, and Straight Education Network (GLSEN) promote positive images of LGBT people in the mass media and educational institutions. Additionally, most organizations that primarily focus on changing state and federal laws—such as the Human Rights Campaign, Lambda Legal, and state Equality groups—sponsor educational programs aimed at increasing the cultural visibility and acceptance of

LGBT people. Many of these groups also march as contingents in Pride parades.

In many cities, groups organize alternative marches for specific LGBT populations. Dyke Marches, Trans Marches, and Black and Latino Gay Pride events are all established events held in many cities that focus on these populations. Like the larger Pride parades, these events make LGBT people visible and challenge their cultural and legal marginalization. However, each of these events adds a specific focus for one group that has experienced its own marginalization within LGBT community. Historically, middle-class white gay men have played leading roles organizing and participating in Pride—leaving women, transgender individuals, people of color, and the working class to feel excluded.[22] In response to this, some groups have pushed for greater inclusion in Pride, while others have shifted their efforts to organizing alternative events.

Dyke and Trans Marches consciously look different than Pride parades. They are no-frills marches following the familiar image of a protest in which participants march in a block chanting slogans such as, "2, 4, 6, 8—how do you know your daughter's straight?" While the events started in reaction to Pride parades, Dyke and Trans Marches are affiliated with Pride and recognized as official Pride activities in many cities, including Atlanta and Salt Lake City. In other cities like New York, these events are organized without any ties to the local Pride parade. Black and Latino Gay Prides take the form of a parade with floats, music, and a festive atmosphere but with a focus on African American or Latino LGBT people, respectively. Or, as a friend once said to me about Black Gay Pride, "It's pretty much just Pride . . . with more Black people." Black and Latino Gay Pride parades are organizationally separate from Pride, but do not explicitly oppose Pride events. While I did not study these events specifically, I do consider the effect of these alternative events on the work of Pride parades.

As an academic, there are two aspects of Pride that I find particularly interesting. Unlike most mass demonstrations that academics study, Pride gives casual participants a central role and focuses on changing culture instead of state laws and policies. More so than other protests, Pride really belongs to the marchers and spectators that participate. While paid and volunteer organizers do tremendous work year-round to take care of the financial, legal, and organizational details of putting on a large event, they give remarkably little direction about the events' message or the behavior of participants.[23] In New York City, for example, any contingent that wishes is free to march as long as they communicate a positive message about queer sexuality and gender. Participants thus construct Pride's messages, in contrast to the top-down list of demands that is often issued by organizers of many protests. Additionally, while traditional protest marches often mark a clear boundary between marchers who are part of the movement and bystanders who are not, at Pride there is a remarkable blurring between the role of marcher and spectator. Participants may begin the day watching the parade, then join in when a group with which they are familiar marches by. Spectators will hold signs declaring their support or wear costumes as part of a joyful embrace of queerness. By studying Pride, then, we can learn more about the impact that participants can make in public demonstrations.

In my view, Pride parades are directed much more at changing culture than politics. They make only the vaguest demands for change in the political arena of laws and government-secured rights. To some, as I discuss below, this means that they are not protests at all but are better thought of as community festivals. I argue that Pride parades are protests with a different target than traditional social movement demonstrations. Rather than state laws and policies, Pride parades seek to change the heteronormative cultural meanings that render LGBT people symbolically inferior to heterosexuals. With their playful displays and festive atmosphere, Pride parades challenge us to think critically about what we deem a protest that aims for serious social change. To understand the significance of these two aspects better, I turn now to what sociologists know about how to change the world.

How to Change the World

Boil it all down, and changing the world is about changing behavior. Environmentalists want individuals to reduce their use of fossil fuels, feminists want employers to pay women as much as men, and hippies want everyone to just mellow out. Each of these groups of activists (except maybe the hippies) creates a sustained social movement in order to effect behavioral change on both personal (micro) and institutional (macro) scales. They may enlist the government to pass a law mandating equal pay that will legally compel employers to pay their female and male workers the same amount. Or they may sponsor "Bike to Work Day" to promote the benefits of leaving the gas-guzzling car at home and commuting with minimal environmental impact. The specific tactic that activists choose to deploy, as well as its overall success, is affected, some would even say determined, by the activists' political, economic, and cultural circumstances.[24] Pride is one kind of tactic, a cultural protest, in which participants communicate myriad messages in an effort to make the world a better place by changing the way people treat their LGBT neighbors.

To effect large-scale behavioral change, most social movements have an ultimate goal, devise strategies to achieve this goal, and then stage collective action tactics in line with these strategies.[25] Ultimate goals are the broad changes a movement would like to see, such as an end to nuclear weapons or the preservation of the nation's forests. Strategies are well thought-out plans of action, and tactics are what people do on the ground to carry out these plans. For instance, one goal of the labor movement is to improve working conditions for wage laborers. One strategy to achieve this goal is to increase laborers' ability to determine these conditions through collective bargaining. Organized worker strikes are a tactic that the labor movement uses to force owners to recognize and bargain with collective labor unions.

Identity movements are those whose ultimate goal is cultural equality for a social group that is defined by a shared sense of self that is based on categories like race and ethnicity, gender, and sexual orientation.[26] Cultural inequality is the pervasive idea that a group of people is inferior due to one of these shared identities. It is expressed when individuals treat members of this group unequally with or without an institutional stamp of approval from the state.[27] On an interpersonal level, individuals may discriminate against their fellow citizens by denying them employment, housing, and consumer goods; or they may use personal slights, insults, and harassment that convey a group's inferiority in the eyes of others. For same-sex couples, this can mean being fired after publicly revealing their relationship or having a local bakery refuse to bake their wedding cake. It may also mean having friends and neighbors deny their marital status and thus treat them as unequal to opposite-sex married couples. On an institutional level, the government may sanction unequal treatment by specifying different rights based on group membership. Many see laws prohibiting same-sex marriage as denying gays and lesbians the same rights and privileges of legal marriage that straight citizens enjoy.

Since unequal treatment by individuals comes in many forms and is shaped by social entities—the state, formal institutions, and private citizens—activists face a strategic dilemma. Should they pursue cultural equality by trying to change the laws that define legal and illegal behavior—that is, go through the state—or by trying to change those cultural meanings and attitudes that guide our decisions about how to treat one another?[28] Strategies pursued by feminist activists in the 1960s through the 1980s give us an example of this choice. One group, liberal feminists, worked for cultural equality primarily by fighting to change laws, while another, radical feminists, created alternative communities that promoted the cultural idea that women are truly equal (or even superior) to men.[29] The first was a state-based strategy, rooted in the logic that the government holds tremendous power over individual lives and, with laws that support rather than undermine women's equality, women would no longer be held back from achieving parity with men.[30] The second strategy bypassed the state with the logic that its power to affect cultural equality is limited.[31] Instead, this strategy reached out to women (and men) directly to free them of the cultural idea that women are inferior to men. Through consciousness-raising groups and grassroots projects like feminist bookstores and domestic violence shelters, radical feminists tried to "be the change [they wished] to see in the world," offering alternatives to challenge the ideas and institutions that encourage the inferior treatment of women.

Theorists of social movements debate these strategies. For them, the question is who in society has power over individual behavior, and thus, what social entities can lead the way to more equal treatment. Charles Tilly, Doug McAdam, and Sidney Tarrow, leading scholars of social movements, argued that in the modern state, the government holds more power over individuals than any other social entity, but also enables social movements with the opportunity to pursue change.[32] Democratic governments allow citizens to petition for change and guarantee their right to free assembly, giving social movements the motive, opportunity, and ability to seek social change through state action.[33] Thus, liberal feminists campaigned for laws to insure that women and men who work the same jobs are paid equally. With its power to regulate wages, the state can prohibit one way that women are treated as inferior. Under this framework, while cultural equality is the ultimate goal for identity movements, they pursue strategies to compel state action that will enforce equal treatment.

By contrast, theorists of new social movements and multi-institutional politics contend that, particularly in Western industrial countries, there are cultural spheres of social life that are at least partially independent from the state.[34] The multi-institutional model asserts that power is located in many institutions, including education, business, religion, and the state.[35] For instance, while same-sex couples could not legally marry in many states in the U.S. before 2015, they were recognized as married by many religious denominations and businesses. For multi-institutionalists, this recognition is a strong force that moves the needle towards LGBT cultural equality, even as state laws sometimes push in the other direction. New social movements theorists go one step further, arguing that culture has power over individuals in society even outside the work of formal institutions like religion. In this view, recognition of same-sex marriage by fellow citizens—attending a gay wedding for example, or using the language of "spouse" to refer to partners in gay couples—is also a force for cultural equality. Within these frameworks, social movements are not limited to state-centered strategies. They can pursue, and hopefully achieve, social change by starting with those individually-held attitudes or institutional policies that guide citizens' treatment of one another. Collective behavior therefore does not have to target the state to be contentious.

Once they have decided on a strategy to achieve their goal, activists then employ tactics. These are discrete collective actions like marches, rallies, labor strikes, petitions, and letter-writing campaigns. Tactics may target the state, an institution like a corporation or university, or the broader culture. Recently, in my state of North Carolina, progressive activists have targeted the Republican-controlled state government with rallies at the General Assembly building in the state capitol to protest a host of new conservative laws. Protests like this, either as a march or a stationary rally, are the epitome of state-targeted tactics. Activists take to the streets en masse to show political power and demand attention. Their action communicates to politicians and to fellow citizens that their cause is important enough to disrupt everyday life and that state action is supported by a significant constituency.[36] In addition to this direct pressure, activists may see their message amplified by coverage in news media and, thus, bring indirect pressure on state actors.[37] They will attempt to frame their message in a way to maximize public support, as when North Carolina liberal activists called their protests "Moral Mondays" (they held rallies each Monday of the three-month long legislative session) to call attention to what they saw as the immorality of new state laws.[38] In a democracy, public support is a powerful message that promises political consequences for lawmakers' inaction.

Researchers consider a broader range of movement strategies to show how activists employ tactics to challenge the cultural underpinnings of individual behavior and demonstrate political power. While campaigning to change a specific law, activists may use their identities in strategic ways to challenge the cultural meanings that underlay government policies.[39] For example, women activists with a group called "Go Topless" collectively march without shirts to protest both the legal and cultural prohibition on women baring their breasts in public.[40] Similarly, LGBT activists sometimes consciously emphasize their difference from heteronormative society—by dressing in drag or showing same-sex affection—when protesting laws that treat LGBT people differently than their straight counterparts (e.g., marriage laws). In doing so, they communicate political power through their presence and cultural power through their deliberate defiance of heteronormativity.

Most research continues to focus on state-directed strategies and tactics, even as a large majority of the scholarship includes analyses of how these tactics also target non-state institutions and culture. But to some activists, the road to equality does not lead through the government and they pursue strategies and use tactics that bypass the state altogether. Labor activists, for example, may target corporations with work strikes and boycotts that apply economic pressure on corporations in order to force changes in the direction of economic equality. Similarly, marriage equality activists may stage public same-sex weddings to counter the cultural imagery equating marriage with a bride and a groom.[41] In these examples, activists do not petition the government to change the laws that shape citizens' behavior; instead, they primarily target other influences on this behavior, such as businesses or cultural images.[42]

When tactics challenge culture, they engage in a rich symbolic contest over the meanings of cultural symbols, language, and codes of behavior. This may take the form of rejecting current symbols associated with a group or reinterpreting symbols of powerlessness with a message of power and action. In one example of rejection, feminist activists protested women's cultural objectification at the 1968 Miss America pageant by throwing "beauty aids" like bras, girdles, curlers, and makeup in a "freedom trashcan."[43] Without these tools of objectification, women were free to be seen and treated as full persons, not merely pretty images. In an example of reinterpretation, sociologist Joshua Gamson showed how the AIDS activist group ACT UP reclaimed the pink triangle.[44] This symbol was used by Nazis to mark homosexuals and thus, signified a dark and oppressive period in gay history. ACT UP transformed the pink triangle into a symbol of power and a call to action by using it to brand their advocacy work. They wrote the words "SILENCE=DEATH" on the pink triangle to call on gay men and lesbians to fight back against a horrific and stigmatized disease, instead of silently accepting death. By reinterpreting this cultural symbol, ACT UP challenged gays and straights alike to approach queer sexuality with respect rather than disdain. Like ACT UP's pink triangle and feminists' "freedom trashcan," cultural tactics seek to change culture by challenging current conceptions and offering alternative meanings.

The examples above are clearly contentious actions, aimed at seriously trying to challenge a part of the existing social order. With their frequent playfulness and use of drama, though, sometimes it is unclear whether a cultural tactic is a contentious, social movement protest or a benign community celebration.[45] Indeed, at first glance, many may view Pride parades as frivolous public parties, more like a Mardi Gras celebration than a march on Washington. To clarify the boundary between protest and uncontentious public event, sociologist Verta Taylor and her colleagues developed a framework of three criteria based on their studies of various LGBT movement tactics.[46] Drawing from new social movements and multi-institutional politics, they understand power as diffuse in society and not limited to the state. This means that social movement tactics do not have to primarily target the state to be effective. For specific tactics, then, the first criterion is that they *contest* an existing social order—whether it is the order of the state, or the order imposed by rigid cultural categories. For example, scholars Leila Rupp and Verta Taylor illustrate how drag performances contest the heteronormative gender binary by highlighting male bodies in feminine dress.[47] The second criterion is that this contestation is *intentional*; it does not happen by accident while participants are pursuing other goals. A crucial part of the famous (but apocryphal) story of feminists burning their bras is that it was an intentional act to challenge restrictive feminine beauty standards, not a convenient way to dispose of old bras.[48] Third, participants need to have a *collective identity*, or a shared sense of self that binds them together as a group. Social movements are about people working together for social change, so while we may occasionally find ourselves walking in coordination with others around us, what makes it a protest march is that we act as a collective.[49]

A final part of explaining social change is to understand the people involved in social movements. Activists can contribute to a cause in many ways—by leading organizations, donating money, articulating movement demands in writing, distributing literature, planning tactics, and participating in protests. A simple way to classify activists is to divide them into two groups: "organizers" who devise strategies and plan tactics and "participants" who carry them out. Scholars tend to focus on organizers who spend a significant amount of their time on movement activity. These leaders debate strategies, weighing chances for success against resources required. When activist groups decide to carry out a protest that fits into their strategies, it is organizers who acquire permits, recruit speakers, issue demands, secure funding, and mobilize supporters.[50] Essentially, organizers do a lot of the day-to-day work of social movements, and it is by and large this work that is the focus of existing scholarship.

When it comes to mass demonstration tactics, participants play an essential but understudied role. Protest marches and rallies require participants to consciously break the intangible rules that govern their everyday lives—rules that tell them not to block traffic, not to raise one's voice, indeed, not to complain about one's lot in life.[51] Once they take the step to attend a protest, most participants do much more than passively follow organizers' plan for action. They chant, make signs that range from poignant to hilarious, and put on creative displays to express dissatisfaction and demand change. While organizers lay the foundation for a given protest, participants breathe life into it by bringing their creativity, their energy, and their passion for the cause. By studying an event like Pride from the point of view of participants rather than organizers, I hope to show a different understanding of protest tactics. Where organizers might regard a protest march as an opening move to let politicians know they're paying attention, participants may see it as an essential way to voice their grievances. Similarly, while organizers may feel the need to articulate a clear, concrete target of a protest, participants may chant against the harder-to-pinpoint cultural oppression that affects their daily lives.

Empirical work on tactics that bypass the state is still in its infancy, but Taylor's framework gives us clear criteria with which to understand cultural tactics. Contestation, intentionality, and collective identity are all essential aspects of social movement tactics regardless of their target. Without a clearly visible target, sociologists particularly struggle with how activists protest culture. Atlanta's Pride Band had a clear target when they turned up the volume and drowned out counter-protesters, but if the evangelical group had not been there, they would still be making a statement. When they marched down the street, decked in rainbows and playing Lady Gaga, and when spectators cheered them on, the Pride Band and the parade in which they took part communicated a broader message—that queer identity is a thing to be celebrated rather than condemned. This book paints a fuller picture of this idea by explaining how Pride challenges established cultural meanings.

How to Change Culture

What exactly does it mean to challenge culture? The answer requires us to first define the concept of culture itself. "Culture" is the shared set of meanings we use to make sense of and act on the world.[52] Culture includes the morals and norms that guide what we should and should not do, the symbols and language through which we communicate ideas, and the complex meanings with which we describe the relationships between ideas. Meanings coalesce into cultural codes, which are the big ideas that guide how we understand and value features of our world.[53] For instance, by defining heterosexuality as normal and desirable, the Western heteronormative cultural code interprets queerness as abnormal. People have used the terms "gay," "homosexual," and "queer" to describe individuals whose primary romantic attraction and sexual behavior is with those of the same sex and often to communicate the moral judgment that these individuals are flawed. Their language and behavior have solidified cultural meanings that link homosexuality with social deviance by labeling it alternatively as sin, criminality, or mental illness.[54] In a nutshell, culture is that part of the social world that makes connections between phenomena and interprets their meaning.

Culture stands in contrast with the state. In this context, I define the state as a formal political community with a centralized government that has the monopoly on the legitimate use of violence.[55] In the U.S., the state is comprised of all three branches of federal government that make, enforce, and interpret our laws along with state and local governments and a host of institutions that the government controls such as public education and the military. The state is responsible for a great deal of the social order in our lives by defining legal and illegal behavior, regulating business and transportation, and, of course, by taxing our income, property, and purchases. Effecting change in the state means altering its laws, regulations, and composition (by electing new leaders), while changing culture means replacing old meanings with new ones. The former is political change; the latter is cultural change.

Culture keeps us in line through its moral, not physical, force. As we internalize cultural meanings about the features of our social worlds, we are motivated to act in accordance with these interpretations.[56] For instance, those who learn that women should be sexually conservative may chastise those who are not by shaming them with name-calling. Similarly, culture provides us with the language and symbols we use to communicate with one another.[57] Those searching for a word to describe a woman who has many sexual partners will find no shortage of terms, virtually all of which communicate a negative judgment, such as the all-too-common "slut." Meanwhile, the words used to describe men with similar behavior, such as "stud," are much more positive. Thus, culture affects our actions both by shaping our internal beliefs and by providing the language, symbols, and codes of meaning that make certain actions possible.[58]

Since culture affects behavior internally and externally, we can say that it exists both in individual minds and in the world. In the mind, culture is each individual's internalized set of norms, values, attitudes, and views on the world.[59] These internalized beliefs then motivate individual action, prompting us to treat our elders with greater respect, say, or to offer assistance more readily to someone of our own race than to someone we perceive as different. Individuals are socialized to believe some things and not others, but they can also change their minds with new information and experiences. One way to change behavior, then, is to start with culture in individual minds by persuading people to change their attitudes. When white people no longer believe that African Americans are inferior, for example, they will not treat them as such.

In another sense, culture resides in the world as explicit language, symbols, rituals, and meanings.[60] These external meanings provide us with the tools to justify our actions, such as when a man uses readily available "slut" language to shame a woman. This sense of culture is the property of a collective; it is the set of agreed upon meanings that individuals use to communicate with one another.[61] We as individuals are then constrained by our culture to a particular set of meanings, which we use to justify action. Since culture in the world is "out there" instead of "in here," an individual cannot influence it on her own, and thus, persuasion is not an effective means of change. Rather than working to change the minds of individuals, a second way to change behavior is to offer new language, symbols, rituals, and cultural codes of meaning to challenge the old ones.

These two dimensions of culture cannot be fully separated. As an intangible set of meanings, culture cannot be pinned down and approached objectively. We make tangible cultural products for all to consume, such as works of art and literature, but even these can only be fully grasped through subjective understanding. In fact, this difficulty in capturing meaning prompted the sociologist Robert Wuthnow to urge scholars to drop the project altogether and focus instead on observable features of cultural products, such as the common themes found in children's books.[62] However, this approach necessarily limits us to a narrow range of research. The paradox of culture is that it is both subjective and social.[63] That is, while meaning is understood in the individual mind, making it subjective, it operates between individuals, making it social. Speaking of culture as in the mind and in the world demystifies this paradox by specifying two ways that culture affects action—through internal values and attitudes that motivate individuals to act and external codes of meaning that make certain actions more or less socially desirable. For activists concerned with changing the actions of many, this framework identifies places to start.

One option for activists is to start with culture in the mind and work their way out to culture in the world. With an inside-out model, activists target individuals with messages to persuade them to change their attitudes about a subject like homosexuality.[64] They may argue from a scientific standpoint that homosexuality is innate, or publicize stories of committed long-term gay and lesbian couples to counter common perceptions about the nature of homosexuality. When people adopt new attitudes, they change their behavior to match these attitudes—by treating LGBT neighbors with greater respect, for example, or by speaking of homosexuality in more favorable terms. This change in culture in the mind then works out to cultural change in the world as new attitudes and behaviors reach a critical mass. As more and more people believe that homosexuality is a valid human variation, they develop new language and symbols to communicate their beliefs, such as using "gay" as a positive descriptor rather than a synonym for "stupid." Similarly, with critical mass, the behaviors of those motivated by changed attitudes will become the community norm so that neighbors sanction one another for the negative treatment of LGBT people. The new language, symbols, and behavioral norms signify a changed cultural meaning in the world to interpret homosexuality as a positive sexual expression.

The outside-in model takes the opposite approach. Activists start with culture in the world by challenging prevailing meanings and attempting to replace them with new ones.[65] Here individuals are not the target of protest; activists do not attempt to change their attitudes. Instead, activists target the language, symbols, or behavioral norms that justify some actions while making others undesirable. The AIDS activist group ACT UP, for example, took this approach when it adopted the pink triangle as a symbol of power and action. Rather than targeting individuals' attitudes towards LGBT people, they targeted a collective symbol associated with the group. By reinterpreting this symbol of powerlessness under Nazi oppression to one of power in the face of adversity, ACT UP promoted a new vision of what it means to be gay in the world. This new symbolic meaning then supports individual actions that are in line with it, as LGBT people become inspired to stand up to inequality and opponents lose some of the justification to deny them equal treatment. With an initial cultural change in the world, individuals do not necessarily *believe* that they should act in a new way; instead they are compelled to because their old actions are no longer justifiable under the new meaning. As they become accustomed to new symbols and behavioral norms, individuals will then internalize cultural meanings, resulting in changed cultural attitudes in the mind. Working on culture from the "outside in," activists do not attempt to persuade individuals; rather, they target the meanings embedded in the language, symbols, and behavioral norms that buttress individual attitudes in the world.

In each model, activists disseminate new messages to challenge those in the dominant culture. For instance, feminists may recognize that both cultural codes of meaning in the world and individual cultural attitudes communicate that women are not as good at math and science as men. They will counter this by offering the message that women are, indeed, quite competent in these fields. This message may come in the form of arguments with comparative evidence of test scores, images of women scientists and mathematicians, or celebrations of the achievements of prominent women in these fields. The difference between the two models lies in the target of this messaging—that is, at whom (or what) activists direct their message. When targeting individuals, activists will try to persuade others, while being sensitive to the concerns of those who are skeptical of their claims. The aim here is to reach individuals and change their minds about what women can do. By contrast, when targeting culture in the world, activists publicize new meanings hoping that they will catch on and supplant the old. Rather than attempting to convince individuals, they assert their preferred meanings in the world as truth, bypassing individual attitudes. Though the meanings in the form of symbols and dramatic displays may turn some individuals off, they offer a new interpretive possibility for use by the media, elites, and ordinary citizens.[66] What activists *do* to change culture, then, is to create and disseminate messages through various social movement tactics.

Like the literature on targeting culture with activism, research on how to enact cultural change is only just beginning. By using the concepts of inside-out and outside-in cultural change, we can learn more about what activists do and what tactics may be most effective. Looking at the incident between the Atlanta Pride Band, spectators, and evangelical counter-protesters, we see a model of changing culture from the outside-in. The band did not blast the chorus of Lady Gaga's "Poker Face" in an attempt to persuade anyone—and certainly not the counter-protesters—that their negative assessments of LGBT people were wrong. If anything, this likely strengthened the evangelicals' view that LGBT people seek pleasure over godliness. Through the band's strategic display and spectators' cheering stamp of approval, participants made a sharp symbolic contrast with counter-protesters' condemnation. By turning up the volume on their celebration of LGBT identity, these Pride participants challenged the meaning of queer sexuality and gender promoted by counter-protesters and attempted to replace it with their own. If successful, members of the public would then associate "queerness" with celebration rather than condemnation. This cultural meaning in the world then works its way into the mind, transforming individual attitudes about LGBT people. This book investigates many more scenes at Pride parades across the country to determine both the target of participants' action and their strategic model to pursue change.

Let's Not Forget That It's Fun

For all the high-minded talk about changing the world, another thing is blaringly obvious about Pride parades: they are a hell of a lot of fun. When I saw the Atlanta Pride Band turn to face the evangelical protesters and belt out Lady Gaga, I laughed and cheered along with the rest of the crowd. Remembering the scene still brings me joy. It is typical for LGBT people and straight allies to make Pride into a daylong event. Depending on how early the parade starts (most step-off around noon), friends will meet for brunch or a house party near the parade route. Afterwards, marchers and spectators alike continue the revelry at local bars or at festivals organized by the committees who put on the parade. Gay-friendly bars and clubs often host special Pride parties the nights before and after the parade, with drink specials, drag shows, and other entertainment. LGBT people and allies hang rainbow flags in front of their houses and greet one another with "Happy Pride." Parades themselves are joyful as marchers and spectators cheer, dance, and show affection for one another.

The fun of public demonstrations has two sides: one side faces outward to the larger society as part of the events' contentious message, while the other side faces inward to participants themselves as they grow closer to one other by having fun together.[67] Dramatic play has long been a part of social movement tactics, from civil rights activists dancing before riot police, to Yippies staging a mock political party convention in 1968 in which they nominated a pig for president, to anarchists in 2001 catapulting teddy bears over a fence at international trade negotiations.[68] Each protest painted its opponent as absurd, using creative play to promote a new meaning of the situation at hand. The anarchists in 2001, for example, recast trade negotiators' desire for privacy as an undemocratic prohibition on citizen input. By lobbing their "stuffed comrades" over the fence that separated protesters from government officials, their action dramatized the lengths negotiators went to avoid public comment on their proposed trade deal.[69] Humor is one way that activists offer new meanings to replace the old ones that they have rendered ridiculous.

A similar use of fun is to demonstrate a new way to be in the world. Cultural theorist Johan Huizinga wrote that when we play, we step out of reality to act out new ideas.[70] Having fun in a new way—counter to one that is prescribed by society—can be a method to urge society to change.[71] In this way, fun is prefigurative, meaning that it acts out the world that activists hope to make a reality. In this vein, the 1990s London group Reclaim the Streets held large dance parties that blocked off city streets to highlight the importance of public spaces in which citizens can socialize, make connections, and have fun.[72] Or the Critical Mass rides staged by bicyclists since 1992, in which hundreds of riders take over streets in major cities with the message that "We are not blocking traffic, we are traffic!"[73] With both tactics, activists enacted their own vision of a good city—a place with numerous free public spaces or one where streets are safe for bicycles—and this vision contested the dominant culture (in these cases, neoliberal trends toward privatization and increased use of cars). Fun is thus a way to convey a contentious message, whether directed at the state that privatizes public space, institutions like corporations who seek to buy that space, or cultural meanings in the world that value the automobile over the more environmentally-friendly bicycle.

Such playful tactics can be controversial among activists. To some, play undermines the gravity of social movements' claims. Rather than challenging the dominant order, critics charge that playful tactics instead communicate frivolity, demonstrating to society that activists are merely having a good time and therefore, their demands are not to be taken seriously. According to some commentators, tactics like Critical Mass, Reclaim the Streets, and Pride are just sideshows to the "real" protest of solemn actions, such as the iconic 1964 March on Washington. A few critics of anti-globalization "protestivals" like those of Reclaim the Streets even argue that playful protest actually reinforces the existing power structure by allowing a small, contained "safety valve," in which citizens can express their frustrations and then return to their normal lives.[74] As we will see throughout this book, fun has long been both a strength and a source of controversy for Pride as LGBT advocates consider its place in pushing for meaningful social change.

The other side of fun is the way that sharing a good time brings people together. During civic and religious holidays, we take a break from work to gather with family, friends, and neighbors. Sociologists understand these special days as times to reestablish bonds and renew our commitment to community values.[75] On the Fourth of July, for instance, Americans get together with backyard cookouts and fireworks, remembering the importance of community and their shared commitment to the American ideals of freedom and equality.[76] During other holidays, community values are reaffirmed more directly by, for example, expressing gratitude on Thanksgiving or remembering military service members on Memorial Day. During "tension management" holidays, the sense of community is reinforced by collectively breaking the cultural norms that give order to our daily lives.[77] Thus, on Halloween, the normal rules of what is proper are suspended: adults can dress up as cartoon characters, boys can wear make-up or dresses, and death becomes a source of frivolity.[78] These holidays offer an opportunity to let off the tension that builds from regularly following social norms, leaving us recharged and able to recommit once the holiday is over.

Of course, in a diverse society, it is rare (if not impossible) for everyone to come together equally. Class, race, and gender inequalities allow some the privilege to have fun during holidays, while others are reminded of their subordination.[79] While some middle-class men relax with a game of football on Thanksgiving, for instance, the women of the house are expected to do the work of cooking the celebratory meal. Meanwhile, many working-class Americans are not even afforded the luxury of the national holiday—including, for example, the employees of retail chains who are called in to work to help prepare their stores for Black Friday sales. The LGBT community mirrors the larger population in its class, racial, and gender diversity, raising the question of whether Pride events bring people together across social categories or merely exacerbate existing divisions.

For those who are able join in, getting together to commemorate the past, to honor our heroes, or to simply have a good time is an emotional experience. We *feel* closer to one another by participating together in rituals. The classic sociological theorist Emile Durkheim called this "collective effervescence," or the heightened emotional state that comes from experiencing the same emotions together.[80] Anyone who has attended a football game, political rally, or religious service can relate to the phenomenon. It is certainly fun to cheer on your favorite sports team alone in front of the television, but it is exponentially more exciting to cheer them on with thousands of others in person at the stadium. As sociologist Randall Collins explains, rituals produce this emotional energy by drawing two or more people together with a shared focus of attention and mood.[81] At a football game, then, fans direct their attention on the game being played while feeling elation or dejection, depending on how well their team is playing. They then feed off one another, producing more emotional energy. Collective effervescence is a positive experience even when the shared emotion is sadness at a funeral or anger at a political rally. This is because we each take a bit of the emotional energy produced by the collective whole, giving us confidence from knowing that we are connected with others.

Protest demonstrations include an element of collective effervescence, which has the effect of binding together participants.[82] More broadly, sociologists recognize that participants' emotional experience is an important aspect of social movements—so much that one may even trace activists' strategic decisions to their emotions of anger, shame, fear, or pride.[83] However, with a focus on state-directed protest, most sociologists have studied the solemn side of emotions in social movements: how outrage draws people to activism, for instance, or how activism fulfills protesters' emotional need to have an impact on the world.[84] Even when the emotions are positive, like collective effervescence, they carry the weight of their larger purpose to change the world. Fun, by contrast, is marked by its lightness. The whole point of fun is to enjoy oneself simply for one's own sake. In doing so, we throw off the normal constraints of society and lose ourselves in collective joy.[85] At Pride, though, even fun serves a purpose.

In this book, I take fun seriously. I explore whether participants challenge cultural meanings when they have fun at Pride and whether they do this intentionally. I also address the possible tension between having fun as an inward-focused way to bond with others and relieve stress and having fun as an outward-focused direct challenge to the world. Sociologists often judge such internal community-building as separate from a movement's external goal of social change, but at Pride, these seem to be one and the same. Throughout this book, I consider the role of fun at Pride parades, whether it adds to or even *is* the message of Pride, how it may hinder this message, and whether, for some participants, Pride is simply a party without larger significance.

The Research

When I tell people that I research Pride parades, their first question is often, "Have you been to the parade in San Francisco?" Some have attended the parade themselves and tell me it is quite grand, while I suspect that others presume that any study of LGBT Pride must include the city so well known for its thriving gay culture. I did not study San Francisco Pride, however, for the same reason that I did not research the parades in Boston, Los Angeles, Houston, or Miami: my focus is not solely on large, well-known parades. I am interested in the Pride phenomenon across the country and this includes small parades far from big cities and medium-sized parades in regional hub cities. I wanted to know whether modest events in Fargo, North Dakota or Burlington, Vermont have anything in common with the grand spectacle of New York City Pride. To do that, I had to travel to parades of all sizes and in all parts of the country.

Before hitting the road, I delved into Pride's history, focusing on its first six years. In a great stroke of luck, at New York City's Pride parade

I met a man who had marched in the first-ever Pride event in 1970. He put me in contact with a few fellow pioneers, who then put me in contact with others, and through this snowball sampling, I was able to interview eleven participants from the 1970 Pride events in New York City and Los Angeles. To these interviews I added contemporary news reports and editorials from the *Advocate*, a leading gay periodical of the time that is still in publication today.[86] I searched all issues of the *Advocate* from June 1969 through August 1975, pulling out articles that discussed the Stonewall riots and Pride parades. Through historical and sociological analyses of this time period in the LGBT movement, I constructed a narrative of how Pride became the phenomenon that it is today.

During the summer and fall of 2010, I attended six unique parades. First up in June was Salt Lake City, home of the conservative Mormon Church, followed by New York City, where today's parade draws one million people. In July, I flew to San Diego and attended Pride in the eclectic Hillcrest neighborhood, then headed back east to Burlington, Vermont where same-sex marriage is legal and it seems that all forty-three thousand residents are gay-friendly. In August, I travelled to the small Midwestern hub of Fargo, North Dakota where I met one teenager who had driven an hour from his rural home so he could be around other LGBT people for a day. Finally in October when the Southern weather cooled down, I went to Pride in Atlanta, where the city itself has a large LGBT population but the state of Georgia is far from welcoming.

While not representative in a statistical sense, these six parades reflect the vast diversity of Pride parades across the country. When I began this project, I collected a list of all Pride parades in the U.S. along with information on their size (number of marchers and participants) and years in existence. I added information about the demographics and cultural climate of parades' host cities, including their racial and ethnic diversity, median income, same-sex marriage laws, and regional public opinions about homosexuality. I then selected one parade from five different size groups, plus New York City. I chose parades from different regions of the country with a diverse range of racial and ethnic populations, median incomes, and cultural climates.

In addition to historical work, this book is based on my ethnographic fieldwork at these six parades, including interviews with fifty participants—marchers, spectators, sponsors, and volunteers—who I met along the way. Like all ethnographies, I immersed myself in each event by talking with participants, watching as floats and marching contingents went by, and walking along the parade route to experience each unique section. I arrived early as marchers prepared their displays and spectators attended house parties and I stayed until parades were over and the crowds dispersed. I noted interesting and amusing sights (from signs to t-shirts), songs, and chants from both Pride participants and counter-protesters. I recorded all these observations with audio field notes and candid pictures. When I returned home, I typed up notes along with my impressions of each parade and their connections to sociological ideas of protest, social change, and culture. Unlike the subjects of most ethnographies, however, the phenomenon that I observe lasts for only a few hours. I discuss the challenges of this "ethnography of the ephemeral" in appendix A.[87]

Along with observing the sights and sounds of Pride parades, I interviewed fifty participants. Research assistants canvassed crowds before, during, and after each parade and conducted brief surveys with participants. They gathered contact information and simple demographics (age, race and ethnicity, gender identity, sexual orientation, income, and education) from marchers lining up, spectators watching, volunteers helping to keep the parades running smoothly, and sponsors attending as representatives of their companies. Following specific criteria, research assistants approached all different kinds of people—from glam drag queens and leather-clad lesbian motorcyclists, to more mainstream families with children and church members handing out water to passersby (for quotas, see appendix A). They did not approach counter-protesters who visually objected to the parades' purpose and messages, focusing instead on those who supported Pride.

When I returned home from each parade, I called participants and interviewed them over the phone. They told me about their experiences at Pride, why they went, who joined them in attendance, and what they thought about Pride parades in general. With these interviews I am able to tell the stories of those who attend Pride, some to have a fun but meaningful day out with friends, others for a rare chance to be among supportive and accepting LGBT people and allies, and most to proudly celebrate who they are. I am also able to show common themes in participants' understandings of the Pride experience. Despite their individual paths to Pride, participants emphasized its cultural messages of visibility, support, and celebration.

Plan of the Book

Pride Parades tells the story of Pride in two parts. In part 1, I describe how gays and lesbians established the event in the early 1970s as a parade to affirm gay identities. I start this story at the beginning: June 28, 1970, when roughly five thousand gays and lesbians (and surely a handful of straight allies) marched through the streets of Manhattan, West Hollywood, and downtown Chicago in the first-ever Pride events. These events were a curious mix of protest march and parade—more festive than a typical protest, but with more contention than a standard parade—and marked the largest public gatherings of out gays and lesbians in history.[88] The first parades were so successful that immediately afterward, participants started planning for the following year. Through archival newspaper reports and personal interviews with participants at these first events, I show how the first parades initiated the model of protest that characterizes Pride today by targeting cultural, rather than political change.

After the new and exciting Pride events of 1970, the phenomenon grew in size and crystallized in form throughout the next five years. Pride organizers in New York, Los Angeles, and Chicago balanced the interests of activists, entertainers, businesses, and unaffiliated gays and lesbians as more and more people participated in their events. Seeing successful Pride marches in these cities, community leaders in Boston, Atlanta, San Francisco, San Diego, Dallas, and Detroit held their own events. The new class of parades drew from the models of New York and Los Angeles while adding their own spin on Pride according to their specific goals and resources. Meanwhile, as the phenomenon grew, organizers and participants faced questions over representation, commercial influence, and frivolity— issues that are still debated today. In chapter 2, I describe how Pride established itself in its first six years as an annual parade promoting visibility and acceptance of the gay and lesbian (and later bisexual and transgender) community.

In part 2, I fast-forward to 2010 and examine contemporary Pride parades. Pride today communicates messages about queer sexuality and gender that run counter to the heteronormative code of meaning that privileges heterosexuality as natural and moral. Chapters 3 and 4 describe the similarities and differences among contemporary Pride parades in my study. While varying greatly in size and local cultural climate, Pride parades share common messages that promote visibility, support, and celebration of LGBT identity. As a cultural protest, Pride parades deliver these new cultural meanings through both the words (signs and slogans) and actions (cheering, dancing, and staging such a parade) of participants. The promotion of these meanings signals a mainly outside-in, as opposed to an inside-out, model of cultural change. While pursuing a common model of cultural change, each parade promotes visibility, support, and celebration using symbols and messages adapted to their local cultural contexts. Additionally, through their variation, Pride parades deal differently with three issues that began in the phenomenon's early years. With still-unsettled debates, Pride parades wrestle with provocative displays, commercialization, and maintaining a sense of purpose amid the festivity.

Pride parades are not just about challenging cultural stigmatization; they are also about building the larger LGBT community. Parades bring the small, sometimes hidden LGBT segment of the population together both physically and emotionally—giving many a welcome reprieve from everyday hostile culture. In chapter 5, I show how Pride's messages of visibility, celebration, and support work simultaneously to challenge external power and foster community.

I conclude this book by looking to the future of Pride. Over forty years since the first parades, the Pride phenomenon continues to grow. Every year, established parades grow larger and new parades are founded. Moreover, LGBT people are finding greater cultural acceptance as the stigmatization of homosexuality and gender transgression lessens. If the need for LGBT activism dissipates with this change in culture, will Pride parades become more like St. Patrick's Day events—benign celebrations of caricatured identity—or will they continue to push boundaries? I answer this question by looking to what Pride parades tell us about collective protest for cultural change.

PART I

Pride Then

1

From "Gay Is Good" to "Unapologetically Gay"

Pride Beginnings

The first march was very much in keeping with how I saw myself politically. Something new and unique to my experience. It was unique because this was the first time in my life that I marched for myself. I marched for my freedom, I wasn't marching as an advocate for someone else's freedom, civil rights for instance—that was uniquely different. That I saw that my identity as a gay man was worthy of political formulation, worthy of a march up an avenue in America in 1970, so that was unique, and I saw progression in terms of my own development, in terms of how I saw human rights and the rights of people, so that was uniquely different.
—Steven F. Dansky, marcher at Christopher Street Liberation Day, 1970

In 1970, Steven F. Dansky was no stranger to activism.[1] A young, progressive man living in New York City, he had marched for civil rights, women's liberation, and economic justice. For the past year, he had been an active member of the Gay Liberation Front (GLF), a radical group committed to broad social change with gay rights at its core. For Dansky, with his activist background, the Christopher Street Liberation Day (CSLD) march in New York City—also known as the first Pride parade— could have been just another protest, complete with angry chants and fists in the air. Instead, Dansky described the march as "something new and unique to [his] experience" because for the first time, his identity as a gay man took center stage and was "worthy of a march up an avenue in America." In contrast to when he marched for the rights of African Americans, women, or the poor, this time he marched for himself, for his own identity. And unlike the past year's activism with GLF, at CSLD,

Dansky was part of a grand gathering of gays and lesbians, who by their sheer numbers made a bigger, bolder statement than GLF had been able to make in their smaller demonstrations. Moreover, Dansky and his fellow participants made their statement in a new way, by having fun and celebrating their identities.

On the other side of the country in Los Angeles, Pat Rocco was not exactly what you would call an activist—he was more fabulous than that. As a performer and filmmaker, Rocco was prominent in the gay social scene of the late 1960s and 1970s, which made him a leader in the gay community. When other community leaders organized Christopher Street West (CSW)—a parallel event to be held simultaneously with CSLD in New York City—Rocco got on the phone and reached out to everyone he knew, urging them to go to the parade. He and his creative friends brought a new brand of activism to the event by celebrating gay identity with a grand parade in West Hollywood. The events in New York City and Los Angeles looked different, but had the same central purpose: proclaiming the cultural worth and dignity of gays and lesbians.[2] These events also had the same pitfalls as the others. Lesbians and people of color struggled to be fully included and some in the community criticized Pride's celebratory nature as a distraction from the seriousness of gay oppression.

I talked to Steven F. Dansky, Pat Rocco, and nine other women and men who marched in the first events of what came to be known to the world as "Pride." Along with a smaller march in Chicago, the events were held on June 28, 1970 and collectively drew roughly five thousand marchers and an equal number of spectators. While Chicago's event continues as one of the nation's largest parades today, I focus here on the marches in New York and Los Angeles because they were significantly bigger at the time.[3] Drawing on interviews with the pioneers of these first parades, scholarly accounts, and news reports, letters, and editorials published in the leading gay periodical of the time, the *Advocate*, this chapter tells the story of these first parades. The events commemorated the Stonewall riots of a year before, when patrons of a gay bar in New York City fought back against routine police harassment. These riots galvanized gays and lesbians across the country and motivated them to fight for cultural equality with renewed energy and optimism. Though gay and lesbian activists had begun changing tactics a few years prior,

Stonewall marks the symbolic moment in LGBT history when gays and lesbians took to the streets to demand equality without compromise. With festive marches to mark the anniversary of Stonewall a year later in New York City and Los Angeles, gay and lesbian activists pivoted movement activism away from targeting the state and culture in the mind toward targeting culture in the world.

CSLD and CSW were unique in tone as well as message. Instead of an angry march or a solemn vigil, participants staged moving celebrations that, for many, were downright fun. The myriad artists, performers, church members, and social service workers in Los Angeles's gay and lesbian community, in particular, put on a parade to publicly revel in gay identity. While some believed this open revelry would ultimately hurt the cause of gay cultural equality, many found the demonstration both personally liberating and publicly effective. Participants on both coasts experienced, some for the first time, the thrill of holding hands in public with same-sex partners, while being surrounded by so many others who showed pride in being gay. They also confronted fears of violent backlash at such public displays, fears that were thankfully unrealized. This open celebration of gay identity contested the dominant heteronormative cultural code that interpreted homosexuality as shameful. These inaugural events of what would later evolve into Pride solidified the gay and lesbian movement's turn toward bolder activism targeting both culture and the state, while also laying the foundation for the grand events—and the controversy that can surround them—that continue today.

Setting the Stage for Pride

Pride has a little known precursor: the Annual Reminder. On the Fourth of July each year from 1965 to 1969, activists silently picketed Independence Hall in Philadelphia to bring attention to gay rights.[4] Participants followed a strict dress code of jackets and ties for men and dresses for women with the intention of presenting themselves as normal, respectable, and non-threatening. They held signs like the one shown in figure 1.1, declaring, "Homosexuals should be judged as individuals."[5] Marching silently, activists sought to change the public perception of gays and lesbians as socially deviant and instead show that they deserved equal treatment by the government and their fellow citizens.

FIGURE 1.1 Homophile activists at the Annual Reminder, Philadelphia, July 1968. Photo by Kay Tobin © Manuscripts and Archives Division, The New York Public Library.

The Annual Reminder was indicative of most gay and lesbian public activism of the time, which pursued narrow political goals and emphasized gays' similarity with heterosexuals. Demonstrating at sites like Independence Hall, homophile activists, as they were called, drew on American civic values to pressure the state for equal treatment. To show that they deserved equality, activists fought dominant stereotypes of gays and lesbians as perverts and sexual predators entirely at odds with "respectable" society. By dressing in conservative clothing and adopting a solemn demeanor, they presented homosexuality as a small, isolated aspect of identity that did not hinder gays' ability to be good citizens and neighbors.[6] Rather than challenging the heteronormative cultural code of meaning, with its binary gender roles and compulsory heterosexuality, homophile activists stressed that being gay did not mean breaking with traditional femininity or masculinity.[7] In this way, activists targeted culture in the mind, asking individuals to change their minds about gays and lesbians and come to regard them as good people worthy of respect. They did not challenge the cultural code in the world that defined homosexuality as inferior to heterosexuality, but instead targeted the individual attitudes that guided people's treatment of gays and lesbians. Activists hoped that by changing individual attitudes, particularly those belonging to influential professionals, they could bring about change in the state and to the institutional policies that discriminated against gays and lesbians.

Early organizations—such as the Mattachine Society for (mostly) gay men and the Daughters of Bilitis for lesbians—had what may strike the twenty-first-century observer as fairly modest goals: to provide social support outside the bar scene and to educate professionals in the medical and psychological communities about gays and lesbians.[8] Both groups drew their names from fairly obscure historical references, signaling the careful approach of their founders.[9] With names that masked their identification with homosexuality, groups could organize gays and lesbians under a cloak of safety while still communicating their true purpose to those "in the know." Homophile activists targeted straight professionals with the logic that if these influential citizens tempered their rhetoric about gays' inherent sickness, then the mainstream would not see them as a threat to its moral and social order. Scholars describe the homophile movement as "accommodationist" because activists did not challenge negative policies and cultural meanings head on, but rather attempted to forge a safe compromise in which they could live unmolested.[10]

Homophile activists' accommodationist strategy was a first attempt at creating a more livable society for gays and lesbians. In the years leading up to CSLD and CSW, gays and lesbians experienced a stark disjuncture between the opportunities afforded by Western society and its cultural and legal censure of homosexuality. By the 1960s, many gays and lesbians in the Western world had the structural ability to organize their lives around their same-sex desires.[11] Free of a social structure that required close family connections for economic survival, gays and lesbians (as well as countless straight people desiring an alternative to the traditional relationship model) could pursue the sexual and romantic relationships that they wanted. Though possible, such a path was not easy.

The heteronormative cultural code was (and still is) a set of meanings that interprets heterosexuality as both natural and good. Without an accompanying code of tolerance, as the one we see today, gays and lesbians were widely condemned by clergy, health professionals, and politicians alike as abnormal and even dangerous to society. Gays and lesbians appeared in the public eye only through stereotyped images as effeminate, sex-crazed men or butch, possibly predatory, women.[12] Socialized with these cultural meanings, straights and gays alike generally believed that homosexuality was detrimental to individual souls and collective society. Adding to this cultural stigmatization, the American legal system treated homosexuality as an illegal sexual act, making the social lives of gays and lesbians subject to police harassment.[13]

Thus, as more and more gays and lesbians experienced their homosexuality as a source of personal fulfillment, they faced public messages telling them that it was a moral, psychological, and civic failing. Many believed these messages, understanding themselves as essentially damaged but knowing that change was impossible. In seeking accommodation, homophile activists hoped to reduce some of the cultural and legal sanctions faced by gays and lesbians. At the same time, they built extensive communication networks through which gays and lesbians shared their visions for a culture in which they could live openly and proudly. Though many put on a mask of heterosexuality in their daily lives—a strategy that today we would call being "in the closet"—they increasingly saw as possible a day when they could take off this mask.[14] Homophile organizations worked to connect gays and lesbians with one another through newsletters and social events, thus providing spaces where they could experience their sexuality as a positive, socially affirmed identity.[15] Meanwhile, these formal organizations were not the only game in town, as gay and lesbian bars flourished in San Francisco, New York, and other large and even small cities.[16] Bars drew working-class and gender-transgressive gays and lesbians who were marginalized both by larger society and by the middle-class homophile movement. There, too, gays and lesbians came together, as their desire grew for a society in which they could live openly, feeling proud instead of ashamed of their sexuality.[17]

During the 1960s, many gays and lesbians like Steven F. Dansky were active in the civil rights and women's movements. They gained both inspiration and practical training in mobilization, movement organization, and protest tactics from these experiences, learning to fight back against social oppression. Meanwhile, growing out of New Left ideology that traced racial, gender, and class inequality to cultural roots, gay liberation ideology identified heteronormativity, not same-sex desires, as the cause of gay and lesbian oppression. Rather than a source of difference and even inferiority, gay liberationists saw homosexuality as a powerful challenge to restrictive Western culture. Heteronormative culture and attendant institutions like marriage and the traditional family, they claimed, repressed everyone, straight and gay alike, by allowing only a narrow range of sexual and gender expression.[18] By pursuing same-sex relationships and playing with gender roles, gays and lesbians broke with this repressive culture and could thus lead the way in its cultural overthrow. Taking up the New Left's emphasis on the psychological damage brought on by repressive culture, gay liberationists promoted pride in one's gay identity as personally fulfilling. The act of "coming out" publicly as gay or lesbian thus took on both personal and political dimensions.[19] With the lofty goal of cultural upheaval, gay liberation ideology nonetheless had a lighter side by emphasizing the pursuit of pleasure.[20] To be truly free, liberationists argued, individuals needed to be allowed to have fun in whatever way suited them without risk of sanction from the state or the culture.

For gay liberationists, the source of gay and lesbian inequality was not their exclusion from institutions or discriminatory laws, but rather a culture in the world that prescribed rigid norms and underlay state and institutional inequality.[21] Gay liberation ideology quickly developed into two branches: *gay power* favored working in coalition with other marginalized groups for a broad attack on oppressive powers, while *gay pride* focused on bolstering the public visibility of gays and lesbians. In the following chapter, I detail how this split led to conflicts between Pride participants as the phenomenon grew. For now, though, gay liberation ideology served as a cultural resource that emboldened gays and lesbians to demand profound social change. Thus, by 1969, many gays and lesbians had both the cultural and material resources with which to challenge their cultural inequality in a new way.[22]

The influences of gay liberation ideology and 1960s civil rights activism came together in the slogan, "Gay Is Good," coined in 1968 by veteran activist Frank Kameny. Inspired by Stokely Carmichael's "Black is

Beautiful," "Gay Is Good" similarly sought to reclaim a long-denigrated term by associating it with positive qualities. In line with gay liberation ideology, the new slogan called on culture in the world to change by adopting a new meaning of homosexuality. And like civil rights activism, "Gay Is Good" called on gays and lesbians to fight back against their oppressors and refuse to accept the inequality imposed on them. As Kameny wrote to fellow activist Dick Leitsch when proposing the slogan, "We will get there [to an equal society] a lot faster if we encourage our own people to hold up their heads, look the world in the eye and say 'Gay Is Good'—without ANY reservations—and . . . face the world with solidarity and self-confidence."[23] Kameny urged gay and lesbian activists to take a bolder stance and demand changes in both the culture and the state laws that underlay their continued mistreatment. Signaling the shift in the movement that would soon bring about the first Pride events, the 1968 National Conference of the Homophile Movement, a coalition of gay and lesbian activist groups across the country, adopted "Gay Is Good" as their official motto.[24]

Many gays and lesbians in 1969—more so white gay men than lesbians or gays of color—had the means to support themselves economically, interpersonal connections with others like them, commercial spaces in which to socialize, and resources with which to assert their social power, but they faced intense harassment from police and cultural disregard. They lived happy and productive lives, but were maligned by mainstream society as criminals, sinners, and mentally ill.[25] Though organizations like the Mattachine Society and Daughters of Bilitis had actively worked for social change since the mid-1950s, they had not made the tangible progress that gays and lesbians anticipated. In 1969, gays and lesbians had no legal protections, which meant that they could be fired from their jobs and denied housing for being gay. Widespread cultural attitudes in the mind meant that most Americans regarded them as sinful and dangerous.[26] Laws made homosexual sex illegal in most states and some ordinances made it effectively illegal for gays to congregate in bars.[27] Many gays and lesbians felt that the strategy and tactics of the accommodationist homophile activists were not effecting change quickly enough. In reality, as it would later become clear, this work was providing the foundation for what was to come—and all the movement needed was a spark to change course.

FIGURE 1.2 Veteran gay activist Frank Kameny marches in first pride parade proclaiming "Gay Is Good," June 1969. Photo by Kay Tobin © Manuscripts and Archives Division, The New York Public Library.

The Stonewall Spark

After midnight on June 28, 1969, police raided a gay bar called the Stonewall Inn. The official reason for the raid was that the bar was serving alcohol without a license; the catch was that the New York alcohol commission would not grant licenses to bars that served gays.[28] Police raids on places where gays congregated—mostly bars and cruising areas—were common.[29] Rather than scatter to avoid arrest, as police raid victims typically did, Stonewall patrons fought back. They turned the tables on police and barricaded them inside the bar. As police reinforcements arrived, so did other gays and lesbians in the area and the raid became a full-blown riot. Riots continued for three nights in a row, ceasing during the daytime for everyone to regroup and starting again as night fell.[30]

Stonewall patrons who started the riots were not the upstanding, well-dressed citizens who participated in the Annual Reminder. They were drag queens and "hustlers" (young male prostitutes) who flaunted their femininity and gay sexual energy.[31] They did not fit into main-stream "respectable" society and they did not care. On June 28, 1969, many of these individuals had endured enough harassment both from the police and society at large—and they fought back without compromising their identities. One drag queen, when threatened with a police officer's nightstick, countered with a sexual proposition. Hearing her crude suggestion, "the cop was so shocked he hesitated in his swing, and the queen escaped."[32] Later, a group of drag queens formed a chorus line and faced down police with Rockettes-style high kicks. They chanted:

> We are the Stonewall girls
> We wear our hair in curls
> We wear no underwear
> We show our pubic hair
> We wear our dungarees
> Above our nelly knees![33]

Through three days of rioting, drag queens led the way in standing against police harassment by refusing to apologize or moderate who they were. Moreover, they resisted with humor and dramatic flair, fighting back by making their opponents look ridiculous.

Drag queens and hustlers were joined by less marginalized gays and lesbians who lived in the area and were able to immediately publicize the riots in both mainstream and gay press.[34] This cooperation in itself was significant, since those who were working-class and flaunted mainstream norms were largely excluded (and excluded themselves) from homophile activism.[35] Rather than downplay their contributions, however, *Advocate* writers put the bravery of feminine gay men and drag queens front and center. Even though they represented the most disparaged aspects of the gay community, they were willing and able to stand up for themselves. One writer pointed out that "those usually put down as 'sissies' or 'swishes' showed the most courage and sense during the action. Their bravery and daring saved many people from being hurt, and their sense of humor and 'camp' helped keep the crowds from getting nasty or too violent."[36] Feminine gay men and drag queens were the heroes of Stonewall. Not only did they bravely fight police harassment, they did so in their own way and showed they did not need to change to be whole. Significantly, these contributions were celebrated by the established gay and lesbian leaders who produced the *Advocate* and headed activist organizations. Historical accounts written years later document the bravery of lesbians as well, and some credit one lesbian's resistance to arrest for initiating the violence.[37] However, since men outnumbered women as Stonewall rioters, community leaders, and *Advocate* readers, contemporary accounts focused most attention on them.

Community leaders paved the way for the demonstration that came to be known as Pride to target culture by interpreting Stonewall as more than a narrow issue of police harassment. *Advocate* writers portrayed police officers as representatives of broad cultural disregard, so that when they raided the Stonewall Inn, they were acting for an oppressive heteronormative culture. One writer, for instance, called frequent police raids "injustices dealt out . . . by the straight establishment."[38] While gay activists did indeed challenge the discriminatory actions of the police, this writer, by referring to the state as the "straight establishment," identified the heteronormative cultural code as the underlying justification to apply state power against the gay community. Another reported an overheard conversation between two police officers during the riots:

> One said he enjoyed the fracas. "Them queers have a good sense of humor and really had a good time," he said. His "buddy" protested: "Aw, they're sick. I like n—— riots better because there's more action, but you can't beat up a fairy. They ain't mean like blacks; they're sick. But you can't hit a sick man."[39]

The second policeman articulated the dominant cultural view of the time that homosexuality was a mental illness and that gays and lesbians should be treated and cured.[40] By quoting him, the *Advocate* reporter highlighted not just police behavior but also the cultural attitudes that informed such state-sanctioned action. As interpreted by gay and lesbian community leaders, the institutional power of the police was that of heteronormative, mainstream society, and this society actively oppressed gays.[41] According to gay liberation ideology, this heteronormative cultural code was the true culprit of gay inequality.

Community leaders saw Stonewall as a spark that inspired gays and lesbians across the country to stand up to cultural oppression. Though movement activism had been shifting in a bolder direction in the years prior, leaders interpreted Stonewall as the catalyst to kick this approach into high gear. The poet Allen Ginsburg observed that gays and lesbians he met in New York City "no longer [had] that wounded look."[42] The desire to live in the world with pride instead of shame that had been fomenting for years in gay and lesbian bars and through their quietly expanding communication networks was finally bursting out into the public sphere. Instead of trying to carve out a narrow space in society where they could live in peace, as homophile activists had done, gays and lesbians would now demand full acceptance.

Participants who I talked to reflected on the new optimism and motivation they observed. Nikos Diaman, who marched in the Christopher Street Liberation Day (CSLD) event in New York as a young gay man, observed:

> I was joyous about the change and attitudes on the street. The people that I met in [New York] when I first came back had a lot of guilt. But the men that I was meeting after the Stonewall, they started the liberation word, that's more optimistic and freer about sexuality.

For Diaman, Stonewall sparked a personal change among gay men he met. For Tommi Mecca, a radical activist living in Philadelphia, Stonewall inspired a more militant attitude toward mainstream society:

> I think it was that spirit, that spirit of rebelliousness, of defiance because you know, you've got to remember that in the early '70s we had everything against us, nobody liked queers, nobody except a few fringe Quakers and Unitarians. Basically, religious groups thought we were the devil, the same with government, just about everybody. So what I saw in New York that first time I went to the Pride march, I saw the spirit of defiance, the spirit of "fuck you, we don't care how you think about us, we don't care you want to lock us up in jail or some psych ward, you are wrong and we are right."

Both men described a changed attitude toward a hostile culture. They refused to accept the message that gays and lesbians are mentally ill, sinners, or criminals and were motivated to publicly fight to make homosexuality culturally accepted as valid human difference.

Stonewall was not the first time that gay patrons fought back against police harassment. In August 1966, patrons of San Francisco's Compton's Cafeteria rioted when police tried to arrest them. On New Year's Day 1967, patrons and LGBT community members spontaneously demonstrated outside Black Cat Tavern in Los Angeles to protest the police raid of the previous night. What made Stonewall different was not the details of the raid itself, but the ability of activists to turn the riot into a catalyst for change. Through their years of work building communication networks among gays and lesbians, establishing gay periodicals such as the *Advocate*, and cultivating relationships with the mainstream press, community leaders were able to extend the initial, spontaneous riot into a sustained three-day event by mobilizing the wider gay and lesbian community.[43] They publicized the riots by calling on contacts within mainstream media and promoting the message in gay periodicals that Stonewall signaled a turning point in gay and lesbian activism across the country. By drawing on existing movement infrastructure, activists made Stonewall into the spark for cultural change.[44]

Preparing to March

Stonewall was reactive; gays fought back when attacked. In the press, at activist meetings, and in their everyday lives, gay community leaders debated what to do next. There was a spark in the community, a desire for more radical action, but many were concerned that this spark would breed militancy and violence. While some argued that violence would be both effective and justified, most leaders feared that a militant response guided by anger would be an overcorrection to the accommodationist stance of homophile activists, arousing backlash instead of substantive change.[45] Young gays and lesbians in particular had not joined the waning homophile organizations, but now seemed to have caught the Stonewall spark—and some activists wanted to harness this new energy in a positive direction.

Radical activists formed the Gay Liberation Front (GLF) in the months after Stonewall to pursue a broad overhaul of what they viewed as a culture of oppression not only towards gays and lesbians but also towards straight women, non-white minorities, and poor people.[46] Rather than combating negative stereotypes with middle-class, normative images of gays and lesbians, as homophile activists had done, GLF activists promoted an ideology that called for confronting oppressive powers and publicly declaring pride in their gay identities.[47] They quickly established chapters in many cities, including Los Angeles, and staged myriad protests. GLF activists had a range of ideas about how to confront oppression, with some preferring militant action against police and others wanting to use humor and drama to push back against cultural meanings.[48] For instance, one tactic GLF used to confront culture was to stage "gay-ins," in which gays and lesbians gathered in public to sing, dance, and generally "hang out." Like Pride, gay-ins challenged heteronormativity by publicly displaying gay identities without shame or apology.[49] In other demonstrations, GLF employed traditional protest tactics by rallying in front of police stations to demand an end to harassment.

Martha Shelley, a young lesbian who had become disappointed with the more modest stance of the homophile group Daughters of Bilitis, remembers:

> [We were] marching down the streets, arm-in-arm, shouting, "Power to the people. Give me a 'G,' give me an 'A,' give me a 'Y.'" Shouting at the top of our lungs. Dressed in whatever wild and freaky costumes we felt like. Forget the nylons, unless you were a drag queen, I guess.[50]

At GLF demonstrations, activists like Shelley made their big gay presence impossible to ignore. Unlike previous homophile activism, demonstrators did not try to fit in with dominant cultural norms, choosing instead to emphasize their difference. Inspired by civil rights activism they demanded, rather than asked for, change in the way gays and lesbians were treated by the state and their fellow citizens. Drawing on gay liberation ideology, they understood this unequal treatment as rooted in the cultural positioning of homosexuality as deviant from the heterosexual standard. Their goal was to shake up the culture that simultaneously ignored and oppressed gays and lesbians.

The Annual Reminder went off as usual one week after Stonewall, on July 4, 1969, but this year, many of the picketers refused to follow the strict dress code and march single file in a circle. Instead, a group of demonstrators broke ranks and held hands, gleefully showing affection with same-sex partners.[51] This was a major departure from the tone and message of the Annual Reminder because it flaunted exactly that behavior—the overt display of homosexuality—that homophile activists sought to downplay. In light of this new vision for gay activism, at a fall planning meeting in November 1969, the Eastern Regional Conference of Homophile Organizations (ERCHO) considered a resolution to change the Annual Reminder:

> [We propose] that the Annual Reminder, in order to be more relevant, reach a greater number of people, and encompass the ideas and ideals of the larger struggle in which we are engaged—that of our fundamental human rights—be moved in time and location.
>
> We propose that a demonstration be held annually on the last Saturday in June in New York City to commemorate the 1969 spontaneous demonstrations on Christopher Street and this demonstration be called CHRISTOPHER STREET LIBERATION DAY. No dress or age regulations shall be made for this demonstration.
>
> We also propose that we contact homophile organizations throughout the country and suggest that they hold parallel demonstrations on that day. We propose a nationwide show of support.[52]

The resolution was adopted, and planning began in New York for what would eventually come to be known as the first Pride march on June 28, 1970.

Across the country in Los Angeles, organizers planned to commemorate Stonewall with a march on the same day. Like their counterparts in New York, they envisioned a public display of gay identity without the regulations on dress and decorum that characterized the Annual Reminders. Planning started in May 1970, but organizers ran into a roadblock when they applied for a parade permit.[53] The police commission (responsible for granting such permits) demanded that organizers take out a bond for $1.5 million in the event that there was violent backlash to their parade and properties were damaged.[54] Comments made by commissioners revealed that their view of gays and lesbians was exactly that which the parade meant to challenge. Police Chief Davis, for instance, said, "We would be ill-advised to discommode the people to have a burglars' or robbers' parade or a homosexuals' parade."[55] Echoing the New York police officer who said that gays should not be beaten when they

riot because they are mentally ill, the Los Angeles police commission expressed the dominant cultural view that homosexuality was an individual defect rather than the basis for group identity. To the commission,
homosexuality was no more a characteristic to celebrate than burglary;
both were criminal and detrimental to society.

The initial denial by the Los Angeles police commission of a parade
permit is significant because it reveals the cultural meaning that underlay
gays' and lesbians' legal inequality. The Civil Rights Act of 1964, a major
victory for civil rights activists, recognized race, sex, color, national origin,
and religion as protected identities and thus established legal equality for
these culturally defined minority groups.[56] Homosexuality was not included, which both reflected and reinforced the dominant cultural understanding that it was not a legitimate basis for group identity. Los Angeles
activists' first battle, then, was to combat this culturally informed action by
the state and obtain a permit to grant them the legal right to stage a parade.

Organizers succeeded in getting a permit after filing suit against the
commission. In his ruling, Judge Schauer said that the right of gays to
demonstrate was equal to that of other minority groups. He wrote:

> Whether it is a group of Negroes demonstrating in Jackson, Mississippi,
> for civil rights, or a group of homosexuals demonstrating for equal rights
> in Hollywood, wherever people are attempting to demonstrate peacefully
> to petition their government for redress of grievances, it is the duty of the
> police that are paid by the taxpayer—including the demonstrators—to
> protect them from intervention by hoodlums, and not attempt to keep
> them from exercising their constitutional rights.[57]

The judge ruled that the commissioners' opinion of the group did not
matter for their constitutional right to demonstrate. He upheld gay and
lesbian equality under the law to receive police protection as they exer-
cised their constitutional rights. Though this ruling did not establish
a wide-ranging legal precedent that would protect gays and lesbians
from discrimination in the future, it did provide official support for the
activists' cultural message that gays and lesbians are a legitimate group
who deserve cultural esteem and legal rights. Of more immediate significance, Judge Schauer's ruling allowed gays and lesbians to take this
message to the broader public by granting them the legal right to a mass

demonstration. By winning the court case, activists could contest the cultural underpinnings of the police commission's original decision rather than fighting the narrower issue of the state's discriminatory treatment of gays and lesbians. In other words, the demonstration could be about more than what the state did; it could also directly target heteronormative cultural meanings in the world.

Planning committees in each city were made up of different types of community leaders. In New York, planners were like Steven F. Dansky: members of activist groups that were working in traditional ways for political and cultural change. These groups, from New York, Philadelphia, Washington, DC, and other major cities, had been conferencing together and planning the Annual Reminders in Philadelphia since 1963 under the name East Coast Homophile Organizations (ECHO, later called ERCHO).[58] As the name suggests, the coalition was comprised of groups that had been working mainly with the pre-Stonewall homophile strategy of narrow public goals and accommodationist tactics. They were joined by newer groups with a more outspoken and uncompromising liberation approach, such as the GLF, which caused some tension. Tommi Mecca, who planned Philadelphia's first Pride march in 1972 and participated in NYC's march in 1971, described this tension:

> There was always friction there between [newer groups] and the homophile people because the homophile people weren't as sold on this idea of coming out of the closet and really being out there and using your real name and all of this stuff and we were . . . I think [homophile activists] saw the writing on the wall, saw that we were the future and that was really smart on their part because we were, we were very much a part of the present and the future.

Though employing different strategies, nearly all groups involved in planning Christopher Street Liberation Day in New York were activists with at least some experience in the disruptive marches and demonstrations that characterized 1960s activism.[59]

By contrast, three strong gay community leaders did much of the organizing work for Christopher Street West in Los Angeles. These three were Morris Kight, head of the Los Angeles GLF chapter; Rev. Troy Perry, who founded the Metropolitan Community Church in 1968 to serve gays and lesbians; and Rev. Bob Humphries, head of a gay welfare organization called the United States Mission. Along with Pat Rocco, these men were prominent both for their social activities and their activism. According to Del Whan, a young lesbian who was active with the militant group GLF, Kight believed that in order to be successful, the parade must include a broad community coalition. So while the planning committee in New York was made up entirely of the activist segment of the gay and lesbian community, the Los Angeles committee included people involved with social service, religion, and the arts in addition to activism.

The different backgrounds of planners in New York and Los Angeles meant that each committee envisioned the coming event with diverse ideas about what it could be. In New York, activists drew on their experiences fighting for better legal and cultural treatment of racial minorities, women, poor people, and gays and lesbians. They were familiar with the drawbacks of homophile demonstrations like the Annual Reminder that sought to convey an image of respectability to sway public opinion. They were inspired by the possibilities for disruptive direct action, which could force bystanders to pay attention by literally stopping traffic and making a scene. Essential to both these possibilities and drawbacks of collective action was the image of protest as a mass demonstration by a group of people demanding change. At the same time, planners in Los Angeles drew from a wider range of experiences in collective behavior, some aimed at protesting injustice, but others at entertaining the public, enriching them spiritually, or alleviating their health concerns with direct service. For years, performers like Pat Rocco had been challenging the notion that homosexuality is shameful by celebrating gay life in song and film. Their broader base of experience allowed Los Angeles planners to imagine creative ways to challenge negative understandings of homosexuality.

Despite their diversity, community leaders in both New York and Los Angeles envisioned what we would come to think of as the first Pride marches in many of the same ways. Central to all was the idea of celebrating the Stonewall riots and carrying on the new spirit of open, bold, and defiant declarations of sexuality. Organizer Morris Kight in Los Angeles described the planned event as "a love-in . . . entirely peaceful and non-violent . . . which is the essence of love."[60] The official title of the event was "Christopher Street West: A Freedom Revival in Lavender," which speaks more of a celebratory event than a defiant protest. The permit, too, was for a parade that included "decorated floats, marching bands, riders on horseback, and possibly a small elephant"—not your typical protest march.[61] The *Advocate* described New York's planned event as a "freedom march," referring, perhaps, to the Freedom Rides of the civil rights movement or to the expected feeling of liberation that participants would experience by marching openly on city streets. On both coasts, activists planned a demonstration that would put the diverse gay and lesbian community on display to demand greater cultural and legal freedom to live openly.

In contrast with the Annual Reminders, which were held at Independence Hall in Philadelphia, CSLD and CSW would be staged on city streets with cultural importance and no relation to the state—Fifth Avenue to Central Park in New York and Hollywood Boulevard in Los Angeles. Moreover, with no dress code and the inclusion of all who wished to participate, these demonstrations would emphasize displaying the gay and lesbian community as they are and without regard to looking "respectable." These differences from the Annual Reminders signaled a shift in both target and tactics. While for some the narrow goal of CSLD and CSW was an end to state oppression in the form of police harassment, the participants and organizers sought to accomplish this not by directly targeting the state but instead by targeting the broader cultural meanings that justified state oppression. Tactically, organizers planned events to make visible gay and lesbian diversity and to joyfully defy the cultural code that classified sexual and gender difference as wrong.

The Big Gay March

On June 28, 1970, participants in New York and Los Angeles were excited but nervous as the time to step off in the parades approached. Christopher Street Liberation Day in New York was scheduled to depart at 2 p.m. from the heart of the gay neighborhood near the site of the now-boarded up Stonewall Inn and travel up Fifth Avenue to Sheep's Meadow in Central Park. Three thousand miles away, Christopher Street West participants prepared to parade down Hollywood Boulevard at 7 p.m. In Los Angeles, Pat Rocco had called everyone he knew (which was quite a long list) to urge them to come to the event.[62] Many responded enthusiastically and planned to be there with bells on, but others were afraid to march for fear of repercussions with their jobs and families. Their fears were not off-base. One year after Stonewall, police harassment was still frequent and supported by laws that made it difficult for gays and lesbians to congregate without fear.[63] Losing one's job for being gay was a constant threat, heightened by a 1969 incident in which San Francisco activist Gale Whittington was fired from his job at States Steamship Company after appearing with his lover in the periodical the *Berkeley Barb*.[64]

Two participants in New York's CSLD told me about their fears that day. Nikos Diaman was active with the GLF in New York and before stepping off, he said,

> I was a little bit apprehensive because I didn't know what would happen. If there would be violence directed towards us, etcetera. It was a little scary but I was with friends and I had my friends. We had organized a brunch in the morning and then we left to march.

Likewise, Stephen F. Dansky, also in New York, reflected:

> In 1970 when we first marched, we were illegal sexually, hospitalized for mental illness as part of a diagnosis that was given by the American Psychiatric Association in the Diagnostic Manual, which also is used for diagnoses. We could have been arrested for so-called sodomy. . . . So when the first march occurred, we were not legitimate. We were legitimate for ourselves, but not legitimate for the world . . . The fear that I had on that very first march, I had no way of knowing whether we would make it, whether we would be attacked. There was a lot of violent protest against us. And we were victims of violence as we continue to be, but even more so in that era.[65]

Though it was police harassment that led to Stonewall a year earlier, Diaman and Dansky were not afraid of the government that day. Instead, they were afraid of how their fellow citizens would treat them as a group of out and proud gays and lesbians. They worried that police would not or could not protect gay and lesbian marchers from economic or physical violence. Indeed, these fears were underscored by the initial insistence in Los Angeles that organizers take out a $1.5 million bond if an uncontrolled violent backlash destroyed property along the parade route.[66] Fortunately, their fears went unrealized as marchers in both New York and Los Angeles were met by mostly supportive crowds. There were no reported incidents of violence or arrests.

Christopher Street Liberation Day, New York City

With clear skies above and seventy-five degree weather, Diaman, Dansky, and three thousand others stepped off at 2 p.m. to celebrate Christopher Street Liberation Day in New York. At first glance, the event appeared to be a protest march like all the others in the socially active 1960s and '70s. Marchers chanted gay liberation slogans such as "2, 4, 6, 8—gay is just as good as straight" and held signs calling to "smash imperialism." Most were dressed in everyday clothes, not the suits and dresses of the Annual Reminder. Going beyond a typical protest, participants added festive elements, including

> colorful pennants of purple, red, green, and yellow. . . . Day-Glo signs reading "Gay Pride" were present everywhere. . . . Attire of the marchers ranged from flamboyant costumes, with laces, burnooses, and capes, to torn shirts and jeans, with a sprinkling of suits. A few drags came in complete makeup and walked the entire three miles in high heels.[67]

While the march in New York featured these festive parade elements, it did not include others like floats, music, or other entertainment. Coming from activist backgrounds, organizers and marchers stuck with what they knew, presenting themselves as proud gay people through their signs, chants, and displays of affection.

Just as they had one year before at Stonewall, gays and lesbians took to the streets to show that they were, in participant Perry Brass's words, "unapologetically gay." This time, their demonstration spread beyond Greenwich Village and through downtown Manhattan. Unlike the protests that many had taken part in before, they did not make specific demands to change government laws. Instead, by being "unapologetically gay," they challenged a culture that condemned homosexuality. According to long-time lesbian activist Martha Shelley,

> The most important thing was to be out in public, to say that we were not going to take it anymore, to say that we were not going to let the police

beat us up and cower in the closet. And a lot of people could get behind that, people who didn't have a political view . . . that it was gay people being out in public and refusing to cower in fear and refusing to buy the idea that we were inferior, mentally disordered, sinners, that we were as happy with ourselves or would be as happy with ourselves if we weren't so beaten up by people as anybody else. That was something that any gay person could get behind.[68]

Shelley and her fellow marchers sought a world in which they could live openly gay lives. While their message referenced police harassment, it was broader than this—addressing the heteronormative cultural code that defined gays and lesbians as inferior and thus sanctioned their unfair treatment by police. By marching on public streets and declaring their sexuality, marchers contested this code by demonstrating that, just as their chant announced, "gay is just as good as straight."

Just like at Pride today, participants had fun marching together on public streets. They felt elated to be surrounded by so many other gays and lesbians in broad daylight. They laughed, held hands, and kissed as they paraded along.

FIGURE 1.3 Three women smile and hold hands at CSLD, June 1969. Photo by Kay Tobin © Manuscripts and Archives Division, The New York Public Library.

Having protested before, the participants were familiar with the feelings of collective effervescence—the heightened emotions that people feel when engaged in ritual action together. But at CSLD, their emotions were even stronger because this time they were marching for themselves. For the first time for many, they got to openly show themselves as gay, displays of affection and all. According to Paul Guzzardo,

> It was very exciting because it was a gay one. You know, lots of gay guys and women that were marching together and that was what made it so exciting. And after being oppressed for so many years—this was just so liberating, I couldn't believe it. To walk down the street and say, "This is who we are." [It was] just really great.

At the same time that participants challenged culture by refusing to censor their gay identity, they also felt the freedom that came from standing up in defiance. Guzzardo said it felt liberating; Perry Brass described the feeling as a "contact high" from being around so many people experiencing such elation at the same time.

The uplifting emotions that Guzzardo and Brass describe are important parts of protest that scholars often overlook but that have come to characterize Pride. By having fun together, protesters are able to imagine new ways of being in the world—ways that are not permitted in their existing cultural meanings and social structures.[69] Within gay liberation ideology, gays and lesbians were oppressed culturally by not being granted the physical or symbolic space in which to freely enjoy their own sexuality.[70] When they took their pleasure-seeking activities "out of the bars and into the streets," as many chanted, gays and lesbians envisioned for both themselves and the world at large what open, liberated sexuality could be. Though some interpreted this festivity as detrimental to the cause of gay equality because it might have detracted from the oppression that protesters hoped to expose, many saw this open celebration as a step toward true equality.

Christopher Street West, Los Angeles

Later that same Saturday, on the other side of the country, one thousand people gathered as the Christopher Street West (CSW) parade travelled along Hollywood Boulevard in Los Angeles. While New York was a cultural protest march with a festive flair, Los Angeles was, in the words of the *Advocate*, "a full-blown parade," with floats, music, animals, and spectators. The *Advocate* detailed the scene:

> Flags and banners floated in the chill sunlight of late afternoon; a bright red sound truck blared music; drummers strutted; a horse pranced; clowns cavorted; "vice cops" chased screaming "fairies" with paper wings; the Metropolitan Community Church choir sang "Onward Christian Soldiers"; a bronzed and muscular male model flaunted a seven-and-a-half-foot live python . . . Sensational Hollywood had never seen anything like it.[71]

Just as New York had done hours earlier, Los Angeles put the gay community on full display. The difference was that it drew from a wider range of the community including activists, artists, and churchgoers. Festivity was everywhere as contingents put on a range of displays to celebrate and make gay identity visible.

Parade participants showed their fabulous gay selves. Two church groups, the Metropolitan Community Church and United Brotherhood Church, displayed their Christian faith by singing hymns and constructing a cross covered in flowers. The Grand Duchess (a drag queen) from San Francisco was "resplendent in jewels and furs" and rode in a convertible while waving to spectators.[72] As the Duchess showcased her defiance of cultural gender norms, another group gleefully flaunted heterosexual norms. Contestants in the *Advocate's* "Groovy Guy" contest (a regular feature of the periodical) showed off their sculpted chests and presented themselves as sexual symbols to be admired by other gay men. Other participants challenged stereotypes to show that gays are a varied group. One man "drew delighted whoops all along the parade route" as he walked with two Alaskan Huskies and a sign that said "Not All of Us Walk Poodles." Another group was decked in leather and rode Harley-Davidsons, showing that some gay men also follow traditional masculine norms.[73]

GLF activists made use of the parade format with street theater that dramatically illustrated gay oppression by the state and challenged its underlying cultural condemnation. Highlighting the way police unfairly targeted gay men, activists dressed as cops with "vice" badges and chased "a gaggle of shrieking 'faeries' wearing gauzy pastels."[74] In another display, a man rode on a float next to a large jar of Vaseline as a way to embrace gay sexual behavior in the face of cultural disapproval.[75] Activists also held signs typical of a protest march, with slogans such as "The Nazis Burned Jews, the Church Burned Homosexuals" and "Stop Entrapment." With theatrics and signs, activists targeted the police specifically for their role in bar raids, like at Stonewall and broader cultural meanings that supported this harassment.

Los Angeles participants celebrated their sexuality, however it manifested. In doing so, they challenged the heteronormative cultural code that defined heterosexuality as normal and good while condemning homosexuality as deviant. This code underlay cultural norms that prohibited the open display of gay sexuality through same-sex affection and required gender conformity in dress and manner. Heteronormative meanings supported stereotyped cultural images of gay men as effeminate and weak and lesbians as mannish and predatory. Moreover, heteronormativity encouraged unequal laws and police treatment by defining homosexuality as an individual defect unworthy of civil rights protection. By defying these norms and countering stereotypes, Los Angeles participants contested the heteronormative cultural code in the world. They offered new images of gays and lesbians that were, above all, proudly and happily gay.

In true parade fashion, CSW drew a crowd. According to those I talked to and reports from the *Advocate*, spectators were a mix of gay supporters and curious straight onlookers. Pat Rocco described the scene at the parade route:

> We stepped out onto Hollywood Boulevard and we were in shock. There were so many people. So many people. This is how I described it: Hollywood Boulevard is probably, it's four lanes. . . . The first people gathered at the sidewalk, then there were people behind them and behind them until they reached the storefront. And that wasn't good enough; there wasn't enough room for people who showed up so they formed a row in front of the curb. And another and another. I would say that there were maybe twelve to fourteen feet left for the parade to go down. Just a little bit. We were just shocked—the number of people who showed up. And they

weren't throwing vegetables, they weren't doing jeers, they were actually in support. And this is non-gay men and women. And of course, our gay brothers and sisters, those who felt they would come out and not be seen, they were there in support. The shock of the number of people is what hit us at first. And the reception is what hit us second.

Rocco perhaps exaggerated their numbers slightly, but spectators did indeed gather to watch the parade. The *Advocate*, too, reported that negative reactions were rare compared to cheers and applause in support of those in the parade. Del Whan, who marched in the parade with a GLF contingent, said that "most of the spectators looked like they belonged in the street with us," meaning that she identified them as fellow gays and lesbians. Others on this busy commercial street were likely attracted by the nearby spectacle. Whan reported interaction between marchers and spectators, saying that, "We urged them on, yelling, 'Join us! Join us!' And some did." Rocco, who had called nearly everyone he knew in the weeks leading up to the parade, speculated that many on the sidelines wanted to be part of the parade but were fearful of repercussions from families and employers. The parade format allowed for various levels of participation, from putting oneself on full display on top of a float to cheering from the sidelines. Unlike New York's march that afforded scant roles to those on the sidelines, the Los Angeles parade incorporated spectators into the demonstration as supporters of its celebratory messages.

As in New York, Los Angeles participants had a great time. Del Whan said she felt elated and noted that others both marching and in the crowd showed their excitement by cheering, smiling, and clapping. Rocco said that he was "in seventh heaven . . . We walked down the street so proudly and often so tearily, just so amazed of the whole concept of that first parade ever. Our attitude and elation were boundless." Participants in Los Angeles shared New Yorkers' enthusiasm for the event, describing it as a liberating experience because they were open about their sexuality in a collective demonstration. Added to that, the cheers from a supportive crowd excited them even more. With a visible, festive parade, gays and lesbians communicated both to themselves and to mainstream society that their sexuality was cause for celebration.

Pride Makes Its Mark

In both message and tone, these precursors to Pride were a far cry from the old Annual Reminders. Those demonstrations presented gays and lesbians as respectable citizens who diverged from their straight neighbors in only one relatively small way. They were romantically attracted to their own sex, yes, but in every other way they conformed to social norms of good behavior. They followed masculine and feminine norms as gay men dressed in suits and ties and lesbians donned conservative dresses. Instead of the radical, disruptive demonstrations that were increasingly common among 1960s leftist activists, homophile activists staged silent, conservative pickets at the symbolic home of American liberty, Independence Hall in Philadelphia. Their choice of this site reflected their public strategy of appealing to professionals within government and institutions, asking for small legal and policy changes to make their lives a little bit better. They tried to change individual cultural attitudes by educating members of the public about gay and lesbian respectability, rather than confronting the heteronormative cultural code of meaning that informed these attitudes.[76] With signs asking for dignity and respect, they made a plea to be included in American society. While this was certainly a brave message for the time—picketers did, after all, insist that their sexuality was unchangeable and did not make them bad people—the message was that American culture in the world did not need to change to accommodate gays and lesbians. Likewise, the tone of the Annual Reminder was reserved. Photographs show picketers with solemn expressions as they demonstrated in silence. The Annual Reminder was not a time to celebrate; it was a time for discipline. Picketers were careful not to offend anyone by indulging in displays of same-sex affection or anything else that would mark them as different from their straight neighbors.

By contrast, Christopher Street Liberation Day in New York and Christopher Street West in Los Angeles were jubilant, boisterous affairs. Though they differed in appearance, the two events had in common the open displays of gay and lesbian sexuality, with little regard for making these images palatable to mainstream cultural attitudes. Inspired by social movements of the 1960s and gay liberation ideology, seasoned activists applied disruptive tactics to the cause of gay cultural equality.

The Stonewall riots of 1969 provided the spark that kicked this new wave of gay activism into high gear. In New York, commemoration of Stonewall took the form of a protest march with festive elements to celebrate gay identity; in Los Angeles, participants put on a parade to make their identity visible. For the first time, gay people marched for themselves *as* themselves, without downplaying the sexuality or gender nonconformity that mainstream culture condemned. The marchers embodied the new gay liberation ethos of pride by literally parading in celebration of their identities. As they marched together in this open display, many had a feeling of euphoria as they found the openness both liberating and fun.

The events were not without their problems. White gay men played a much more prominent role in both the planning and the execution of the marches than did lesbians or people of color. With greater economic and social capital, white gay men dominated gay and lesbian social life and activism at the time (and often still do).[77] Though not equal, all three women that I spoke to said that there was better inclusion of women at all levels of planning and participation at these events than at any other movement action of which they had been part. Male marchers also noted that men and women worked more collaboratively on the two Pride events than they had in the past. Still, Pride organization and participation was dominated by men; it was not an easy fix for gender problems. Likewise, gay people of color were largely absent from Pride. This reflected their marginalization in society at large as well as overt discrimination within the gay community.[78] I did speak to one New York participant, Roberto Camp, who is Mexican-American. He described a "very close brotherly, sisterly kind of interaction" at CSLD among gay men and lesbians from many ethnic backgrounds. He cited the participation of Puerto Ricans and African Americans in the march as evidence of inclusion. From this scant evidence, it appears that gay people of color were welcomed, but relatively few participated and racial and ethnic diversity was not a focus of organizers.

The festive parade elements and provocative displays were points of contention at both events. Many felt that floats, drag queens, and Groovy Guys distracted from the serious message of gay equality. In New York, this issue came up at planning sessions as organizers debated inviting non-activist groups such as bars to participate. According to Perry Brass,

There were other people who thought, well, if we do this, suppose the bars want to take it over and want to have floats and go-go boys. And we said, Martha [Shelley] and Bob [Kohler] and other people said no—this has got to be a political march, we have got to bring politics into this, it is going to be most of all a conscious raising event, which is what was so important to us at that period. . . . And so we wanted this march to be a consciousness-raising event, we didn't want it to be splashy, we didn't want floats, we didn't want disco music, we didn't want any of that kind of stuff, we wanted banners, if there was going to be music, we were going to provide it, none of the amplified pop crap, we would have whistles and drums of our own. This was going to be just the idealism of young people of that period.

For Brass and other activists, festive elements like amplified music and dancers would take away from the march's contentious message and thus make it less effective.

Along with distracting from its call for change, some argued that the more provocative displays like the jar of Vaseline would hurt the positive image of gays and lesbians that homophile activists had worked so hard to promote. The *Advocate* printed a letter from a reader who believed that Los Angeles's parade did more harm than good:

By showing us off as a group of silly freaks, those queens sure lowered our public image to the level public opinion has had it set for years. How can we make demands for equality, based on our rights as normal citizens, when our public image is constantly destroyed by flamboyancy and poor taste?[79]

To the writer of this letter, participants did not take bold, brave action by parading their sexuality in the open. Instead, they hurt the chances for equality by lowering public opinion of the gay and lesbian community. That is, rather than challenging the heteronormative cultural code of meaning in the world, some argued that provocative images risked hardening individual cultural attitudes in the mind about gays and lesbians. Ruth Weiss, who marched with GLF in the Los Angeles parade, agreed that images of gay men flaunting their homosexuality were bad for the cause of equality, but she blamed the media that published such pictures. To her, the media chose to focus on those images that would be most offensive to mainstream readers, rather than giving an accurate representation of the parade as a whole.

Most participants and writers, however, defended the parade. Readers responded to the original letter by arguing that legal rights should not be based on one's conformity and that it was those most marginalized—drag queens and effeminate gay men—who fought hardest during the Stonewall riots.[80] One writer asked, "Why do gays have to be blackmailed to suppress their own in catering to public prejudice?" and "Why reject our own, identify with our oppressors, discriminate against queens just because their lifestyles are not our bag?"[81] For these writers, Pride was about challenging negative cultural meanings even at the expense of narrower political goals and modest aims to change individual cultural attitudes.

More than just a difference of opinion, this debate reflects the divisions within gay and lesbian community. During the homophile era, working-class and younger gays and lesbians largely stayed away from homophile organizations in favor of the social life available in bars. Those involved in gay bar culture eschewed the modest, "respectable" image promoted by homophile activists in favor of more overt and varied displays of sexuality (at least in the relative safety of bars). Moreover, gay liberation ideology elevated the open celebration of sexuality to a movement goal. The struggle for gay liberation was a struggle for the space to play, for the freedom to seek pleasure in all its forms without restriction from either the state or culture in the world.[82]

At CSLD and CSW, the many segments of the gay community—"old guard" homophiles, newly radicalized gay liberationists, and the marginalized drag queens, hustlers, and butch lesbians who had found a home in gay bars—came together to put on a public display, and their cooperation was certainly not easy. As we will see in the following chapters, Pride planners and participants, often coming from different segments of the gay and lesbian community, have continued to debate the issues of festivity and provocative displays throughout Pride's history.

Scholars mark the 1969 Stonewall riots as the time when the gay and lesbian movement went from publicly seeking modest political and civil accommodation to broader cultural change in the world. While activists did not abandon strategies to bring about change through state action, with Pride, they established a tactic to target cultural change directly. On each coast, this tactic looked a bit different. In New York, organizers and marchers like Steven F. Dansky were politically active for a host of progressive causes and put together a festive event in the form of a political march. In Los Angeles, entertainers like Pat Rocco joined with religious leaders, social service providers, and activists to put on a parade, complete with floats. In both formats, participants threw off the suits, dresses, and polite behavior of the Annual Reminder, put on jeans and tie-dyed shirts (or went shirtless to show off their muscles), and proclaimed they were "unapologetically gay."

2

"Unity in Diversity"

Pride Growth

The parade in Los Angeles won't have begun to tap its potential until there are at least twenty times that many marching; until far more than three or four gay businesses are
represented; until the Metropolitan Community Church
can find a way to produce, in the streets, not just the trap-
pings of an ordinary parade, but the regenerating fervor, the
Pentecostal excitement of communal love, that has made the
church such an exhilarating experience; and until Gay Lib
also can produce more than just a march with a few shock-
ing displays—until it can produce on the streets the process
of liberation.

—Jim Kepner, activist and writer for the *Advocate,* 1971

After what would become known as the first Pride events in June 1970,
gay and lesbian community leaders declared them a resounding success.
Christopher Street Liberation Day (CSLD) in New York and Christopher Street West (CSW) in Los Angeles drew more people than planners
expected, while marchers and spectators alike felt a new kind of joy from
publicly showing themselves as gay and unashamed. All involved breathed
a sigh of relief that the demonstrations were not met with violence. This
new form of protest mixed with festivity was certainly not without its
critics. Some thought the events were too flashy and that the open and
sometimes stereotypical displays of gay identity would hurt equality more
than it would help. Despite these concerns, community leaders in New
York, Los Angeles, and Chicago started planning for 1971, while gays and
lesbians in other cities talked about holding their own Pride events.

Gay and lesbian Americans in 1971 lacked both legal rights and cultural esteem, but they finally saw change on the horizon. Years of ho-

mophile organizing and a flourishing underground bar culture had prepared gays and lesbians to come out and fight for legal and cultural equality. No longer willing to put on a mask of heterosexuality, many adopted gay liberation ideology that called for open, prideful display of their sexual identity. Emboldened by Stonewall, gays and lesbians largely dropped the homophile strategy of pursuing modest political change with tactics like the Annual Reminder that required activists to conform to heteronormative standards of dress and behavior. Instead, they broadened the targets of their activism to include contestation of culture in the world. The marches in 1970 were the expression of a new vision of gay and lesbian activism, one that directly confronted a culture that denigrated homosexuality. Gays and lesbians now demanded that society change to accommodate them, making room in the culture for sexual and gender difference. Events in New York and Los Angeles signaled this change as gay people like Stephen F. Dansky, Martha Shelley, and Pat Rocco marched for themselves as themselves. With thousands of others, they proudly affirmed their identities with displays of affection and signs declaring "Gay Is Good," and in a break from earlier homophile demonstrations, planners did not put any restrictions on how marchers presented themselves.

The new energy and vision expressed in the Christopher Street marches inspired new activists to join the cause of gay and lesbian cultural equality. Young people like Nikos Diaman in New York were inspired by the defiance of Stonewall rioters to join with others and demand a change in society's treatment of gays and lesbians. But this surge of activism brought with it divisions about strategy as activists debated the best way to achieve equality. Sociologist Elizabeth A. Armstrong described three main activist camps within the gay and lesbian social movement in the early and mid-1970s.[1] The first two, "gay power" and "gay pride" came out of gay liberation ideology which identified the heteronormative cultural code as the source of gay and lesbian oppression. With a close alliance to New Left understandings of all oppression as interconnected, "gay power" activists called for complete cultural overhaul, arguing that gays and straights alike needed to free themselves from oppressive social institutions including the family, religion, and gender.[2] They saw race, class, gender, and sexual inequality as linked and advocated partnering with other movements

to push for broad-based social change. Also drawing from gay liberation ideology, "gay pride" activists were inspired by the successes of the
civil rights movement to conceive of gays and lesbians as a distinct minority group defined by their sexual difference from the heterosexual
majority that, like racial and ethnic minorities, deserved equal political rights and cultural legitimacy.[3] These "gay pride" activists sought
to change both the heteronormative cultural code and eradicate the
discriminatory laws that oppressed gays and lesbians. Still others, "gay
rights" activists, wanted to continue the narrower strategy of the homophile movement and push for modest legal and institutional change
by presenting gays and lesbians as respectable members of society who
did not threaten the heteronormative order.[4] Following gay liberation
ideology, which regarded homosexuality as publicly, not just personally, significant, both gay power and gay pride activists recast all gays
and lesbians as activists by emphasizing the individual experience of
"coming out" as a contentious act.[5] Those who did not join a movement group looked for ways to publicly show their gay identity, and
Pride planners in particular tried to maximize their participation in
collective demonstrations. By contrast, gay rights activists were more
narrowly focused on pursuing the public interests of gays and lesbians
and did not find it necessary to include all who identified as gay in
movement activism.

   "Infighting," as scholars call it, is when activists within the same
movement fight over strategy and tactics.[6] Scholars have often thought
of infighting as destructive to a social movement. By fighting with one
another, activists would divide their supporters and undercut one another's progress toward social change.[7] Diversity in strategy and tactics,
however, can be productive as well, prompting activists to engage in
crucial debates that clarify what their movement truly is about.[8] Fur-
thermore, activists do not necessarily need to come to a complete consensus. They may instead form separate organizations, each with their
own niche, as gay rights activists lobby politicians for legal change, while
gay power activists stage dramatic street protests that agitate for cultural
change.[9] The diverse visions for social change certainly presented a challenge in the years after the 1970 marches, but it was this diversity that
led to its unique format as a participant-driven parade targeting culture
for change.

Writing in the *Advocate*, Jim Kepner articulated the prevailing vision of what Pride could be. Indeed, planning committees and journalists at the *Advocate* used the label "Pride" to name these events in most cities (with the exception of New York, Los Angeles, and San Francisco, which used "Christopher Street" and later "Gay Freedom Day" in San Francisco). This common labeling illustrates the prevailing vision of a unified Pride phenomenon with iterations across the country as each city drew from a shared idea to stage its own event. As gay and lesbian activists moved forward with the ultimate goal of cultural equality and a bold strategy to target both culture and the state, Kepner imagined Pride as an event to bring out all facets of the gay and lesbian community. In addition to the myriad businesses and community organizations that he talked about in the epigraph to this chapter, Kepner said,

> Until every drag queen and female impersonator in Los Angeles is out there to flaunt their feathers—and every gay biker as well; until the parade can show—with a force of numbers that will drown out all the petty bitching—that Gays are indeed all kinds: characters and conformists, preachers and truck drivers, hairdressers and Marines, butches and swishes, male and female, black and white, hip and square, radical and conservative, hewing to no single stereotype, whether it is the stereotype of the respectable middle-class image many want us to put forward, or the stereotype of the swish which they are so afraid of.[10]

By showing gay and lesbian diversity loudly and proudly, Kepner believed that gays and lesbians would free themselves from a hostile culture while challenging the fears, misconceptions, and stereotypes that underpin such hostility.

However, though many agreed with the broad outlines of Kepner's vision, the three main activist camps—gay power, gay pride, and gay rights—butted heads on the specifics. In line with the desire of gay pride and gay rights activists to tap into gay and lesbian community resources, Kepner envisioned strong business participation in Pride parades. Gay power advocates, however, saw gay and lesbian inequality as just one piece of a larger system of oppression with capitalism at its heart—and thus rejected even gay-owned businesses as part of this system that they sought to overthrow. Likewise, gay pride activists who were more specifically focused on liberating gays and lesbians joined gay power activists in supporting Kepner's desire to bring together all kinds of gays and lesbians, even those "butches and swishes" who deviated markedly from mainstream social norms. Conservative gay rights activists, by contrast, wanted to publicly put forward only the most palatable image of the gay community in order to persuade skeptical individuals that gays and lesbians were worthy of greater acceptance.

Throughout the early 1970s, gays and lesbians in an increasing number of cities worked through these debates as they put on annual events. They did not resolve them all—in fact, debates over provocative displays, commercialization, and festivity remain today—but they did establish a format and target for Pride that enabled gays and lesbians to show their community's "unity in diversity." By 1975, the gay and lesbian community had developed Pride's format as a parade to contest cultural meanings through the open affirmation of gay identity across the country. The parade format allowed each contingent to put on its own display, be it a gay power call to "smash imperialism" or a gay pride celebration of drag performance. By targeting culture in the world, Pride encouraged creative displays of gay identity that incorporated fun and drama to offer new, positive messages about homosexuality. Though by no means perfect, this format and target drew participants from across the gay and lesbian spectrum, each incorporating their own visions of a better world. Meanwhile, as Pride crystalized as a cultural protest, other gay and lesbian activists targeted the state by working to change discriminatory state laws and practices and targeted institutions with campaigns to challenge the negative treatment of gays by religious, media, and medical institutions.

When people think of a Pride parade today, or when organizers put on a Pride event in a new city, they draw on a common idea.[11] Pride is a culturally meaningful phenomenon that was developed by planners, community leaders, and ordinary gays and lesbians, as they debated movement strategy and balanced competing interests while putting on Pride events from 1970 until 1975. Though Pride has by no means been static in its growth since 1975, and while it continues to vary along with local contexts, much of what we recognize today as Pride was established in these early years. It is this phenomenon that I describe in the remainder of the book.

1971: Focus on Growth

The inaugural events of 1970 set a precedent for Pride as a different kind of protest in target and tone. While including demands on the state to end police harassment, Pride pivoted to target the heteronormative cultural code that supported unequal treatment by the state. This code of meaning equated homosexuality with deviance and drove many to be publicly quiet and privately ashamed of their sexuality. Gays and lesbians in New York and Los Angeles went "out of the closet and into the streets" to publicly declare their sexuality as a way to challenge this negative cultural code in the world.[12] Pride participants' collective, public declaration of homosexuality was also festive in tone: they did not grudgingly admit to being gay, they celebrated it.[13] Such open celebration fit with the gay liberation ethos to regard gay identity as a source of power and pride rather than a hardship to be endured. As Pride grew, it strove to fulfill the vision articulated by Jim Kepner in his 1971 *Advocate* piece: to bring out all facets of gay and lesbian community in a grand display that would liberate participants and, indeed, American culture at large.

The 1970 events gave gays and lesbians two visions of Pride. Organized by a coalition of gay power, gay pride, and homophile gay rights activists, Christopher Street Liberation Day (CSLD) in New York was a festive march that incorporated parade elements like colorful pennants and costumed participants into the familiar form of a protest march. Participants marched in a block while chanting and holding signs calling for change. In Los Angeles, entertainers and community advocates—counted as activists by their newly politicized gay identity—joined with members of movement groups to stage Christopher Street West (CSW), a full-blown parade complete with floats, convertible cars, music, and spectators. In the early 1970s, Pride planners and participants debated these formats while working to put on events that fulfilled Kepner's vision. On the one hand, a simple protest march was a familiar venue for presenting demands for change. New York's CSLD drew on this form while charting new territory with a festive message that made broad demands for cultural change. But as more people got involved, they had different ideas about how to communicate the message that they were "unapologetically gay" and that mainstream society had better get used to it. Some wanted music, others wanted theater, and some wanted both staged on big, decorative floats. On the other hand, a parade was a culturally familiar format that allowed for myriad displays in a festive procession. Los Angeles's CSW incorporated chanting activists, dancing performers, and a singing church choir in its 1970 parade. The downside with the parade format is that it is not usually used for protest, so many worried that the entertaining, carnival aspects of the event might threaten the contentious, change-oriented messages of Pride. Along with this debate over the form that Pride should take, planners tackled conflicting ideas about the appropriate role for businesses and how best to represent the diverse gay and lesbian community. Those planning Pride events needed to find a way to make infighting productive, to bring together the broad spectrum of gays and lesbians in an event that allowed each facet to show their own vision of liberation.

As they planned for 1971, community leaders in New York and Los Angeles, along with those in Chicago, Boston, and San Jose tried to grow the Pride phenomenon as an annual demonstration by the gay community. Editorialists at the *Advocate*, the leading national gay periodical, promoted participation by writing, "We urge every homosexual who possibly can to take part—march, cheer, yell, or whatever. Experience the thrill of freedom, pride in yourself, and love—in a way that few of us have ever felt before."[14] Gay liberation ideology is evident in this quote, as the author encourages readers to march not just to effect social change, but for the psychological fulfillment that comes from openly showing one's pride. Despite tensions between gay power and gay pride activists as both strands fought for control of the post-homophile gay movement, this conflict was largely absent from Pride.[15] After the euphoria of the 1970 events, leaders wanted to reproduce those successful events and continue the good vibes. As a result, they largely avoided tackling the question of what form Pride should take and instead chose the one they thought would best grow the phenomenon.

Christopher Street demonstrations in New York and Los Angeles thus looked much the same in 1971 as they did in 1970. In New York marchers followed the same route as the year before, beginning in Greenwich Village near the site of the now-closed Stonewall Inn and proceeding up Sixth Avenue to Central Park. The march grew in size from 1970, with anywhere between five thousand participants as estimated by the

New York Times to the planning committee's optimistic figure of twenty thousand.[16] Similar to the Pride events of 1970, a mix of activists and unaffiliated gays and lesbians from New York and other East Coast cities marched joyously in their everyday clothes while chanting, "2, 4, 6, 8—gay is just as good as straight" and "3, 5, 7, 9—lesbians are mighty fine."[17] The *Advocate* reporter Breck Ardery noted a more relaxed atmosphere than during the inaugural march, as participants harbored fewer worries about violent backlash from either the police or their fellow citizens.

Like its 1970 parade, CSW in Los Angeles "had more of the aspect of a Shriners parade—complete with clowns, outlandish costumes, and a deft baton twirler—than a militant civil rights march."[18] The parade was bigger and grander than the previous year, with two thousand marchers and up to fifteen thousand spectators. Also like in 1970, Los Angeles's 1971 parade drew participants across the spectrum of the gay and lesbian community. The Metropolitan Community Church (MCC), founded as a Christian community specifically for gays and lesbians by parade organizer Rev. Troy Perry, entered the largest float at fifty-five feet long, covered in roses. It included amplified music and singing by the MCC choir. The Society of Pat Rocco Enlightened Enthusiasts (SPREE), a community and arts group, sponsored another float that featured music and young, attractive men wearing swim suits. Contingents from local Gay Liberation Front (GLF) groups marched and put on their own displays, including a banner that read "Sucking is Better than War" and a large caterpillar figure, dubbed the "cockapillar," that was fashioned to resemble a penis.

Many, particularly gay rights activists who favored a more image-conscious homophile strategy thought these displays were offensive and detrimental to the gay and lesbian cause. Tony Robles, owner of a gay bar in the San Fernando Valley, said that because of the two displays, "the efforts of the entire homophile community have been set back years."[19] Critics like Robles charged that, instead of challenging the stereotype that gays are sexually depraved, the "sucking" banner and the "cockapillar" reinforced this detrimental image. Though the actors making this argument have changed over the years, this was the start of a long-running debate about how to present the LGBT community at Pride. On the one side, some argue that provocative, even sexually explicit displays challenge negative cultural codes that classify homosexuality as inherently unsavory. On the other, critics urge Pride planners and participants to take cultural sensitivities into account and restrict displays that may cause offense. I argue that provocative displays can indeed be productive in challenging cultural meanings, but as we will see in chapter 4, Pride participants today tend to moderate their displays in response to their local cultural climates.

The debate over provocative displays reflects disagreement over the most effective strategy to achieve the goal of large-scale change in how gays and lesbians are treated. Those in favor of provocative displays pursue an outside-in model of cultural change, targeting cultural codes of meanings in the world with displays that flip these meanings—by showing homosexuality as a source of joy and fulfillment rather than shame. By contrast, critics endorse more of an inside-out model that targets cultural attitudes in the mind, attempting to persuade individuals that gays and lesbians are misunderstood. The inside-out model avoids an approach that might be misconstrued as offensive or cause individuals to harden their attitudes against equality, while the outside-in model welcomes it as a way to introduce competing meanings to culture in the world. With their high aspirations to include all types of gays and lesbians, from the conservative businessman Tony Robles to the radical gay power activists in the cockapillar display, Pride planners in the years to come worked to incorporate both of these models for change.

In Chicago, what began in 1970 as a small and simple two hundred-person march grew to a grander parade in 1971, in the fashion of Los Angeles's event. There were a few bar-sponsored floats, trucks with amplified music, and decorated cars along with marchers who waved flags and showed affection with one another.[20] Unlike New York and Los Angeles, Chicago's 1971 Pride event did not follow the trajectory of its previous year when the demonstration was more militant and state-directed as activists marched to the city's Civic Center to demand an end to police harassment.[21] Instead, Chicago planners drew on the models of New York and Los Angeles to stage a celebratory march that primarily targeted culture and included many parade elements. As in other cities, leaders worked to balance the diverse strategies of gay power, gay pride, and gay rights activists and to not let infighting divide them. At the event's pre-march rally, student leader Jack Baker urged participants to "keep our anger in the right direction" by fighting against heteronormativity and state repression, not against one another. According to *Advocate* reporters John Tackaberry and Bob Fish, such admonitions were successful as diverse gay and lesbian participants in 1971 showed camaraderie among diverse members of the gay and lesbian community while advertising their pride in gay identity.[22]

Gays and lesbians in Boston adopted the Pride idea of a public celebratory march uniting gays and lesbians by hosting a week of activities culminating in a march. Their march shows how, in 1971, the vision of what Pride should look like was still in flux. While other Pride events were notable for targeting culture, Boston's route included three concrete state and institutional targets—by proceeding from police headquarters to St. Paul's Episcopal Church and ending at Boston Common, in front of the Massachusetts State House. Anti-gay culture in the world still loomed as a target, as planners selected locations that they saw as embodiments of this culture.[23] During a rally following the march, participants focused more explicitly on culture with a "closet-smashing" demonstration. After a man joyously emerged from a large brown closet, activists then destroyed the structure to dramatize the oppressive nature of the cultural pressure for gays and lesbians to stay "in the closet" by not revealing their homosexuality.[24] This dramatic display embodied the liberationist message that public declaration of gay sexuality would lead to both personal fulfillment and social change. Like other Pride events, the march in Boston protested negative cultural codes with a public demonstration that was sprinkled with color and festivity. But unlike those events, Bostonians targeted three concrete representatives of anti-gay culture and alternated its festive tone with a more somber one.

In Boston Pride 1971, we see gays and lesbians working through the visions of gay power, gay pride, and gay rights activists to flesh out what Pride could be. Recall that during the 1960s gay activists and thinkers developed gay liberation ideology, which identified the heteronormative cultural code as the source of gay and lesbian oppression and urged them to defy this code by proudly declaring their sexual identities. This ideology spawned two strands: gay power activists wanted to work in coalition with other oppressed groups to overthrow racist, sexist, classist, and heteronormative culture writ large; while gay pride activists focused more narrowly on cultural and political change that would create a society in which gays and lesbians could live openly. From these two strands, planners conceived Pride as a collective demonstration of gay identity to challenge heteronormativity. However, gay power and gay pride activists advocated different strategies toward the state and other institutions such as churches. While the former wanted to demolish these entirely, the latter found common cause with homophile gay rights activists who sought discrete policy changes. These activists even saw some institutions as potential allies, so that they embraced the support of gay-friendly churches where gay power activists rejected institutionalized religion as inherently oppressive. Rather than destroying the collective, community-wide nature of Pride, this infighting spawned an event that incorporated cultural, state, and institutional targets. Boston Pride created space for each of these three groups to carry out their brand of activism. Gay rights and gay pride activists were able to protest unequal treatment by the state and the church by rallying at sites of power, while gay power advocates could confront the heteronormative cultural code by symbolically smashing the closet. Meanwhile, casual gay and lesbian participants were able to come out for the day and have fun proudly declaring their identities. Though this worked well in 1971, the disagreements over strategy quickly became too fraught; Pride honed in on culture as its main target for the parade, and included other targets for its ancillary events.

In New York, Chicago, and Boston, the 1971 Pride parades concluded Gay Pride Week, a week of events that included activist workshops, social dances, and state- and institution- targeted demonstrations. In New York, the GLF hosted a workshop on gay radio communication and a legal clinic, while the Gay Women's Liberation Front sponsored a sing-along and two other groups had dances.[25] On the Thursday prior to Sunday's parade, five hundred people participated in a candlelight vigil march to City Hall to demand passage of a bill that would guarantee legal protections for gays and lesbians.[26] In Chicago, one hundred people staged a mass "kiss-in" at the city's Civic Center Plaza to protest the upcoming trial of two activists charged with public indecency for kissing in public two months earlier.[27] The next day, nearly one thousand gays and lesbians attended a Gay Pride Week dance. As many did in the other two cities, Boston's gay groups held workshops throughout the week leading up to the Pride march that covered issues affecting the community, such as gay relationships, sexism, "coming out" as gay, and activism.[28]

The Gay Pride Week events served two important functions in constructing the Pride phenomenon. First, Pride events attempted to bring together all facets of the gay and lesbian community, including all types of activist and community groups, businesses, and gays and lesbians not involved in formal groups. This was—and continues to be today—a tremendous undertaking, given the diversity of people and interests in the gay and lesbian community. In addition to gay power, pride, and rights activist strategies, individuals and groups came to Pride with a desire to educate fellow gays and lesbians about important social and political issues, to create forums to share artistic work, and to let loose and have a good time in a venue that was not a dank gay bar.[29] The events leading up to Pride parades gave groups the opportunity to host all types of events and allowed individuals to learn, socialize, and protest in a host of different venues. Second, Gay Pride Week allowed the parades to concentrate on cultural protest by creating spaces for other types of social movement activity. Gays and lesbians could have fun and build solidarity while socializing at dances, then learn about social movement tactics and organization at workshops. They could make specific demands of the state and formal institutions at demonstrations prior to the celebratory parades. With both of these functions, groups could host events that suited their priorities and individuals could attend those that fit their interests. The Pride parades themselves were relieved of the burden of meeting everyone's agenda, freeing them to concentrate on being fabulous cultural protests. In this way, Pride could incorporate diverse people and interests without the need to fully agree on every aspect of the event.

The year 1971 was one of growth for the Pride concept. The two flagship events of 1970, CSLD in New York and CSW in Los Angeles, followed much the same form as they had the previous year, but drew more participants both as marchers and spectators. In Chicago, community leaders put on a Pride march with five times as many participants as in 1970 while abandoning their more traditional state-directed protest form in favor of a cultural protest march with many festive parade elements. Meanwhile, gays and lesbians in Boston incorporated the focus on cultural inequality while still making claims on the traditional protest targets (the state and formal institutions). In 1971 Pride was establishing itself as an annual festive demonstration for gay and lesbian cultural equality, but its format was still not solidified.

1972: Growing Pains

The year 1972 was a defining year for Pride as gays and lesbians faced crucial questions over what they wanted the event to be. Conflicts over outrageous displays, inclusion, and whether Pride should take the form of a march or a parade came to a head in New York and Los Angeles.[30] In New York, activists who wanted a more serious, change-oriented march fought with bar owners who wanted to advertise and entertain by entering floats. In Los Angeles, conservative members of the community withdrew their support of the parade because of what they deemed the offensive sexual displays of previous years. Lesbians in both cities pressed for inclusion in the official planning process and for more decision-making influence on the goals and format of the events. While infighting in social movements can derail collective action, it also forces productive conversations about the image and direction of the movement.[31] For Pride, conflicts forced community leaders to confront divisions among gays and lesbians in order to create an event that would showcase all facets of the community. As they debated the practical issues of including bars and floats in the event and setting limits on provocative displays, gays and lesbians clarified their stances on the larger issues of community image, inclusion of subgroups, festivity, and commercialization. Within a few years, Pride committees would settle on a format for Pride that balanced the interests of most factions, but they would continue to struggle with setting limits on displays, adequately including all members of the LGBT community, incorporating businesses, and balancing serious purpose with a fun atmosphere.

At the same time that these flagship Pride events struggled, gays and lesbians in six new cities caught Pride fever and organized their own demonstrations. Most prominently, community leaders in San Francisco overcame their initial resistance to the Pride concept and came out with a bang. They put on what the *Advocate* described as "one of the all-time gay parade spectaculars" complete with floats, music, and conflict-free participation from a wide spectrum of the gay and lesbian community.[32] While planning committees—both of new Pride events and those in their second years—had less infighting than those planning New York's and Los Angeles' events, they too faced challenges of including diverse community members and choosing the format and tone to best convey their demands for change.

Debating Pride's Format in New York

Even before Pride was born, the prospect of a public demonstration including the entire gay and lesbian community was simultaneously seductive and fraught. The cultural and legal oppression that kept gays and lesbians invisible to the straight majority also kept them hidden from each other. When they did find ways to socialize, it was in small groups based on affinity and often segregated by class and race.[33] Gay men who liked leather and motorcycles got together with others who shared their interests, while those who expressed themselves by wearing drag formed separate social networks. Likewise, professional gay men, lesbians who followed a butch/femme dynamic, and lesbians who rejected this style socialized almost exclusively among one another, creating their own networks, venues, and culture.[34] Since its inception with the homophile groups Mattachine Society and Daughters of Bilitis, gay and lesbian organizing sought to build connections across these micro-cultures and to craft an understanding of homosexuality as a shared identity that united a diverse group.[35] Activists reasoned that if they were going to successfully challenge the broad cultural stigmatization of homosexuality, they needed to bridge the divides between various gay and lesbian factions to present a united front. While Pride Week events preceding the 1971 parades in New York, Los Angeles, Chicago, and Boston allowed for groups to put on myriad events, Pride planners wanted the parades themselves to bring people together in a community-wide public demonstration. As planners debated Pride's format, then, they tackled the bigger issues of inclusion, commercialism, and movement strategy.

The divide was particularly great between gay men and lesbians.[36] Until women made material, legal, and cultural gains as a result of the feminist movement in the 1970s, platonic socializing between women and men was rare in American culture. Among gays and lesbians, this division was more acute since the few social venues where gays congregated were primarily for sex and romance and they did not seek one another out for romantic relationships.[37] Moreover, due to society-wide gender inequality, gay men had better employment opportunities and higher wages and thus greater social autonomy than their lesbian sisters. This freedom meant that men had greater ability to come out as gay. Many gay men moved to cities to pursue sexual relationships and create rich social lives.[38] Lesbians often had a different experience; many discovered and went public with their homosexuality when they became involved in activism, meaning that for some the identity of "lesbian" and "activist" were intertwined.[39]

With different lived experiences and levels of social autonomy, gay men and lesbians had both different priorities as activists and unequal power in activist organization. Gay men dominated gay and lesbian activism, at times showing overt sexism to lesbians. Del Whan, a lesbian activist in Los Angeles, noted that in her chapter of the GLF, there were only four lesbians to about forty gay men. Those lesbians who were involved in gay activism, like Whan, often had to fight to have their voices heard. Moreover, gay men and lesbians sought different strategic outcomes for their activism. While gay men wanted to end police harassment and overturn anti-sodomy laws, lesbians sought to address wage inequality and violence against women.[40] These priorities, along with experiences of sexism, prompted many activist-minded lesbians to align more with straight women in the feminist movement than with gay men in the male-dominated gay and lesbian movement.[41]

As a mass demonstration of gays and lesbians, Pride was able to make a big public statement. Gays and lesbians disagreed, though, on what this statement should be. Gay men were on the whole more in favor of communicating the gay liberationist message that homosexuality is a source of joy and pride, countering the cultural meaning of homosexuality as a sin that brings only shame. By contrast, lesbians for the most part wanted the event to adopt a serious tone and message that would highlight their unfair treatment at the hands of the state and fellow citizens. Such a statement would target the state and cultural attitudes, with the goal of persuading individual politicians and members of the public to take up the cause of gay advocacy. Carefree festivity, they feared, would undermine the demand for change by reinforcing negative stereotypes. Infighting prompted gays and lesbians to clarify their visions for Pride and to ultimately fashion the event as a parade to communicate multiple messages.

In 1972, the debate over what statement gays and lesbians should make with Pride centered on the practical question whether it should take the form of a march or a more festive parade complete with floats and commercial contingents. Writing to the *Advocate* that year, Boston activist Allen Young observed, "It is not a mere coincidence that most of the attempts to make the parades more grandiose are being made by men, while most of the demands for simplicity are coming from lesbians."[42] Indeed it was not. With less social autonomy and often stronger activist identities, lesbians involved in Pride wanted the event to immediately tackle those issues with which they were most concerned. They did not see the utility in floats and other parade elements for achieving social change. Ruth Weiss, a lesbian activist in both New York and Los Angeles, spoke of festive aspects as mere spectacle that distracted from Pride's serious demand for social change. To her, "guys wearing speedos, women going topless . . . are simply a sell-out to the patriarchy." Weiss connected this "sell-out" to the commercial interests of business sponsors who advertised at Pride with scantily clad participants—an issue I discuss in detail in chapter 4. In the opinions of Weiss and many other lesbian activists, these displays had no redeeming value by way of challenging heteronormative cultural meanings. There were, of course, plenty of gay men who shared their views and allied with them in pushing for a less festive tone to the events. As the planning for 1972 Pride events got under way in New York and Los Angeles, lesbians in both cities insisted on playing a greater role than in past years. With their influence, planning committees in New York and Los Angeles saw "a resurgence of a long-standing controversy over whether the parade should be simply a mass march or more traditional in form."[43]

Those pushing for a parade form saw it as the best way to fulfill two goals shared by gay power and gay pride activists. First, a celebratory parade encourages gays and lesbians to publicly revel in their gay identities. The notion that gay sexuality is a source of pride rather than shame and as such is a thing to be celebrated was central to both power and pride strands of gay liberation. Advocates believed that it was this bold cultural message—directed both toward culture in the world and participants themselves—that was missing from the earlier homophile movement. Second, a parade offers a way to include the many facets of the gay and lesbian community. Just as Pride Week allowed each group to fashion its own event, each contingent in a parade puts on its own show. Whether they want to show off their sculpted bodies, chant and raise their fists against police harassment, sing praises to God as gay Christians, or advertise their bar with music and dancing, a parade allows space for each of these performances.

By contrast, a mass march requires greater agreement about a central message and list of demands. Leaders first decide on this message, and then organize participant displays to communicate it. While such focus may communicate the urgency for change that many lesbians, in particular, argued was necessary, this top-down control inevitably leads to a loss of participants who disagree with the message. That is, the requirement for a unified message can, though not always, engender the kind of infighting that derails collective action. Instead, the parade format assigns a greater role for participants to drive the overall meaning by inviting each contingent to communicate its own message. Taken together, contingents showed "unity in diversity," communicating that gay identity is varied but that the community was united in celebrating homosexuality.[44] In a commentary in the *Advocate* about this dilemma, Jim Kepner wrote, "The parade will and must constitute a market place of messages, not a single message, unless that single message be that there is unity rising out of our diversity."[45] For those who advocated a parade form, state-directed messages could be part of Pride but would not be the whole of Pride's message. A single contingent could, for instance, march with a banner and chant, advocating for the passage of a non-discrimination ordinance, but the entire Pride parade did not have to be about this ordinance.[46] The events could also include messages, whether subtle or overt, directed at religious institutions, mass media, and cultural imagery.

New York City was ground zero for the debate over what form Pride should take. In its first two years, Christopher Street Liberation Day took the form of a march while incorporating parade elements like colorful decorations and a festive tone.[47] By 1972, though, with the parade model in full swing in Los Angeles and pressure from local bars and the financial sponsorship they could bring, New York found itself pushed more in the direction of a parade. Meanwhile, lesbians and some gay men urged the planning committee to resist these influences. While parade defenders argued that Pride should be a celebration of gay and lesbian life, detractors looked at the events in Los Angeles and saw frivolous entertainment devoid of either political or cultural contestation. Gay power activists, including many lesbians, were particularly concerned with limiting the influence of bars since they viewed any kind of commercialism—even bars that catered to gay patrons—as part of the very power structure from which gays needed to be liberated.[48] As Nikos Diaman in New York put it, for him and his fellow GLF members, it was "more important how we treat each other as people rather than buying stuff." To gay power activists like Diaman, business interests and social change were simply incompatible and thus allowing bars to participate in Pride could only corrupt the whole endeavor.

New York planners reached a compromise in which all groups were welcomed to participate in the march but floats were not allowed.[49] In parade fashion, however, each contingent had the freedom to put on their own display. Women's groups led the march by linking arms and singing "When the Gays Go Marching In." Behind them, bars participated with banners (but not floats), alongside activists, religious groups, and a number of marchers dressed in drag. A few prominent figures joined in, including Dr. Benjamin Spock of child-rearing advice fame and Michael Pesce, a Democratic nominee for New York State Assembly. This was the first time Pride saw this type of participation, in which people well-known outside of their connection to the gay community marched to show their support of gays and lesbians.[50] In another first, Jeanne Manford marched with her son, Morty, holding a sign that read "Parents of Gays Unite in Support for Our Children." After many gays and lesbians reached out to her, asking that she talk with their parents, she decided to begin a support group.[51] That group became Parents and Friends of Lesbians and Gays (PFLAG), which now has affiliates in 350 communities in the U.S. and abroad, with over 200,000 members.[52] PFLAG affiliates still march in Pride parades and are among the most popular contingents.

While resisting the commercialism and, to some, the frivolity that came with floats, New York's 1972 demonstration did inch closer to a parade form. Like Christopher Street West in 1970, New York included a much broader spectrum of the gay and lesbian community than the activist groups that made up its inaugural march. With the ability to decide on their own displays, these new participants conveyed a host of messages, some aimed at celebrating gay life and others at demanding concrete change in how gays and lesbians were treated, particularly by the police. Straight allies visibly participated for the first time and communicated their own messages of support for gays and lesbians. Though still nominally considered a march, New York's Pride in 1972 had the diversity of messages and festive atmosphere that characterize a parade. Together these messages showed that gays were diverse, proud, and not going anywhere.

Debating Visibility in Los Angeles

Pride was—and still is—a massive coming out of the gay and lesbian community. In the first two years of Pride, demonstrations in New York, Los Angeles, Boston, and Chicago enabled participants to make their gay identities publicly visible in a way that no previous collective events had done. With the rallying cry "out of the bars and into the streets," gays and lesbians broadcasted their intention to live openly, making their sexuality a public and visible identity rather than a private desire reserved for hidden spaces. Since homophile activists took their first steps toward gay visibility, however, the gay and lesbian community wrestled with competing views on how to represent itself to mainstream society. Drawing on a gay liberation ideology that flaunted heteronormative culture for both social change and personal fulfillment, gay power and gay pride activists wanted to show the nonconformity of gays and lesbians. By showcasing drag queens, butch lesbians, and "fairies" (effeminate gay men) who loved themselves and one another, they strove to challenge the heteronormative code of meaning that prescribed only misery for those who rebelled. Like their homophile forerunners, though, gay rights activists feared backlash if the community presented too radical an image of itself and instead urged caution. With a greater focus on targeting cultural attitudes in the mind, they advocated for presenting a modest image that could persuade individuals to rethink their perceptions of gays and lesbians.

Rejecting the image-conscious dress code of the homophile movement's Annual Reminders, Pride planners let participants put on whatever display they wished as they marched the streets. This move was especially important to gay pride and gay power activists who viewed mainstream

cultural norms as an essential culprit in the oppression of gays and lesbians. But after overtly sexual displays appeared in CSW's first two parades, many in Los Angeles—particularly those advocating a gay rights
strategy—felt it was time to place some limits on what could be entered in
the parade. They worried that displays like the oversize jar of Vaseline in
1970 and the "cockapillar" of 1971 did more harm than good by confirm-
ing the stereotype that gays are oversexed and devoid of propriety.[53] As
planning got under way for Los Angeles's 1972 parade, the gay rights legal
aid group HELP, which had a Tavern and Guild Division representing gay
bar owners, pushed for guarantees that similar provocative displays would
not be part of the upcoming parade. Pride planners were sensitive to their
demands because, in addition to wanting to include this important segment of the gay and lesbian community, they did not want to alienate bar
owners and the financial support they brought to the parade.[54]

Planners—most of whom advocated gay pride or gay power
strategies—saw any formal restrictions on parade entries as contrary to
the parade's mission to make gay identity visible in all its forms. To planning committee leader Del Whan, restricting the expression of Pride
participants simply reproduced the repression that gays and lesbians experienced in broader society: "This is a liberationist parade. Some gay
people stand in the way of gay liberation, and it's unfortunate. Many
times they are more obstructive than the heterosexuals."[55] As a gay
power activist, Whan wanted Pride to further her goal of overturning
heteronormative culture, which meant encouraging free expression even
if—especially if—it offended mainstream cultural sensibilities. Similarly,
Morris Kight, head of Los Angeles gay power group Gay Liberation
Front (GLF) and a key CSW in Los Angeles organizer in 1970 and 1971,
thought that any censorship would go against the spirit of Stonewall,
which Pride commemorated. "To compromise that totally into an exclu-
sionary affair," he said, "would be no credit to the veterans of Christopher Street. Gay has been the subject of total exclusion for four thousand
years. It behooves us to break up that habit of exclusion."[56] As we saw
in chapter 1, the Stonewall riots of 1969 were notable for the prominent
participation of feminine gay men and drag queens—individuals who
had been previously discouraged from visibly participating in homophile demonstrations. Since its inception, Pride was meant to be a demonstration of gays as they are without compromise to what was palatable

to mainstream culture. For Whan and Kight, censoring any displays meant excluding members of the gay and lesbian community and presenting only a whitewashed picture of gay identity. Such a move would be both ineffective and anathema to the inclusive spirit of Pride.

In the end, the Los Angeles planning committee issued guidelines for parade entries but did not place formal restrictions on what could or could not be displayed. The guidelines urged parade contingents to consider the impact of their entries on the effort to build solidarity within the gay and lesbian community and to think about the messages that their displays sent to both gay and straight people. Planners asked contingents to keep in mind the goal of building a sense of pride in gay sexuality.[57] Despite this concession, HELP, the group that led the push for formal restrictions, withdrew support for the parade. Los Angeles in 1972 did manage to avoid provocative displays, but—due to the prolonged infighting and, perhaps, the *Advocate*'s intent coverage of it— the parade drew fewer participants than previous years. The *Advocate* marked its size at four hundred marchers and five thousand spectators, compared to two thousand marchers and fifteen thousand spectators in 1971.[58] With its smaller size there was only one float this year, sponsored by the arts and entertainment group SPREE (Society of Pat Rocco Enlightened Enthusiasts). As in previous years, contingents were made up of activists groups, community service groups, and the gay religious group Metropolitan Community Church.[59]

When a social movement experiences infighting, factions work out big conceptual issues about the strategic direction of their movement through debates over small practical issues.[60] In New York, gay men and lesbians with different views on inclusion, commercialism, and movement strategy argued over the practical matter of whether to move toward a parade format by including floats and bars. Similarly, as Los Angeles planners worked to balance gay rights activists' demand for a formal restriction on provocative displays and gay pride and gay power adherents' insistence on open expression, community members worked through the larger issue of strategic visibility. While debate over the big conceptual issues continues today, planners in Pride's early years solved (for the most part) the small practical problems by settling on a parade format in New York and deciding on guidelines, but not formal restrictions, for contingent displays in Los Angeles.

Pride Grows across the Country

As flagship events went through their first growing pains in New York and Los Angeles, gays and lesbians staged Pride demonstrations for the first time in San Francisco; Detroit; Hackensack, New Jersey; Dallas; Atlanta; and Philadelphia. They confronted many of the same divisions over strategy as they discussed the details of planned events, but their debates were less heated as they focused on the initial challenge of staging this large event. Similarly, gays and lesbians in Chicago and Boston came together to grow events now in their second year.

Four hundred miles north of Los Angeles in San Francisco, community leaders put on a parade that involved diverse gay and lesbians, attracted fifty thousand people, and avoided the controversial displays that marred Los Angeles's parade in 1971. Though it was by many accounts a success, to achieve such popularity, the city's first Pride parade intentionally avoided explicit demands for change. Gay and lesbian activists of San Francisco initially resisted commemorating Stonewall with a parade because they felt they were making inroads working with police rather than rioting against them, and thus viewed Pride as ineffective.[61] By 1972, though, it was clear that Pride was catching on, moving beyond the commemoration of one event and becoming a public show of unity and pride for the gay and lesbian community. As such, many decided it was time to get on board and stage their own grand parade.

San Francisco Pride planners fashioned their event after Los Angeles's parade model, complete with floats, vehicles, and music. Many in the San Francisco gay and lesbian community had participated in the 1970 and 1971 parades of CSW, and Los Angeles organizer Morris Kight travelled up the coast to help the city put on its first Pride parade. This close connection may explain why San Francisco's parade looked like the one in Los Angeles. Also in parade form, San Francisco Pride drew throngs of spectators, organized itself around many contingents rather than a cohesive marching block, and passed by a reviewing stand where a panel of judges awarded prizes for best entries.[62]

The grand parade brought together many different groups. According to the *Advocate*, "drag queens, gay businesses, entertainers, religious groups, prison groups, gay organizations, reigning 'royalty,' leather men, radicals, street people, conservatives, lesbians, and 'hunky guys,' were all represented in parade contingents."[63] Planners achieved this diversity by explicitly ruling out any displays or speeches that could have been seen as obscene or contentious. Though gay power, gay pride, and gay rights activist groups were certainly welcome in the parade, it does not appear that they used the venue to provocatively challenge cultural meanings or to demand specific legal change. Committee members planned the event as a celebratory parade and not a protest march as they worried that a demonstration would alienate much of the gay and lesbian community and would fail to draw a large crowd.[64] In making this choice, they were able bring throngs of supporters to the parade but, as lesbian activists elsewhere feared, they may have turned Pride into an entertaining spectacle rather than a contentious, change-oriented demonstration.[65] In an interesting twist from the anti-commercial stance of gay power activists elsewhere, the parade's Grand Trophy (yes, in true parade fashion, this one gave out awards) went to a GLF contingent from Bakersfield that was sponsored by its local Jolly Times gay bar.[66] While gays and lesbians in New York and Los Angeles debated the proper format and participant rules for Pride, San Francisco put on a smooth parade that brought diverse people together in novel ways under its guidelines. In doing so, however, it may have sacrificed the punch of contentious messages that were evident elsewhere. This issue of balancing carefree festivity with serious contestation is one that Pride participants still face today.

Other cities in the U.S. hosted Pride events in myriad forms, most trending toward the New York format of a serious purpose with festive parade elements, and a focus on bringing together diverse subgroups within the gay and lesbian community. Detroit planner Susan Williamson said of her event, "Though this will be a serious demonstration, we do not intend to lose our sense of humor . . . The atmosphere will be festive, with floats and a good bit of camp."[67] Likewise, Pride marches in Chicago, Hackensack, New Jersey, Dallas, and Atlanta also mixed festivity with contention, and were able to bring together diverse segments of their local gay and lesbian communities with minimal conflict.[68] Each of these events drew a few hundred people—up to one thousand in Chicago—and included activist groups, community groups, and like the event in Detroit, "a good bit of camp."[69] There were no reports of provocative displays like those in previous Los Angeles parades.

Atlanta, one of the parades that I focus on in this book, held its first Pride march in 1972.[70] Like other Pride events in their first year, Atlanta Pride brought together about 250 gay and lesbian activists, artists, entertainers, and ordinary members of the community in a festive march. The event had only one vehicle, a truck that carried the Women's Song Theatre as they sang gay-themed songs.[71] Though including floats was a source of controversy in New York, in Atlanta it seems that it was more a question of resources. Floats need to be sponsored by an established, well-organized group with financial backing. Though Atlanta did have a number of activist and community groups, in 1972 there was not one big enough to sponsor a float, nor did a commercial gay bar take on the task. Instead participants took to the streets on foot to, according to GLF Co-Chair Bob Bilderback, "declare to our gay brothers and sisters and the community in general our individuality and self-pride."[72] Like their counterparts in New York and Los Angeles during Pride's inaugural years, community members in Atlanta and elsewhere concentrated on bringing diverse gays and lesbians together in open display. In doing so, they largely avoided the heated conflicts that marked more established events in 1972.

Once again Boston—and now Philadelphia—hosted marches that were a bit less festive and more overtly contentious. Like the previous year, in taking a different form, they show that while the Pride idea was very powerful, what it meant in practice was still in flux. In these two cities, gay and lesbian participants marched to sites of state power—the city jail and the Massachusetts State House in Boston and Independence Hall in Philadelphia—and contested both the state and culture with dramatic displays rather than with humor or festivity.[73] In Philadelphia, several marchers, donning masks and chains, placed a symbolic coffin at Independence Hall to represent shedding their guilt over homosexuality.[74] Like the previous year's demonstration, Boston's parade participants clearly protested state actions while also contesting the cultural code that treats homosexuality as a source of shame and a thing to be hidden.

After three years, the Pride concept had caught on across the country, but there were still many models for what a Pride event could be. In Los Angeles and San Francisco, Pride was unmistakably a parade with floats, music, and entertainment. In this form, the event embodied the gay power and gay pride idea of defying heteronormative cultural oppression by openly affirming gay identity. Guidelines in Los Angeles helped avoid the provocative displays of 1970 and 1971 that angered gay rights advocates, but without formal rules, this faction still worried about the visible image presented of gays and lesbians. They preferred a modest representation that would be more likely to sway individuals to adopt favorable attitudes about gay people. Rules on displays and a parade format enabled a popular event in San Francisco that brought diverse people together, but many worried that the serious message of social change was lost in the spectacle. In most other cities, Pride took a form somewhere between a parade and a traditional protest march, what I call a festive march. Following the lead of New York City, these events in Chicago, Detroit, Hackensack, Dallas, and Atlanta incorporated parade elements like floats with the procession of mainly contingents who marched on foot while alternately cheering and chanting. Once again this format allowed for expressions of pride in gay identity, but resisted charges of frivolity incurred by parades. Finally, two cities, Boston and Philadelphia hosted Pride marches that looked most like traditional protests with fewer festive elements and routes that ended at sites of state power. Community members in these cities did not yet confront disagreement over provocative displays and thus largely avoided the larger conceptual issue of gay visibility.

Through their differences, Pride events were each conceived as mass demonstrations to affirm gay sexuality and make visible gay and lesbian people. Though some events included challenges to state power, all targeted culture for change. All were fun and uplifting for those who marched and those who watched from the sidelines. As Pride grew, planning committees struggled with how to best make a cultural challenge, how to include all segments of the gay and lesbian community, and what role fun should play in the events.

1973–1975: Crystallization

From 1973 to 1975, Pride solidified in form as a parade with a contentious purpose. With this format, community leaders were able to balance the diverse strategies of gay power, gay pride, and gay rights activists as well as divisions between gay men and lesbians. Though the community did not come to a consensus on strategy, as a tactic, the parade format made it possible to air multiple messages within one event as each contingent put on its own display. These varied messages targeted cultural meanings in the world, cultural attitudes in the mind, and specific state and institutional policies, while making visible many different segments of the gay and lesbian community. Through discussions on the practical matter of format, planners and community members shaped Pride into a showcase of the community's "unity in diversity," united as they were by a gay identity that was expressed in diverse ways.

Similar to Atlanta's events in 1972, the question of what form Pride should take became one of resources more than one of intention. Larger, more diverse gay and lesbian communities like those in San Francisco and Chicago staged grander parades as community groups and local bars sponsored floats and decorated vehicles. Smaller communities and those hosting Pride for the first year put on simpler marches, incorporating festivity on a more modest scale through songs, cheers, and the occasional truck with streamers. San Diego, for example, saw its first Pride event in 1974 when a group organized by the newly established gay community center marched without a permit in a show of visibility.[75] However, while the question of format died down, greater concern emerged over how Pride parades could carry a serious message amid the all of the revelry. Though the gay power strand of activism waned, gay pride and gay rights activists continued to struggle over how best to represent the gay and lesbian community. In 1972, planners in New York saw a march-without-floats format as a way to keep Pride serious and oriented toward change. In the following years, those in New York and elsewhere focused less on format and more on how to accommodate all interested contingents. The question became, how could Pride succeed in to bringing out the entire gay and lesbian community—including gays and lesbians who would not normally come to a political demonstration—all without watering down Pride's demand for change?

While the organization of Pride parades in 1972 was marked by conflict, in 1973, it was marked by calm. The CSLD of New York City was a "triumphant procession" of about three thousand marchers and up to twenty thousand spectators. It is unclear whether floats were included that year, but the issue did not appear to be the subject of controversy as it had been in 1972. Gay bars participated heavily, making up half of all contingents, and were joined by the same mix of activists, religious groups, and individual gays and lesbians who marched in years past.[76] Similarly, in Chicago and San Francisco, gays and lesbians from many different organizations and businesses marched, danced on floats, or rode in cars in the cities' parades.[77] Both parades were light on explicitly contentious messages, leading the *San Francisco Chronicle* to conclude that its parade "was not a plea for general public approval as much as a celebration of tolerance already won through public relations campaigns in recent years."[78] Across the country, smaller Pride parades mixed celebration with contention. In Atlanta, two hundred marchers sang "God Bless America," "We Shall Overcome," and chanted "2, 4, 6, 8—gay is just as good as straight," while in Pittsburgh, sixty people urged others to "come out, come out, wherever you are!"[79]

In contrast, Los Angeles did not host a Pride parade in 1973. After all the infighting of 1972, it seems that no one was willing or able to take the lead and try to bring all factions together. According to Troy Perry, head of the MCC, many thought the meetings to organize the 1972 parade were consumed by fights that left little room for actual planning.[80] Morris Kight, also frustrated with the continued tensions, questioned whether staging Pride was the best use of gay and lesbian collective efforts. Activists had recently worked on municipal elections in Los Angeles in 1973 and, as Kight argued,

> An enormous amount of the community's creativity was exhausted in the elections, which have just concluded. No other community in the nation had that going for them. In the cities where Christopher Street celebrations are planned, they don't seem to have that distracting influence. We had it, and I believe that a good many people who have to do with gay community opinion felt that our efforts, if directed towards a major street demonstration, would exhaust us away from the political campaign.[81]

Kight thought that, if given the choice between staging Pride and pushing for political change, activists should choose the latter. Others, including writers for the *Advocate*, disagreed. Martin St. John, who reported the story, pointed out that New York City, Minneapolis, and Detroit all recently had local elections but still held Pride parades. Likewise, the president of the Los Angeles Gay Community Alliance, Gerry Denning, noted that Pride often brings out many gays and lesbians who do not get involved in state-focused politics.[82] In another *Advocate* article, Arthur Evans argued that Pride was still very much relevant because it rejects the cultural message that gays are deviant and instead affirms their self-worth and collective strength.[83] While Kight was ready to move on to other activist projects, many in Los Angeles still found Pride worth the effort.

Kight's view on priorities of the gay and lesbian movement reflects the flourishing of activism in the early 1970s. Pride was the largest and most visible gay collective demonstration that was inspired by Stonewall, but it was certainly not the only one. Activists in many major cities petitioned for municipal gay rights ordinances, pressed politicians to support gay rights, demonstrated against continued police harassment, and confronted mass media outlets on their portrayal of gays and lesbians.[84] In 1973, activists for gay rights won their biggest battle yet, when after years of public confrontation and behind-the-scenes pressure, the American Psychological Association removed homosexuality from its Diagnostic and Statistical Manual.[85] This marked a withdrawal of institutional support for the cultural belief of homosexuality as a mental illness. The role of Pride as a cultural protest then crystallized as activists launched campaigns for gay and lesbian equality on multiple fronts in the early and mid-1970s. While Pride demonstrations still had space for state-directed messages, other tactics targeted the state and major institutions—and thus left Pride to primarily challenge cultural codes about homosexuality.

By 1974, parades moved away from explicitly targeting the state and formal institutions. While groups in many cities organized marches and rallies focused on these concrete targets as part of Pride Week, the parade itself did not make specific demands of the state or formal institutions except through a few scattered contingents. In Detroit, for instance, activists held a rally and march to the City-County Government Building on the Tuesday before Saturday's parade.[86] In New York, activists picketed at St. Paul's Cathedral and at a Brooklyn Orthodox Synagogue during Pride Week (but before the big parade) to protest the opposition of these institutions against a proposed municipal gay rights bill.[87] State- and institution-directed campaigns also motivated new people to attend the Pride parade where, either as spectators or a marching contingent, they could voice their particular concerns. One participant of

New York's large gay Catholic Dignity contingent was quoted saying, "The archdiocese really forced all of us to come out this year."[88] For this lifelong Catholic, the Church's vocal opposition to the proposed municipal antidiscrimination ordinance known as "Intro 2" demanded an equally vocal response. Marching publicly in Pride was a way for this man and others to stand up to the denigration that they had long faced from prominent institutions like the Catholic Church.

Pride was thus a venue for many messages, including but not limited to those demanding legal and institutional change. Many came with the simple message that they were gay and unashamed, others with more elaborate displays that celebrated elements of gay culture like drag performance and camp humor.

While most Pride parades in 1974 seemed to put on events that were both serious in purpose and fun, any contentious messages in San Francisco appeared to be drowned out by frivolity. As the *Advocate* put it, "Frivolity and joy were much more in evidence than militance and social determination."[89] There were a few floats and marching units that called specifically for gay cultural esteem and political rights, but these were vastly outnumbered by contingents that made no explicit call for change. Instead, gay bars and magazines sponsored festive floats, while a dozen entries featured drag queen "royalty," reminiscent of the pageantry displayed at other mainstream parades. The mainstream newspaper *San Francisco Chronicle* charged that, with so few explicit demands, there was little evidence that the parade had any purpose beyond revelry. Some in San Francisco's gay and lesbian community agreed, while others like leader Allen Blade argued that, "If open celebration of your lifestyle, if joy and good times and loving companionship on the streets of a great city, if pride in our own gay businesses and activities is not an important part of the concept of liberation, then somebody needs to do some rethinking."[90] Like Blade, I argue that Pride's displays do constitute cultural protest, but as San Francisco's 1974 parade and some contemporary parades illustrate, the fun aspect of Pride can lead to frivolity when it is not accompanied by cultural contestation.[91] In an attempt to avoid division between gay pride, gay rights, and other activist visions for social change, San Francisco planners in 1974 seemed to avoid contention altogether in favor of a good party.

As the 1975 parades approached, the *Advocate* devoted editorials and commentaries to consider the purpose of Pride. In side-by-side commentaries, writers debated whether Pride was "serious" or "a circus." David Brill from Boston argued that Pride conveys the simple but important message that gay is good. "With apologies to *Love Story*," he wrote, "gay pride means never having to say you're sorry to anyone for being gay."[92] Pride parades make gays and lesbians more visible in American society, he wrote, and they were building awareness that the gay community was much more diverse than the representative white gay men who were often the most visible.[93] Christopher Stone from Los Angeles disagreed, saying that rather than showing diversity, Pride parades present "a small group of self-centered and slightly hysterical individuals" who only reinforced negative stereotypes.[94] He felt that women at Pride were a bit more serious-minded, but were drowned out by male revelers, noting that "television reporters didn't have to add a word to parade footage to make the coverage superb anti-gay propaganda."[95] In the end, Stone charged, Pride only hurt the cause of gay and lesbian liberation.

Other commentators moderated Brill and Stone's arguments. In the gay-pride vein that advocated both cultural and political activism to bring about social change, these critics favored Pride parades but urged for more involvement in both Pride-related events and other types of activism. Commentator George Whitmore acknowledged that Pride is an important annual celebration and public display of protest, but that it cannot be the whole of gay and lesbian activism; the community, he argued, also needs to work for political change.[96] An editorial contended that Pride should continue to show gays and lesbians as they are, even if the resulting displays reinforce negative cultural stereotypes. "Part of gay reality," the editor wrote, "is that some gay men like to wear dresses, some like to wear leather, some like to wear nothing. Some gay women prefer combat boots and hair under their arms . . . Like every other community, we have people who do not conform."[97] According to this writer, it is up to those who defy stereotypes to make themselves visible by participating in Pride. As another editor wrote, "Circus and Serious, unified and fragmented, [Pride is] the closest thing to a national holiday we have yet."[98]

Conclusion

Through the first half of the 1970s, gays and lesbians across the country worked to establish Pride as a simultaneous national holiday and contentious demonstration. Though united in their desire for a society in which they could live openly and be treated with respect, gays and lesbians were divided in how best to achieve this goal. Gay rights, gay pride, and gay power activists each offered different strategies, some focusing on changes in the state and individual cultural attitudes and others envisioning a more thorough cultural upheaval. Through debates over the practical challenges of format and censorship, gays and lesbians clarified their stances on issues of visibility, inclusion, and movement strategy.

The debates about representation, tone, and the gravity of Pride have persisted to the presented day. But by 1975, after six years of growth, Pride was established as an annual parade with themes of public declaration of gay identity, unity among diverse people, celebration, and a continued demand for social change. Like the first events in 1970, the core of the Pride phenomenon was rooted in the actions of gays publicly showing themselves as they are and without apology. As Pride events grew bigger and juggled demands from more segments of the gay and lesbian community, planners struggled to maintain this core. Likewise, each time a group in a new city organized a Pride event, they adapted an increasingly familiar model to their own communities. The first six years of Pride did not see a resolution to all of the issues that such a project presented, but planners were successful in settling on a final format for Pride's celebratory, collective, and public declaration of gay sexuality. From 1975 on, Pride was fashioned as a parade—complete with multiple contingents, decorated vehicles (when possible), and an air of celebration—rather than as a simpler state-directed march.[99]

While Pride has certainly evolved since 1975—with greater corporate involvement, in particular, beginning in the 1990s—it was in the early 1970s that Pride established itself as a culturally meaningful phenomenon.[100] Pride parades have since spread to both big and small cities across the country (and the world) in much the same form as the first parades in 1975. This book explores the sociological meaning of Pride as a collective action, making our focus the contemporary working of Pride rather than its development as a historical phenomenon. In this first part, I have examined how Pride was established as an annual parade to unify gay and lesbian community and demand their inclusion in the wider society. In the second part, I skip forward to 2010 to analyze how communities across the U.S. employ Pride to push for similar goals.

The words of Jim Kepner, as quoted in the epigraph of this chapter, proved to be remarkably prescient. In 1971, Kepner claimed that the Los Angeles parade would not even begin to reach its potential until there were "at least twenty times that many marching; until far more than three or four gay businesses [were] represented."[101] Well, by 2010, with four hundred thousand people marching in or watching Los Angeles's Pride parade and scores of business sponsors, it seemed it had reached this potential, and then some (see appendix C for a complete review of Pride's growth from 1975 to 2010). Moreover, Pride has spread to 116 cities across the U.S. and now draws a total of over six million people. From the early years of establishing Pride as an annual parade to declare gay identity, Pride has grown every year to the massive phenomenon that it is today.

In the next chapters, I jump from Pride's foundational years to consider just what Pride is today in America. Through the lens of six diverse parades, I look at the ways in which Pride contests cultural meanings about gay sexuality and gender transgression and how this varies depending on each parade's local context. I also consider how Pride parades continue to tackle many of the challenges encountered by participants in early parades, such as how to maintain a serious message while staging a fun and festive event and how to fully include all in the LGBT community. In a nutshell, I consider how Pride is doing with regard to the rest of Kepner's vision of the ultimate goal: to "produce on the streets the process of liberation" and to "show with a force of numbers . . . that Gays are indeed all kinds."

PART II

Pride Now

3

"We're Here, We're Queer, Get Used to It!"

Cultural Contestation at Pride

I'm of Irish descent. And I have much more pride in being
gay than I do in being Irish because I think that everyone
likes to be Irish on St. Patrick's Day. But you have to be pretty
brave to be gay on Pride Day.
—Blake, a gay male spectator at the 2010 Pride parade in
Burlington, Vermont

Blake is a gay man in his early thirties living in Burlington, Vermont.
By all evidence his city is very supportive of LGBT people. Vermont
was the first state to change its marriage laws to include same-sex couples through the legislative process rather than by court order, and the
issue has been far less controversial than in most states. Gay couples
can regularly be seen walking hand-in-hand in the city's main business
district without backlash and LGBT families find ready acceptance in
their neighborhoods. Despite this, Blake resisted going to Pride until
2010 because, while he is proud to be gay, he did not want to be quite
so public about it. To Blake, parades like Pride and St. Patrick's Day are
events where identity is on full display. St. Patrick's Day is all about Irish
identity, and even those who do not trace their heritage to the Emerald
Isle "go Irish" (albeit a caricatured version of it) for the day. Similarly,
Pride is all about queer identity; but with continued cultural stigma, it
takes courage to express this identity openly, even in a gay-friendly city
like Burlington. In a culture where homosexuality is still regarded as
inferior, Blake "had to be brave" to proclaim his gay sexuality in such a
public way.

In contrast to Burlington, Salt Lake City is definitely not a city known
for its LGBT population. Utah citizens approved a constitutional amend-
ment banning same-sex marriage in 2004 by a vote of 66% in favor and

34% opposed. A federal court overturned the ban in December 2013 but with an appeal by the state government and a majority of citizens still opposed, the issue remains contentious.[1] Though residents are aware of and can be accepting of their LGBT neighbors, Salt Lake City's culture is dominated by the Mormon Church. With a strong emphasis on the nuclear family and belief that homosexual behavior is sinful, the Mormon Church does not have a place for LGBT people within its communities.[2] While many LGBT people still find accepting networks, those I talked to felt that they were unwelcome in Salt Lake City as a whole.

Across the United States, Pride parades are held in all kinds of local cultural climates, from the liberal and gay-friendly Burlington, Vermont to the conservative Salt Lake City, Utah and everywhere in between. Running through these local climates is heteronormativity, or the cultural code of meaning that defines heterosexuality as the natural model for how men and women interact.[3] Wrapped up in this code is a strict gender binary in which two genders are opposite and complementary with no overlap in social roles, behavioral norms, or even personality types.[4] LGBT people deviate from the heteronormative cultural code in two ways: through sexual orientation (desire for the same sex) and gender transgression (identification with—or explicit display of—qualities incongruous with one's corresponding male/female body).[5] Heteronormativity plays out a bit differently in each community; in Burlington, queer people are tolerated, even welcomed, but feel a current of "otherness" that they cannot quite shake, whereas in Salt Lake City, the value of heterosexual families is shouted from the rooftops and LGBT people are pointedly left out.

Alongside heteronormativity runs an increasingly strong cultural code of tolerance. Public opinion surveys over the last five decades find that Americans have much more tolerant attitudes toward a number of stigmatized groups, especially LGBT people.[6] The shift in support for LGBT political rights, notably same-sex marriage, has been particularly swift and has caused researchers to reexamine old theories of opinion change.[7] Similarly, recent studies of LGBT people and their straight friends and neighbors describe a marked softening in mainstream treatment of LGBT people so that in many places they are able to live openly without fear of outright hostility.[8] Whereas gays and lesbians of the 1970s lived with frequent harassment from police and fellow citizens, many LGBT people are unmolested and even accepted as they go about their daily lives. These changes in Americans' attitudes and behaviors indicate an emerging standard to approach LGBT people with tolerance instead of condemnation—making it possible for LGBTs to live freely and openly.

Though growing tolerance has made LGBT lives much better, it has not reversed the heteronormative cultural code that continues to position queer sexuality and gender as inferior to heterosexuality. While many Americans now tolerate their LGBT friends and neighbors, this acceptance is often limited to those LGBT people who conform to mainstream gender and relationship norms.[9] That is, gays, lesbians, and bisexuals (and transgender individuals, but to a much lesser extent) may be accepted, but only to the extent that their queerness does not disturb the larger heteronormative order. Queer sexuality and gender may be tolerated, but not celebrated or normalized.[10] American culture has come a long way in its tolerance of LGBT people since Pride began in the 1970s, but the persistence of heteronormativity means that cultural equality is far from complete. At each Pride parade I studied, participants confronted heteronormativity by promoting alternative messages about queer gender and sexuality.

A change in culture requires a change in how we define and understand the meaning of certain things. Culture is "located" in two places: it is "in the mind" in the form of our internalized attitudes and values, and it is "in the world" as symbols and meanings that we use to communicate with one another.[11] Achieving cultural equality for LGBT people entails changing both individuals' heteronormative cultural attitudes that judge queer sexuality and gender transgression as wrong or distasteful and the explicit symbols in the world that couple queerness with inferiority.[12] Activists can adopt two models to change culture. They can work "inside-out" by targeting change in individual attitudes or go "outside-in" by attempting to alter the symbols and meanings in the world that inform these attitudes.[13] With both models, activists communicate cultural messages about what things such as queer sexuality and gender mean.

In 1970, participants marched proudly through the streets of New York and Los Angeles to show that homosexuality means strength, love, pride in oneself, and joy. They fought against the norms, symbols, and ideas in mainstream culture that depicted homosexuality to mean moral bankruptcy, mental illness, and criminal behavior. In the budding movement for LGBT rights, gays and lesbians crafted and crystallized Pride as an annual parade to declare gay identity in protest of an anti-gay culture that proscribes invisibility and shame. From the political and cultural backlash of the late 1970s and 1980s to the new cultural visibility of the 1990s to the growing awareness of LGBT lives in recent years—as nearly all Americans encountered same-sex marriage at the ballot box in the 2000s—a lot has changed for LGBT people since 1970. Yet through this changing cultural landscape, they continue to stage Pride events in their struggle to achieve cultural equality. This chapter explores how each Pride parade I studied communicated the messages that queer sexuality and gender should be visible, supported, and celebrated. In chapter 4, I show how these messages differed along with their context.

Visibility

Above all, Pride parades aim to increase the visibility of LGBT people. Early Pride pioneers marched with the rallying cry, "Out of the bars and into the streets," declaring their intention to make their gay presence known. Forty years later, there are many signs of this project's success. LGBT people today have an unprecedented level of visibility—with record numbers of gay, lesbian, and bisexual (though still few transgender) characters in mainstream television and a number of openly LGBT politicians at local, state, and even federal levels.[14] Americans are also more likely to see LGBT people in their everyday lives; a 2013 Gallup poll found that three-quarters of Americans said that they knew someone who is LGBT.[15] In light of such progress, sociologist James Joseph Dean argues that we are now in a "post-closeted era" in which many gays and lesbians no longer need to hide their sexual difference in mainstream society.[16]

Though it is vastly more common to see openly LGBT people today than it was in 1970, public images of queerness are still remarkably narrow. Media representations of LGBT people remain limited to those that fit best within a heteronormative framework: gays, lesbians, and bisexuals—but rarely transgender people—who follow gender norms and traditional relationship models.[17] In their daily lives, LGBT people are often pressured to downplay their sexuality and conform to normative gender presentations, a situation that researchers refer to as "the gay-friendly closet."[18] Indeed, scholars who argue that we are now in a "post-closeted" or "post-gay" era also note that this new embrace of gays and lesbians is generally restricted to those who follow gender norms and traditional relationship styles.[19] Queerness continues to carry with it the stigma of difference and inferiority so that LGBT people feel pressured to hide their sexuality and gender identity. This stigma often remains when one is "out" as LGBT, such that they manage it by avoiding the subject or educating others about sexuality.[20] Thus, though they find varying degrees of social acceptance—and are, in some places, welcomed in a way that would have been unthinkable to Pride pioneers of the 1970s—LGBT people still struggle to be fully visible in a world dominated by a cultural code that privileges heterosexuality.

As queer theorists explain, LGBT invisibility goes much deeper than the denial or condemnation of gay sexuality and gender transgression itself. In fact, there has been a marked reduction of such outright condemnation in the American public sphere. The new code of tolerance relegates explicit statements about the evils of homosexuality to the fringes of public discourse. However, LGBT lives are still persistently left out of public depictions of moral citizens. Such invisibility is the result of a prevailing heteronormative culture, which values heterosexual coupling as the "gold standard" for romantic relationships, families, and individual sexuality. LGBT relationships and families are often not defined as such both culturally and legally, rendering them socially invisible.[21] Though LGBT people appear in the media considerably more today than in the homophile era, LGBT news and television characters are still presented through a heteronormative lens. Characters are alternatively stereotyped and desexualized so that, while present, they still reinforce the primacy of heterosexuality.[22] For instance, sexual desire is all but nonexistent in the relationship of the gay couple Mitch and Cam on *Modern Family* (a show that I love, for the record). Though the inclusion of these characters is indeed a step toward full LGBT equality, by removing their sexuality, the show reinforces a continued discomfort with same-sex desire.

Visibility (or lack thereof) was certainly on the minds of Salt Lake City Pride participants on June 6, 2010. While the city itself has a thriving alternative culture that is quite gay-friendly, it is also home to the headquarters of the conservative Church of Jesus Christ of Latter-Day Saints (also known as Mormon). Church doctrine and culture emphasize family life, believing that God organizes the family form as one man, one woman, and children and that this is the most important social unit.[23] The Church officially condemns homosexual behavior as sinful—and, for that matter, all sexual behavior outside of heterosexual marriage. While Mormons by and large advocate tolerance and compassion toward LGBT people, their beliefs place same-sex relationships squarely outside the category of family.[24] Over half the population of Salt Lake County is Mormon.[25] According to Pride participants, the Church dominates the local culture. Thus, heteronormativity in Salt Lake City has a strong spiritual basis. Many Salt Lake City residents regard traditional gender roles and heterosexuality as moral imperatives, so they both celebrate straight families and condemn queerness. Families are incredibly visible in Salt Lake City, but LGBT families—and often the larger LGBT community –are left out.[26]

Utah Pride participants took over downtown Salt Lake City on a Sunday in early June. The parade was scheduled to start at 11 a.m., and by 10:30 a.m., over twenty thousand people had made their way downtown. There was an air of excitement as marching contingents lined up and spectators settled into their spots. At the parade line-up area, members of a flag drill team called the Righteously Outrageous Twirling Corps (ROTC) prepared their horses and unfurled their American, state of Utah, and rainbow flags. Close by, a female musician tuned her guitar while sitting on a trailer bed. The trailer was pulled by a U-Haul truck with a large handwritten sign that read, "What do lesbians take on a second date?" It is a familiar joke (the punch line: a U-Haul) referring to lesbians' real or imagined tendency to move quickly into serious relationships. Near her, the DC Cowboys, clad only in very short cut-off jeans, boots, and cowboy hats, practiced their country dance routine to a Lady Gaga tune. Behind me I heard a man tell his friend, "This is what I love about Pride!" I assume he was referring to the Cowboys' dancing bodies and, perhaps, the rare open display of gay sexuality on the streets of Salt Lake City.

FIGURE 3.1 The DC Cowboys dancing group performs a short routine on their float in Salt Lake City's Pride parade. Photo courtesy of Jacqualine Müller.

While most spectators cheered the Cowboys and other marchers who strutted their stuff, not all agree that such overt sexual displays are either appropriate or helpful to the cause of LGBT equality. As I will discuss further, sexual displays are a flashpoint for debate over how Pride parades represent LGBT people to the broader world.

While marchers prepared, spectators gathered with friends along the parade route. Most were dressed in shorts and t-shirts, appropriate for the sunny weekend weather. Many marked their LGBT identity with coded styles, such as cargo shorts and short hair for lesbians or close-fit V-neck shirts for gay men. These personal styles have been developed by LGBT people to signal their identity to others within the community. As mainstream awareness of queer sexuality has grown, many outside the LGBT community recognize these markers as well, albeit often in the form of derogatory stereotypes (the "mannish lesbian," for example). Participants also held hands with same-sex partners and flirted with new acquaintances. Some spectators were bolder in their divergence from mainstream norms. Though they were few in number, drag queens strutted down the streets in complete make-up, dresses, and high heels.

Rainbows were ubiquitous. Marching contingents held rainbow flags and decorated their floats with rainbow balloons and streamers. The contingent from Wells Fargo went all out, dressing in each color of the rainbow while holding matching flags. The effect was a human flag made up of fifty people marching behind the company's signature horse and buggy. Spectators wore shirts, socks, headbands, beaded necklaces, and leis, all in rainbow colors. At the end of the parade, a massive, block-long flag was unfurled on a side street adjacent to the parade route. Parade participants played, danced, and took pictures on this giant symbol of LGBT community. The rainbow flag was designed specifically for this purpose in 1978 by San Francisco artist Gilbert Baker.[27] Each color was meant to represent a different aspect of gay and lesbian life such as art, nature, and healing. The flag has also come to represent the LGBT community, similar to how foreign national flags in the U.S. represent ethnic communities. At Pride, rainbow flags, clothing, and accessories were used to make the community visible.

Salt Lake City's LGBT Pride parade started at 11 a.m. with a roar. Like all parades I visited, save Burlington, the Dykes on Bikes had the honor of leading the parade. This group also got its start at a Pride parade, when twenty women motorcyclists headed the 1976 San Francisco Pride parade.[28] With Pride established as an annual event to affirm gay identity, these women joined in order to make visible their own brand of lesbianism, one that included such masculine markers as motorcycles and leather clothing.

In Salt Lake City about thirty women made up the Dykes on Bikes. Some wore leather vests and most had a butch (or, more masculine) gender presentation with short hair and clothing that de-emphasized feminine features. From their physical appearance to their Harley Davidson motorcycles, the women adopted symbols of masculinity in ways that displayed their lesbian identities. With the parade line-up complete and spectators clamoring to begin, the Dykes on Bikes revved their engines to kick off the parade and were greeted with loud cheers.

While Dykes on Bikes showed their identities through actions and styles of dress, other parade participants did so with overt displays of sexuality. Like the DC Cowboys, a number of male marchers and spectators went shirtless. There is certainly nothing remarkable about shirtless men outdoors on a sunny summer day, but at Pride these displays were at least

FIGURE 3.2 Two Dykes on Bikes ride in San Diego's
Pride parade. Photo courtesy of Sarah Tompkins,
Serenity Styles Photography.

partly sexual. All the men I saw showed off their sculpted chests to the
admiration of onlookers, complete with approving looks and occasional
verbal compliments. There was not a beer belly in sight, indicating an
adherence to LGBT subcultural norms of desirability.[29] Interestingly, the
most overt show of sexuality in Salt Lake City's parade came from presumably straight women: dancers from a local strip club. As their float
moved along with the parade, the women danced on poles that held up
two tents. Heavily associated with heterosexual desire as pole dancers
are, their sexual dancing largely fell within a heteronormative understanding of human sexuality as between men and women. However, to
signal the group's (temporary, at least) affiliation with LGBT community, one wore a rainbow tutu on top of her tight tank top and short

shorts. Though this was an explicitly queer event, a parade organizer said they welcomed the group as a sign of broad acceptance for all kinds of sexuality.

In their everyday lives, LGBT people, particularly those in Salt Lake City, are not fully visible. Cultural images in the world of the ideal romantic couple, family, athlete, and citizen are rarely lesbian, gay, bisexual, or transgender. Pride parades challenge this invisibility with the opposite: a big, loud, colorful event staged on public city streets in the middle of the day. The parades made LGBT people impossible to ignore as participants blocked traffic and paraded their identities. Moreover, in Salt Lake City and elsewhere, Pride parades publicly offered images of LGBT people in all the roles—romantic partner, parent, athlete, citizen, even flag twirler—from which they are usually obscured.

Visibility has long been a goal of both Pride parades and of the LGBT movement more broadly.[30] Early Pride marchers used the rallying cry, "Out of the bars, into the streets!" to articulate their hope that by demonstrating openly rather than cowering in dark bars, they would bring new visibility to their community. Similarly, homophile activists staged Annual Reminders to bring a measure of visibility to the LGBT community and the discrimination it faced. Despite the tremendous growth in awareness of LGBT people since those early days, visibility remains a main message of Pride parades today.

Scholars classify two broadly defined strategies that activists use to counter heteronormativity and to make LGBT people more visible.[31] The first—a strategy to promote difference—emphasizes divergence from heterosexual norms, challenging the culture to accept LGBT people on their own terms. In 1970, the inaugural events in New York City and Los Angeles were remarkable for the way that participants openly displayed their homosexuality with hand-holding and declarative signs. In subsequent years, gays and lesbians debated whether this was the best way to present the community at Pride; some argued that participants should moderate their presentations while others preferred highlighting even those aspects of gay and lesbian life that the mainstream may find offensive. The second response—a strategy of sameness—is to downplay differences from heterosexuals by showing LGBT people as virtuous in culturally valued ways—as parents, citizens, and churchgoers—and thus worthy of acceptance into heteronormative culture. This response was typified in the pre-Stonewall Annual Reminders, when homophile activists dressed in suits and dresses and marched silently in front of Philadelphia's Independence Hall. Both of these responses to heteronormativity attempt to make LGBT people visible. The first challenges the culture to expand and make a place for LGBT people while the second emphasizes ways that LGBT people fit into existing culture.[32]

At the Pride parades in 2010, I observed both difference and sameness strategies as two distinct forms of visibility. Defiant visibility communicated that LGBT people exist and that they would continue to be present, regardless of whatever one thinks of them, while educational visibility dispelled misconceptions about LGBT people.[33] Each message attempts to change culture so that the world becomes a more accepting place for LGBT people, but does so primarily through different models. Adopting an outside-in model for cultural change, defiant visibility targets culture in the world by attempting to dismantle its heteronormativity to make room for queer people as they are. Educational visibility, meanwhile, relies on *both* inside-out and outside-in models. When targeting culture in the mind, participants ask individuals to see the ways that LGBT people fit into an admittedly heteronormative culture by communicating messages of educational visibility. These messages also target culture in the world by offering new images of LGBT people, though stopping short of the wholesale challenge to heteronormativity issued by defiant visibility.

Defiant visibility can be summed up by the familiar chant: "We're here, we're queer, get used to it!" With this message, Pride communicates that LGBT people will not change to accommodate or fit into heteronormative culture. Participants were defiant when they made themselves visible as LGBT without regard to how outsiders might judge them. For instance, lesbians in Salt Lake City, Atlanta, San Diego, New York City, and Fargo, North Dakota presented themselves without apology as they wore leather and rode their motorcycles with Dykes on Bikes. Nearly everything about their display—from their masculine or "butch" hair and clothing to their use of the label "dyke"—highlighted their divergence from heteronormative standards. Similarly, ubiquitous rainbow flags, from the temporary tattoos sported by the Speedo-and-bowtie-clad marchers of Queer Utah Athletic Club (QUAC) to the massive block-long flag unfurled at the end of Salt Lake City's parade visibly signaled the presence of LGBT people in the city and the defiance against the norm that heterosexuality rules public space.

From the "cockapillar" in Los Angeles's 1971 parade to the scantily clad members of the DC Cowboys and QUAC in Salt Lake City in 2010, overt displays of queer sexuality have long been a controversial part of Pride parades. By unambiguously showing same-sex desire, Pride participants flaunt the heteronormative cultural standard that makes heterosexuality the only publicly acceptable expression of human sexuality. By summarily rejecting this standard, sexual displays are very much a difference response to heteronormativity. While challenging dominant meanings can be productive, such disregard for mainstream norms may also provoke backlash in the form of hardened attitudes against LGBT people. As they did in the early days of Pride, LGBT people and allies debate the utility of difference and similar approaches to increase LGBT visibility (see chapter 4).

Pride participants invoked defiant visibility when they defended those sexual displays that others may read as offensive or frivolous. Ed, a gay man in Atlanta, said these displays were part of the Pride's defiant message:

> On the one hand, I could see that [de-emphasizing sexual displays would encourage support]. But on the other hand, I guess maybe their point is, yes, we are men who have sex with other men—deal with that.

Although sexual displays, such as scantily clad participants or suggestive dancing on floats, were rare in all parades, they have long been associated with Pride parades. Indeed, during the first few years of Pride, this type of overt sexuality caused some members of the gay and lesbian community to withdraw their support from the project because they believed such displays only confirmed cultural stereotypes about gays and lesbians. In 2010, unlike back then, I did not find strong opposition to sexual displays among the Pride participants I interviewed.[34] With greater tolerance for LGBT people as compared to forty years ago, participants did not worry that overt sexuality would cause intense negative backlash. Though some questioned whether such displays were helpful in achieving full LGBT equality, they did not fear it would significantly damage the cause. Rather than focusing on how sexual displays might influence mainstream attitudes about LGBT people, participants like

Ed found sexual displays to be meaningful because they challenge the cultural code that interprets gay sexuality as shameful, something to be hidden. In other words, participants saw the target of such displays as culture in the world, not culture in the mind.

Participants asserted that Pride's message of defiant visibility was important, even if this message might be misunderstood. Jonah, a gay man from San Diego, defended the importance of defiant visibility:

> Sometimes I think that they [mainstream society] just don't get it a lot. But at the same time, it's still very important that we do it because it's like, no matter what people think of our community, we're not going away. We're here and we're going to have our rainbow parades—whatever they want to think about it. You know, we're going to have our crazy floats and wear our high heels, and you know, do our thing. So I think it's very important for people to understand that, you know, we are a community . . . that loves everyone and likes to have a lot of fun and everything, and we're not going away. We are a part of San Diego.

Jonah described Pride as a way to demand belonging in the larger community of the city. In this light, the Dykes on Bikes and QUAC members in Speedos showed themselves to be just as much a part of the Salt Lake City community as the Mormon Church. Participants acknowledged that some displays are judged negatively, but said these individual opinions were not the point. Pride did not seek to change this view, but instead to assert the rightful place of the LGBT community in culture, despite it. With defiant visibility, Pride challenges the heteronormative code of meaning that casts LGBT people as inferior. Defiant visibility means being present despite any opposition—in fact, in the face of anticipated opposition.

Defiant visibility relies primarily on an outside-in model of cultural change. With this model, activists pursue cultural equality by starting with the meanings in the world that guide individual attitudes. The visible images of LGBT people *are* the message that is offered up in contrast to cultural images that leave LGBT people out. Messages of defiant visibility, like DC Cowboy's overt sexuality or the "cockapillar" from Los Angeles's 1971 march, are often criticized both within and outside of the LGBT community for poorly representing LGBT people. Someone skeptical of

LGBT cultural equality is likely to react negatively to such images because they tap into the heteronormative fears and stereotypes often attached to queer sexuality—the idea that LGBT people are overly interested in sex, for example. But while it may not be effective at persuading a change in individual attitudes (culture in the mind), defiant sexuality poses a compelling challenge to the heteronormative cultural code in the world. Pride marchers and spectators visibly counter heteronormativity by demonstrating that people with male bodies look beautiful in dresses and high heels, that romance and desire exists between women alone, that men are sexual objects for other men, and most of all, that LGBT people exist in society and are not going anywhere. Instead of trying to achieve cultural equality by changing individual attitudes toward gay sexuality and gender transgression, with defiant visibility, Pride participants declare that culture in the world needs to change to make a place for LGBT people.

Participants also displayed a second variation on visibility, which I call "educational visibility." With defiant visibility, participants embody stereotypes; with educational visibility, however, they combat them. In line with the sameness strategy, educational visibility fights stereotypes in order to persuade individuals that LGBT people fit into mainstream culture and thus should be accepted. At the same time educational visibility also targets culture in the world by confronting and seeking to replace existing images of LGBT people. Stereotypical beliefs in the mind and images in the world of LGBT people cast them as incompatible with heteronormative society. Gay men are stereotypically portrayed as weak and feminine (a combination which in itself is troubling), while lesbians are imagined to be angry and mannish. Bisexuals often fight against the interpretation that they are over-sexual and indecisive (because they cannot "choose" one gender) and transgender people contend with ideas that they are bizarre and confused. These stereotypes facilitate perceptions that queer sexuality is incompatible with a mainstream culture that values family, work ethic, and steadiness. Instead of a wholesale challenge of heteronormativity, educational visibility contests the discrete stereotypical beliefs and images of LGBT people that fuel opposition to LGBT inclusion. With educational visibility, Pride makes LGBT people visible as they really are, not as they are caricatured to be.

At every parade from Fargo to New York City, LGBT couples attended with their children, showing themselves to be stable and family-oriented.

In San Diego, there was a special viewing area under a tent for LGBT seniors to bring both comfort and visibility to this often-unnoticed group. Members of gay-straight alliances at North Dakota State University, the University of Vermont, and Emory University, along with many high school groups, marched to show themselves as young, studious, and LGBT. Working against the popular belief that queerness is less prevalent among people of color, parade contingents publicized the racial and ethnic diversity of the LGBT population by marching under banners announcing themselves as "LGBTQ South Asians of Atlanta" and "Being Latino" in New York City. Since the repeal of the military's "Don't Ask, Don't Tell" policy one year after my research, military contingents have been a strong and celebrated feature in San Diego's parade. The visible presence of LGBT military service men and women challenged the stereotype that gays are too weak to serve alongside their straight counterparts. In all of these examples, LGBT participants highlighted the ways that they fit into the mainstream by embodying popular virtues.

Stereotypes are specific ways that LGBT people are "othered" as different from the mainstream. Activists' sameness strategy presents LGBT people as ordinary citizens that are "just like" heterosexuals. At Pride, the majority of spectators at all parades dressed in simple shorts and t-shirts such that, notwithstanding a string of rainbow beads, they looked as if they could be found at any public parade. For many, this reflected the simple truth that they *are* "just like" heterosexuals when it comes to the way that they dress for a summertime parade. As a collective statement, it asks skeptical individuals to question the way they see LGBT people, urging them to see their similarities rather than differences. It also contributes to culture in the world by offering images of LGBT people that already fit into heteronormative society.

In contrast to defiant visibility, which primarily targets culture in the world, educational visibility targets both individual cultural attitudes in the mind and cultural images in the world. Educational visibility draws on widely shared cultural values like family, citizenship, and education and ties LGBT people to those qualities. In other words, harkening back to the homophile "accommodationist" strategy, one aspect of Pride parades is to frame LGBT people as worthy of respect and acceptance. We know from public opinion research that individuals are more likely to express positive attitudes about a subject when it is associated with something that they already hold in high esteem.[35] Thus, Pride participants—like the Atlanta gay dads group who held a sign reading "We're in Your PTA"—showed the ways that they are valued members of society while making clear that they are LGBT.

Much more than other messages, Pride participants directed educational visibility at skeptical individuals who they hoped would see the parade. Blair and Martin, both from Salt Lake City, described how they hoped Pride would influence others.

> BLAIR: I think Pride is important because then other people can see
> how our community is, enjoy what we do and it's not just what ev-
> erybody thinks it is.
> MARTIN: You know, Pride is important for the people who are par-
> ticipating but it's also important for the crowd, the people that are
> watching. To actually see and experience something different, and
> expose little kids to it. That it's not this big scary thing. Especially
> here in Utah, parents teach their kids it's the most wrong thing you
> could ever do—to be gay or lesbian, transgender. I think it just shows
> that it's a fun community and they're proud of who they are. I think
> it's almost most important for not the people participating but the
> people watching outside the community.

By invoking educational visibility, these participants and others argued that if people could only see the LGBT community accurately, they would accept it and support greater cultural equality. Pride parades showed that, instead of "the most wrong thing you could ever do," being LGBT was a source of joy that did not in any way inhibit one's ability to be a good parent, say, or a disciplined athlete.

Participants' goal in demonstrating educational visibility was to show that LGBT people fit into existing heteronormative society. Unlike defiant visibility, which primarily targeted culture in the world, educational visibility targeted culture in the mind. Participants hoped to change individuals' attitudes by exposing them to LGBT people that, in many ways, are "just like them." Important to this goal is the emphasis that Pride parades present a positive and accurate image of the LGBT community. In the logic of defiant visibility, it does not matter whether individuals judge the image of the LGBT community at Pride positively because Pride seeks primarily to challenge culture with new coded meanings.[36] By contrast, the logic of educational visibility finds that there is nothing truly objectionable about queerness and thus, individuals will develop positive attitudes toward LGBT people by seeing them portrayed accurately.

The trouble with the logic of educational visibility is that many people, both inside and outside the LGBT community, *do* find some representations at Pride to be objectionable. Sexual displays, or even more modest displays of affection, make gay sexuality and gender transgression visible to an extent that some do not appreciate. This is not a problem for defiant visibility because the message does not target cultural attitudes in the mind, and thus does not need to be sensitive to individual reactions. But educational visibility targets both culture in the world *and* culture in the mind. It offers new images of LGBT people that defy stereotypes in the hopes that individuals will see LGBT people as equals and accept them into mainstream, heteronormative society. To be successful, educational visibility relies on persuading individuals that their current attitudes are misinformed or misguided. For activists pursuing an inside-out model, this translates into a need to be very conscious of the how demonstrations may be interpreted. As discussed in chapter 1, the more tightly controlled Annual Reminders preceded the colorful Pride parades. Operating with educational visibility, these demonstrations sought to present gays and lesbians as non-threatening, respectable, *normal* members of society in order to dispel the myth that being gay meant being fundamentally different from, and thus dangerous to, society. In order to sell this image, however, organizers set rules on participants' dress and behavior.[37] With far fewer strict rules at today's Pride parades, this difficulty with educational visibility points to a weakness of pursuing inside-out cultural change with a mass demonstration.

A second problem with educational visibility is that, as with the Annual Reminders, promoting a positive image of LGBT people—as defined by dominant culture—requires setting rules that make many in the community feel excluded. Though it may be a trivial matter to ask scantily clad men to cover up, drag queens, transgender individuals, and others with non-normative gender presentations may also be asked to change in the name of educational visibility.[38] For many LGBT people, dress, hairstyle, and other features of personal presentation are a matter of identity; thus, asking them to change these things is tantamount to asking them to suppress their identities. Though I did not talk to anyone who felt personally excluded at Pride, in chapter 5, I discuss the lack of full inclusion of some groups—particularly, transgender and bisexual individuals—which may be partially based on image.

American society has seen a dramatic shift toward cultural equality in the nearly half-decade since the first Pride marches. Due in part to these collective demonstrations of queer visibility, LGBT people today can be open about their sexuality in a way that Pride pioneers could scarcely dream. This shift is not complete, however, as heteronormativity continues to dominate American culture in the world. While LGBT people are often tolerated when they make themselves visible, they are still pressured to conform to heteronormative standards for gender and sexual displays. Pride participants pushed for greater LGBT visibility with two distinct messages. With the first, defiant visibility, participants confronted the heteronormative cultural code head-on, attempting to change culture from the outside-in, so that LGBT people can be visible in whichever way they choose. With the second message, educational visibility, participants advertised the ways that LGBT people already fit into existing heteronormative culture. They directed this message at both culture in the world and culture in the mind with a hybrid model of cultural change.

Support

There is strong political polarization around LGBT rights. By 2010, citizens in thirty states had voted on and passed constitutional amendments prohibiting the recognition of same-sex marriage. Five years later, the Supreme Court overturned all of these amendments by a narrow 5–4 vote. However, in what may be considered a backlash, a number of states have passed "religious freedom restoration acts" that allow business owners and (in some cases) public officials to deny services to LGBT people based on religious beliefs. LGBT people continue to be the subject of political debate at the local, state, and federal levels as politicians offer bills to prohibit discrimination based on sexual orientation and gender identity, to restrict adoption to heterosexual couples, or to mandate pro- or anti-homosexuality messages in public school sex education. Critics working to limit political rights and cultural esteem for LGBT people argue that queer sexuality conflicts with traditional moral standards and contributes to a national moral decline. While politicians increasingly speak out in support of LGBT issues—as of 2015, President Obama and nearly all Senate Democrats have publicly declared their support for same-sex marriage—there are perhaps an equal number of voices condemning such support. In short, even as more voices call for tolerance, continued conflict means that the public sphere is often not a site of support for queer people.

Once again, the roots of condemnation lie in the heteronormative cultural code of meaning. By holding up heterosexuality, with its strict gender roles, as the gold standard for romantic relationships, family, and gender presentation, queerness is positioned as inferior. Historically, this inferiority manifested in cultural meanings that classified queerness as sin, sickness, and criminality.[39] Though the latter two have largely disappeared from mainstream culture—yet more extreme voices still advocate for "reparative therapy" to cure LGBT people of their mental illness—queer sexuality and gender are still regularly characterized as sinful. The Christian Right has been a long opponent of LGBT rights, and arguments against same-sex marriage often point, either explicitly or implicitly, to the immorality of homosexuality.[40] Likewise, a recent poll measured 45% of respondents who believed homosexual behavior is a sin.[41] Even when they do not hold such views themselves, young people overwhelmingly associate anti-gay sentiments with Christianity.[42]

Thus, LGBT activists have long worked to counter the condemnation of queerness that is inherent to heteronormativity. One way they have done this is by enlisting the support of those in culturally respected positions. Early homophile activists lobbied physicians, psychologists, and lawyers with the hopes that they would speak for their cause, reasoning that the vocal support from these (straight) professionals could carry more weight than arguments from LGBT activists themselves.[43] Similarly, since the 1990s, LGBT students and teachers have partnered with straight allies by forming gay-straight alliances in high schools across the country. The involvement of straight allies who presumably have no personal stake in LGBT rights has brought these groups greater legitimacy and influence in school policy and culture.[44] Religious, civic, political, and corporate leaders outside the LGBT community confer symbolic capital—culturally valued honor and respect—on LGBT organizations when they act in support of their missions.[45]

LGBT people and allies in Fargo, North Dakota felt in need of some public support in August of 2010. Though they did not hear the outright condemnation from churches and politicians that is typical in the Bible Belt South, neither did they hear explicit messages of support for queer sexuality or gender. Instead, there was a deafening silence around LGBT issues; queerness was not to be discussed, despite the pressing need of LGBT people for acceptance and support. Cultural disapproval reinforced queer invisibility as well. As a result, LGBT people felt that being open about their identities was simply not acceptable in Fargo.

On August 15, 2010, the downtown area of Fargo, North Dakota was an unequivocally supportive place for LGBT people. Rainbow flags hung from lampposts along the short four-block stretch of Main Street that makes up the city's central commercial district. These flags made queerness visible and communicated support, saying, in effect, "LGBT people are welcome here." According to Warren, a member of the parade's organizing committee, the flags were sponsored by the Downtown Community Partnership, a private group that works to create a vibrant downtown through the promotion of local events. In lending their support by hanging rainbow flags along the parade route, the group signaled the importance of Pride to the area's vitality.

As the parade passed, marching contingents displayed messages of support. The women's soccer team from a nearby college marched in their uniforms, holding a banner that declared "I Love My Gay Teammates." Some wore stickers with the equal sign (=) from the Human Rights Campaign, a national LGBT rights group. Before the parade, the soccer players told me their team had two "out" lesbians and as a group they decided to march to show that, unlike others in their friends' lives, they appreciated sexual difference. A group from the local Best Buy, an electronics chain store, marched and handed out flyers as a way to emphasize corporate support for their LGBT employees and LGBT issues affecting the public in general. The Fargo Moorhead Derby Girls, a local women's roller derby team, skated and cheered while many members' children passed out candy to spectators. Similarly, Planned Parenthood's contingent included kids as well, plus the sign, "Prevention Equals Healthy Families." Each of these groups emphasized their support for the LGBT community over their membership in that community. That is, through both explicit statements of naming others in need of support ("I Love My Gay Teammates") and implicit identification with non-LGBT subjects (sports, business, reproductive rights), many Fargo Pride contingents identified themselves as allies rather than full members of the LGBT community. Thus, while LGBT-identified groups like school gay-straight alliances communicated LGBT visibility, as allies, these groups communicated support for a community to which they did not entirely belong. Though these messages are by no means mutually exclusive in that the same demonstration can communicate both visibility and support, they are conceptually different.

In addition to businesses, community groups, and non-profit organizations, many local churches marched with signs of support for LGBT people. Members of the local Unitarian-Universalist congregation held a sign that read "Civil Marriage is a Civil Right." Congregationalists, Lutherans, Episcopalians, and a spiritual group called the Free Thinkers followed suit, showing support. Ruth, an older member of the Episcopal group, explained her groups' motivation to participate:

> There were probably eight or ten of us last summer who marched with a banner from our church so people would know that it was a church-affiliated group. You know, there's so many negatives associated with a lot of our churches with their Neanderthalic views of sexuality, so it is hard for people to understand a church would support LGBT people. So we were really eager to be known as a group of people from the Episcopal Church who were out and supportive.

Ruth had been supportive of LGBT people since she first became aware of the concept of homosexuality. As a Christian, she felt it was her duty to love all God's children and to speak out for those who were disparaged in society. Christian churches that outwardly condemned homosexuality troubled her, and Ruth felt these churches gave Christianity in general a bad name. While few churches in Fargo broadcast their anti-gay views, some were known to espouse conservative sexual mores that did not make LGBT people feel welcome. For example, a group within Ruth's congregation, known as Integrity, worked specifically on LGBT community issues. Ruth and other Integrity members decided to show their support publicly by marching in Fargo's Pride parade. Along with

FIGURE 3.3 Members of a local Episcopal Church march in Fargo's Pride parade. Photo courtesy of Jagnoor Singh.

other congregations, these church groups offered images of support that countered the strong cultural association of Christianity with anti-gay sentiment.

Perhaps the most potent symbol of support was found in Parents and Friends of Lesbians and Gays (PFLAG). Since Jeanne Manford—who marched with her son in support of his right to be gay—joined other parents of gay children to form PFLAG in 1972, the group has worked to help people embrace their LGBT loved ones. In Fargo, a small group of eight members marched, holding signs declaring "I Love My Gay Son" and "Hate Is Not a Family Value." Their signs countered the Right's political framing of opposition to LGBT rights as "family values." These displays also spoke to the rejection experienced by many LGBT people when they come out to their families. There was a PFLAG contingent at each parade I attended, and they received the strongest emotional reactions of all contingents. I heard loud cheers when PFLAG contingents marched, and saw parade-goers approach individual members to thank them and often receive a hug.

Thus, the second cultural message of Pride parades was public support. In a cultural and political climate where queerness is often coupled

FIGURE 3.4 PFLAG members march, holding signs of support in Atlanta's Pride parade. Photo courtesy of Stan Fong, Atlanta Pride Committee.

with negative judgment, Pride parades actively challenged this rejection with outspoken and visible support. Participants like Deb, an older lesbian in Salt Lake City, described Pride as being "a great display of public affection for gays," notable for its contrast to the everyday experience in which queer sexuality was not embraced. Support was made public for all to see and focused outward at the larger culture. While participants like those on the women's soccer team in Fargo certainly signaled their acceptance of gay teammates on an interpersonal level, by marching in Pride, they also publicized this acceptance to the community at large. Similarly, churches like Ruth's indicated that they welcomed LGBT members in congregation materials and on their website, letting potential LGBT and straight congregants alike know that the church accepted queer sexuality. Demonstrations at Pride went one step further, challenging cultural disapproval by symbolically linking queerness with public support.

While marchers and spectators held signs and banners proclaiming their support, participants said that spectators also made a statement to support LGBT people simply by being there. According to straight ally Jessica in Fargo,

> Participation is huge for Pride parades because I think it's a good way for the community to be driving by or walking by and see a bunch of people all there for one thing and that's support and the rights of the LGBT community. I think participation is huge for how many people are affected and are involved.

Jessica's statement points to how public support primarily targets culture in the world rather than culture in the mind. She imagined passersby who saw the parade being impressed by the large number of people coming out in support of a marginalized group. She did not think that seeing the parade would necessarily change onlookers' minds about LGBT people, but instead, by witnessing the parade, they would receive the message that gay sexuality and gender transgression is worthy of support and not derision.

The participation of churches in all Pride parades signified a particularly potent symbol of support. As I examine in the next chapter, religious opposition varied in character and intensity in each community I studied, but both nationally and in many local communities, conservative Christians are the loudest voices against LGBT cultural equality. Often this vocal opposition comes to Pride in small groups of counter-protesters who hold signs proclaiming homosexuality a sin and warning participants of their doomed fate. I observed such groups in San Diego, Salt Lake City, and Atlanta. Tobias, a gay man in San Diego, saw in these counter-protesters the embodiment of cultural opposition to queer sexuality and gender—a feeling embraced by many Pride participants. He shared an anecdote to illustrate how supportive churches stood up to the anti-gay messages of counter-protesters:

> There was a very poignant moment. Maybe midway through the parade, there's a fire station. And adjacent to the fire station, year after year they have sort of—for want of a better word—a right-winged, religious

zealot sort of collection of people who carry signs like "Fags are Burning in Hell," or what have you. At one point, the Episcopalian contingent came down and had a very large contingent of individuals, and they just stopped and then turned and faced them. That was such a poignant snapshot of the left-right debate that sort goes on in this country. It was really symbolic of not even a direct reference to manifest issues like gay marriage, but then there's also the larger context for that. So I think that that was one particular moment that I really reflected on and that made an impression.

Few scenes provided such a direct contrast between pro- and anti-gay religious groups, but church groups marching in parades tacitly made this contrast by emphasizing the religious basis for their participation. The groups held signs that challenged religious condemnation of queerness by asserting their pro-gay interpretation of religious principles, using phrases like "Jesus Loves Everyone" and "God is Love, No Exceptions." As participants in Pride, church groups offered an alternative message to the one that Christian groups often give in the public sphere, communicating that morality means supporting LGBT people, not rejecting them.

Another group that showed their support publicly at Pride was local and national businesses. In all parades, businesses were involved as financial sponsors and as marching contingents—often, the two went together. Like Best Buy in Fargo, sponsors emphasized company support of LGBT public issues and their queer employees. Many corporate sponsors used slogans on banners and t-shirts that connected Pride with their business. Marchers with a local bar-and-grill in Atlanta, for instance, wore shirts that said "Taking Pride in Our Service," while San Diego Public Defenders held a banner that read "Getting You Off Since 1988." Participants were aware that businesses designed these displays ultimately to increase company sales, but most appreciated their involvement anyway. Dee Ann, a trans woman in Fargo, explained why she liked seeing businesses at the parade:

I love corporate sponsorship and participation because that's a way to get their name out front. There are a lot of people that say, you know, Focus on the Family and that whole crowd, "Oh look, McDonald's is sponsoring gay-this or -that." They take them to task, and that's wrong because so many people in the LGBT community are still semi-closeted, so sometimes those people will actually not step forward and help put out the brushfire.

For Dee Ann and others, marching in the parade or providing financial support for it was a way for businesses to publicly place themselves on the side of the LGBT community. With mainstream recognition, both local and national businesses demonstrate that it is acceptable and even desirable to support queer sexuality and gender to the society at large.[46]

Rather than seeing it as a show of support, critics argue that corporate influence has turned Pride into a market to sell goods to the LGBT community, eroding its effectiveness as a means to push for change.[47] Large Pride parades indeed carry multi-million dollar price tags, which require hefty financial support. Some parades court corporate sponsorship more than others, but all must find a way to pay for the safety, insurance, and cleanup that a large civic event such as Pride entails. As we saw in previous chapters, the role of businesses as financial backers and participants in Pride parades has always drawn criticism. Critics today argue that to successfully court businesses, Pride parades tone down the more contentious, provocative displays in favor of presenting gays and lesbians as eager consumers who pose no threat to businesses' social power.[48]

Empirical research on Pride parades has painted a more nuanced picture of business involvement in Pride. Sociologist Lauren J. Joseph points out that the individual corporate representatives that negotiate sponsorships are ardent supporters of LGBT rights who urge their companies to sponsor Pride over other causes.[49] Some organizers see involvement as a necessary evil to cover the financial burden of Pride, while others view the connections between Pride and corporate sponsors as an important way that Pride challenges LGBT marginalization. In another study, marketing researchers Stephen M. Kates and Russell W. Belk show how participants at Toronto's Pride parade used consumer goods like rainbow flags and t-shirts with gay messages to resist dominant cultural codes about queer sexuality.[50]

Commercialization at Pride is certainly a cause for concern, a point I elaborate on in chapter 4, but my study reveals a less problematic view toward business involvement on the ground. Participants that I interviewed overwhelmingly saw business participation as a positive show of support for LGBT people. They acknowledged that businesses may have the ulterior motive of marketing their products to LGBT consumers, but what mattered to them was that businesses were there as part of Pride, standing on the side of LGBT people and against the stigmatization of queer sexuality. From this perspective, businesses from local restaurants to national corporations like Best Buy lent important symbolic capital to the LGBT community through their participation in Pride. Though their participation is not always an unqualified good, commercial sponsors of Pride were a valuable mainstream voice in support of LGBT people.

Like defiant visibility, the code of public support challenged heteronormativity primarily from the outside-in. Whereas the heteronormative cultural code in the world interprets queerness as deviant, unnatural, and even morally wrong, public support challenges this meaning by endorsing it as a legitimate, respected human variation. Though a few participants hoped their support would influence individual attitudes, such as those of passersby and casual onlookers, most talked about public support in a general sense. Explicit signs—like Atlanta PFLAG's "Hate is Not a Family Value" or San Diego United Church of Christ's "Jesus Didn't Turn People Away, Neither Do We"— promoted acceptance of queer sexuality and gender as a cultural value. Like Ruth, the Episcopalian straight ally in Fargo, participants wanted themselves or their organizations to be "known as a group of people who were out and supportive." Support was communicated as a public show of visibility on the side of LGBT cultural equality. Such displays targeted culture in the world with a symbolic contest over collectively held meanings, not a persuasive campaign to change individual cultural attitudes.

Celebration

Public support is one message to counter cultural disapproval of queer sexuality and gender. Celebration is another. In the American public sphere, politicians, activists, and ordinary citizens debate whether LGBT people can be good parents, whether their relationships are sacred enough to be worthy of marriage, and whether their sexuality or gender identity is reason enough to be fired or denied housing. While many do indeed argue for expanded rights and protections for LGBT people, these debates draw on a heteronormative cultural code of meaning that regards queer sexuality and gender as inferior to heterosexuality. Even those activists and politicians that defend LGBT rights support their position by saying LGBT couples can be *as committed* as heterosexual couples, or that LGBT parents can be *as good* as straight parents.[51] Despite the evidence that children of gay and lesbian parents can actually have *better* outcomes than those of heterosexual parents, the public debate still centers on whether LGBT people adhere to heterosexual standards, not whether they ever exceed them.[52] In everyday life outside of public debate, the cultural script of "coming out" as LGBT regards the act as a burden to be accepted rather than a gift to be celebrated. Increasing tolerance means that many LGBT people can come out and find acceptance much more readily than in previous generations, but tolerance falls short of full celebration.

Though queerness may not be celebrated in the public sphere, heterosexuality certainly is. Heterosexual couples are universally celebrated at weddings, anniversaries, and marriage proposals. First dates and first kisses with the opposite sex are cultural rites of passage. Even abstinence from heterosexual activity is marked by highly gendered Virginity Balls in which fathers "guard" their daughter's sexual purity by standing in for her future male partner.[53] Growing acceptance of queerness has indeed led to public celebration of some celebrity same-sex weddings and viral YouTube videos of wedding proposals, so the heterosexual monopoly on the public sphere appears to be eroding. However, in praising heterosexuality as the "gold standard" for human sexuality, the heteronormative cultural code of meaning stigmatizes the queer sexuality such that public celebration is rare.

In San Diego in 2010, members of the LGBT community were still reeling from public debates over the legitimacy of queer sexuality and gender. Less than two years prior, residents saw same-sex marriage in their state legalized by court order only to be re-banned by popular vote in November 2008. In the intervening months, thousands of gay and lesbian couples celebrated their weddings while same-sex marriage opponents derided their unions as harmful to society. I talked to many participants who pointed to Prop 8 as a sign that their queer sexuality was still condemned by the larger culture. Also on their minds was the debate over the military's "Don't Ask, Don't Tell" policy barring openly LGBT people from serving. With Marine, Navy, and Coast Guard bases, San Diego is home to over one hundred thousand active members of the military, so the issue hit close to home.[54] During the national debate, LGBT people heard themselves described as unable to work with straight counterparts and thus, dangers to unit cohesion. Defenders countered that gay and lesbian soldiers could be "just as brave" as heterosexual ones. While people in the San Diego LGBT community did find some public support, they did not find celebration until San Diego Pride.

In contrast to this dour public talk, the Hillcrest neighborhood of San Diego was a happy place on July 25, 2010. With two hours until step-off, the neighborhood was alive as restaurants hosted pre-Pride brunches, residents near the parade route hosted house parties, and marchers prepared their floats. As I walked to the parade line-up area, I passed two parties on each side of a duplex. At one, lesbians dressed in knee-length shorts, t-shirts, and sandals or sneakers and shared beverages in red Solo cups. Next to them, on the other side of the duplex, three Sisters of Perpetual Indulgence gathered with friends before marching in the parade. Like Dykes on Bikes, the irreverent Sisters are loosely organized groups that join in Pride parades across the country. A cultural protest group, they are men who paint their faces bright white and dress in mock nuns' habits. With their appearance and street performance, the Sisters satirize the Catholic Church's condemnation of homosexuality.[55] Near them, another group gathered for a pre-Pride house party, this one comprised mainly of men identified as "bears." This subgroup within the LGBT community rejects the dominant gay male culture that prescribes thin, chiseled physiques by instead embracing their larger, hairy bodies.[56] I identified the group as bears by the flag they flew in front of the house: an adaption of the California state flag with its bear in the center and a rainbow instead of a red strip at the bottom. Just as a football game prompts a host of tailgate parties organized around a love for the game and team, San Diego Pride was an occasion for each of these varied groups to gather and have a good time being queer. Since the gatherings were public, the diverse groups made the implicit statement that queer-ness is indeed cause for celebration.

As the parade start-time drew near, the route was alive with a diverse crowd of spectators. According to the event's organizers, an estimated two hundred thousand people attend San Diego's Pride parade annually. There was an atmosphere of festivity as spectators greeted one another and anticipated the display to come. LGBT seniors gathered under a designated tent, while families with children secured quieter spots along the route. I talked with a straight couple in their mid-forties who lived in the neighborhood and set up their camp chairs and a cooler to enjoy the colorful entertainment. A group of shirtless young white gay men walked by, followed by two older Latino men holding hands and wear-ing shorts and t-shirts. The wide street allowed plenty of room for spec-tators to walk around and socialize while leaving dedicated space for the parade to run through. The more conservatively dressed participants seemed to enjoy the sights of those with more flamboyant dress, like the eleven- or twelve-year-old girl who approached a leather-clad man for a picture. This man was white with a dark, trimmed beard and wore shorts, two leather straps criss-crossing his bare chest, and a leather col-lar. Like bears, leather men are a subgroup within the LGBT community with their own gender and sexual norms.[57]

San Diego's parade began in the same fashion as Salt Lake City and Fargo: a group of Dykes on Bikes revved their engines and led the parade as crowds cheered. This time, the women motorcyclists were followed by men dressed in similar leather fashion, riding their own bikes. There were over one hundred motorcycles in all, followed by the mounted Gay Rodeo Association carrying various state and rainbow flags. In addi-tion to familiar community groups such as local non-profits, school gay-straight alliances, and churches, San Diego's parade also included many grand floats sponsored by nightclubs featuring amped-up music and shirtless dancing men.[58] Katy Perry's "California Gurls" was a par-ticularly popular song choice, with its lines, "You could travel the world/ But nothing comes close/ To the Golden Coast/ Once you party with us/ You'll be falling in love." Despite its implicit heteronormativity (the lyrics are directed to men who will fall in love with "California girls"), the song set the tone for participants' expression of joy in queer sexuality. A float for the Brass Rail, a local LGBT nightclub, passed by blasting this song, encouraging spectators to sing along and join in the dancing.

The air of festivity extended to crowds along the parade route. Many watched from rooftop and balcony parties hosted by local restaurants and private residences. The route passed by the fire department, where three firefighters watched the parade from the roof. After turning a corner, the route passed a multi-story apartment building for senior citizens. Many gathered on apartment balconies or in front of the building to watch the festivities. Hazel was one of those observers, and she described the parade as an event full of "colors and lots of aliveness" that could "take depression away." She appreciated the message of acceptance and was glad she could take part in this celebration of an often-beleaguered social group. Hazel looked forward to Pride because to her, the day—and, by extension, the LGBT community—was connected with an upbeat, positive feeling.

On its face, there is nothing contentious about celebration. In fact, for a small minority of participants, Pride was simply a fun party without a greater purpose. Scholars of social movements and activists alike worry that unless participants *intend* to make a contentious statement, their actions cannot lead to social change.[59] Since the early days of Pride, commentators have worried that too much emphasis on festivity will erode the event's serious messages about the legitimacy of queer sexuality and gender. If participants attend Pride simply to have fun, perhaps the event will not actively contest LGBT people's cultural inequality. However, as I discuss further in chapter 4, Pride's festive and playful nature fits within a tradition of social movement activism that uses humorous performance to promote a new vision of the ideal society.[60]

Marchers, spectators, sponsors, volunteers, and researchers like me certainly did have a lot of fun at Pride in San Diego that year. It is hard not to enjoy cheering and dancing in a joyous environment. But we could have had just as much fun at a private party. Instead, Pride parades run through city streets for all to see. They are public celebrations of something that is rarely celebrated in the public sphere. This celebration was an important aspect of the parade for participants. Angela, a lesbian in Burlington, and Jonah, a gay man in San Diego, talked about collective celebration at Pride:

ANGELA: Pride is a day for us to celebrate who we are. There are lots of days where we get to be like, hey, I don't get to file my joint tax return or hey, I don't have rights, or hey, I don't have this. So it's a great day as a community to be excited together about who we are.

JONAH: It's like every year there's one day, one day a year where my entire community mobilizes together and is truly proud and confident of ourselves. I think that's very powerful for us to have a day of Pride and being GLBT.

Both Angela and Jonah spoke of Pride as a special day set apart from their everyday lives. They saw celebration of their sexuality—much like with visibility and support—as sorely lacking in the larger culture. Angela referred to her daily life of legal and cultural benefits denied to her as a lesbian, while at Pride being lesbian meant celebrating her identity with others like her. Pride celebrations are meant to be seen. Similarly, Jonah described Pride as a powerful demonstration, during which LGBT people do more than solemnly accept their identities; they proudly celebrate them. In the very places where many participants feel pressure to downplay their sexuality in everyday life, at Pride they made it the subject of explicit, public celebration.

Once again, this message primarily targets cultural meanings in the world. In explaining why celebration was important, participants did not point to individual acts of judgment or discrimination. Rather, they pointed to a broader understanding that their sexuality and gender identity, even when tolerated, is not culturally celebrated. Celebration at Pride is a public display that offers a different message of what it means to be LGBT. Pride attempts to change culture from the outside-in by symbolically linking celebration—rather than condemnation, inferiority, or even more benign tolerance—with gay sexuality and gender transgression. It does not target individual cultural attitudes for change, and in fact, as many participants pointed out, the celebration may even worsen the some opinions of LGBT people. However, participants said over and over again that it is important to celebrate queer sexuality and gender in this public manner. Its significance comes from the way celebration replaces an old, harmful cultural meaning with a new positive one.

Conclusion

Pride parades contest a heteronormative cultural code that devalues queerness by actively promoting the visibility, support, and celebration of LGBT people. Each of these messages speaks to the cultural meaning of queer sexuality and gender. The messages are not political and Pride is not part of a strategy to achieve cultural equality by reforming state laws and policies. Instead, Pride is a protest tactic that directly challenges existing cultural meanings and attempts to replace them with new ones. At each Pride parade, participants enacted the visibility, support, and celebration of and for LGBT people.

All messages challenge culture from the outside-in. By increasing the visibility of gay sexuality and gender identity, showing support for the LGBT community, and celebrating all things queer, participants attempted to establish new cultural meanings and challenge current ones. As these meanings embed in American culture, individual behavior and attitudes will change in response. For instance, imagine a day when the social norm is to celebrate a person's "coming out" as LGBT. We have already seen a change in normative responses around homosexuality—from outright condemnation and attempts to "cure" homosexuality to public expressions of concern, tolerance, and even support.[61]

One message, educational visibility, targeted both culture in the mind and culture in the world with a hybrid model of cultural change. Like the others, educational visibility offered new images of LGBT people in an attempt to embed these in the existing culture in the world to replace those that portray queer sexuality as damaging to society. With an added target of culture in the mind, though, educational visibility also engaged an inside-out model of cultural change. By showing LGBT people who display cultural values of family and citizenship, Pride parades expose members of the public to real LGBT people, individuals with whom they could presumably identify, and as more and more people learn about this community, attitudes toward them will hopefully change. These changed attitudes will then work their way out—as individuals might, for example, change their responses when others come out to them as LGBT, based on their own reassessment of queerness. When enough people change their attitudes and behavior, these become reflected in cultural language and symbols.

Despite their diverse cultural climates, all six parades that I visited promoted common themes. As Blake said, "you have to be pretty brave to be gay on Pride Day"—and participants in each city did just that, and many with flair. Chapter 4 explores how these participants communicated Pride messages differently according to local cultural climates and how variations among parades responded to long-running debates about representation, commercialism, and frivolity at Pride.

4

"Pride Comes in Many Colors"

Variation among Parades

Even in Toronto, people are able to express themselves a little more openly and freely than in New York because [of] the law enforcement and just the general culture. The public are more relaxed about the individuals who chose to maybe express themselves through body art or nudity. Here in Austin [where I live], I mean, we're in Texas, if anyone decides to do that, it's just a little frowned upon.
—Court, gay male volunteer at New York City's 2010 Pride parade

I went to the parades in New York and San Francisco. And I have to say San Francisco has a big gay population over there, so it's pretty big, really long, and its scale is much bigger. They have more rights statements, gay people, that, represent the community, and there are very famous like politicians or movie stars or different people. In New York you can see different cultures that have evolved, too, because New York is a melting pot, they have [an] Asian population, Middle Eastern population, Indian population, all pockets in their parade. Atlanta is pretty much between medium-size and large-size and it increases every year.
—Eugene, gay male participant at Atlanta's 2010 Pride parade

Court and Eugene are both veteran Pride participants. Court helps organize the parade in Austin, Texas, where he lives, and in the summer of 2010, he decided to visit as many cities as he could to volunteer at their local Pride events. With family in Toronto and friends in New York City, when I met him he had participated in both these parades and compared them to his home event in Austin. Eugene lives in Atlanta and has attended the parade there many times. He has never been involved in organizing Pride, but he has been to parades in New York and San Francisco. Both men see the ways that Pride parades challenge culture with the visible presence of LGBT people, but they also point out that participants adapt their displays to their local communities.

Court observed that in cities like Toronto where LGBT people are more accepted, participants have the freedom to celebrate their differences and push cultural norms even further with sexual displays. Meanwhile, in the relatively conservative Austin, Texas, participants are more reserved in their public displays. They make their presence known with a parade declaring themselves as LGBT citizens and allies, but also show they are part of the wider community by not diverging too radically from local norms. Eugene noticed that the look of parades reflects the populations of host cities and the resources of local LGBT communities. With a large gay population, myriad advocacy organizations, and celebrity allies, San Francisco puts on a massive parade with political statements and notable celebrities. Likewise, New York's parade reflects the city's racial and ethnic diversity, while Atlanta is smaller than these two events, matching its smaller population size.[1]

In the previous chapter, I described how Pride messages flip the heteronormative cultural code of meaning on its head. Where heteronormativity makes queerness invisible, LGBT people and allies stage Pride parades to make themselves undeniably visible. Where it rejects LGBT people as deviant, they show public support for the LGBT community. And where heteronormativity prescribes condemnation, or even lukewarm tolerance, they celebrate queerness with the grand festivities of Pride. Nonetheless, the tenor and expression of heteronormativity varies as one travels from place to place across the country. It is accompanied by a cultural code of tolerance that also varies in strength and application. LGBT people find varying degrees of visibility and acceptance across the U.S., from the Castro district in San Francisco—where one is greeted by a giant rainbow flag outside the subway stop—to small cities like the one I studied in the South, where a "don't ask, don't tell" norm about queerness prevails.[2] Some even argue that we have reached a new era of queer social acceptance in which sexual orientation is no longer a defining characteristic of one's identity.[3] Though the Pride participants

I met did not share this mindset, evidence of unprecedented inclusion (in some areas of the country, at least) reveal how cultural challenges are dynamic across time and space. Participants adapt Pride messages to fit their local climates. With different cultural challenges—in San Francisco, LGBT people may work for greater transgender visibility, while those in small cities work to end pervasive condemnation of gays and lesbians—the Pride parade in San Francisco indeed looks very different than the one in the small Southern city that I studied.

Communities also have different resources of people, organizations, and money, all of which they use to put on Pride parades. As Eugene noted, both the scale and diversity of Pride parades in San Francisco, New York, and Atlanta varied with each city's population. Much of the difference between the look of big-city parades like New York's and small town ones like Fargo's can be attributed to the size and character of the population and the resources of the LGBT community. Simply put, with more people, Pride parades in big cities draw larger crowds than their small-city counterparts. Larger populations also have more diversity, enabling big-city Pride parades to make visible LGBT people of various racial and ethnic backgrounds, affinities, and personal styles, and with broad ranges of interests. Moreover, LGBT communities in bigger cities also have established organizations like community resource centers, political advocacy groups, and various non-profits that can help organize and participate in Pride parades. They have the gay bars and clubs and the LGBT-friendly businesses that enter colorful, well-produced floats and donate money for parade logistics. All of these resources contribute to the way Pride parades communicate visibility, support, and celebration.

Local cultural climate—the nuanced cultural meanings of queerness in a given area—and community resources are the two main influences on Pride variation across the country.[4] These factors affected both *how* each Pride parade in my study communicated visibility, support, and celebration and *how much* they emphasized these messages. With limited money and few people, participants in small towns like Burlington celebrated queerness with balloons and handmade signs, while in the big city of New York, they constructed elaborate floats complete with choreographed dancers and amplified music. Similarly, in Atlanta's Bible-Belt cultural climate, a number of pro-gay churches marched to show support for LGBT people, while in the less religious and more tolerant San Diego, politicians found it politically advantageous to demonstrate support by joining the parade. Cultural climate also influenced how much emphasis participants put on Pride's messages. In the relatively harsh climates of Atlanta, Fargo, and Salt Lake City, the parades responded to strident condemnation of queerness with messages of support from churches, businesses, and individual participants. Meanwhile, in the friendlier cities of Burlington, San Diego, and New York, participants worked to move the cultural response to queerness from lukewarm tolerance to full acceptance by openly celebrating LGBT identity.

Variation among Pride parades brings out debates on what messages Pride should communicate and how best to convey them. Since its early days, Pride organizers and participants have struggled to create an event that is an outlet for free expression without sliding into the realm of the offensive, that is financially sound but not dominated by commercial interests, and that has both a festive atmosphere and a serious purpose. Through early infighting over format and other practical issues, planners established Pride as a collective demonstration of the gay and lesbian community's "unity in diversity." Far from resolving debates over representation, commercialization, and frivolity, this early infighting set a precedent for future Pride participants to tackle them anew each time they gather to put on the annual event. Whereas those who plan Pride events continue to struggle with practical issues like courting commercial sponsorship and setting guidelines for participant displays, ordinary participants do not encounter them in the explicit, head-on fashion that scholars consider infighting. Instead, they draw from their grounded experience to put on meaningful displays that they hope will bring about greater cultural equality. Pride is an occasion that brings out different stances on the abstract issues of representation, commercialization (and the involvement of other institutional actors like politicians), and frivolity—stances that reflect both the enduring diversity and desire for unity in the LGBT community.

Organizers, participants, and academics disagree about where to draw the line in these debates. For instance, at what point does the celebration, the fun of Pride, erode its serious message of cultural change? Some felt that point was reached at San Francisco's 1974 Pride parade, when in their report on the event, the *Advocate* commented that, "Frivolity and joy were much more in evidence than militance and social determination."[5] Others champion Pride as a venue for such carefree celebration in an otherwise constraining world. Similarly, there is room to debate the role of businesses in Pride and the wisdom of displays that many may deem offensive. Increasing acceptance of queerness means that LGBT people may feel freer to celebrate and to express themselves as they choose, along with making public demonstrations of support for the LGBT community more attractive to businesses. Such successful cultural change since Pride's early days brings the issues of representation, commercialization, and frivolity to the forefront as never before. Exploring variations of Pride across the country offers a window into the ways communities can approach these issues and an opportunity to take a step back and consider the harms and benefits to each approach.

Visibility

It is hard to imagine a more visible LGBT presence than in Manhattan on Pride weekend in 2010. Roughly one million people attended the two-mile, five-hour long procession down Fifth Avenue and into Greenwich Village, the city's "gayborhood" that is home to the historic Stonewall Inn, the massive LGBT Community Center, and numerous LGBT bars and clubs. Rainbow flags were everywhere—on city lampposts, in front of bars and cafes, and emblazoned on banners announcing Sunday morning's parade. Even the Empire State Building got in on the game, lighting up in rainbow colors from Friday to Sunday. During the parade, marching contingents held banners announcing themselves as "Gay Geeks of NY" and the "Flaggots" (an LGBT color guard). Spectators donned rainbow knee socks, held hands with same-sex partners, and defied gender norms with spiked hair on women or too-tight t-shirts on men. A few participants showed a more radical divergence from heteronormative standards, dressing in full drag or strutting down the street in nothing but a Speedo.

LGBT visibility has been a goal of Pride parades—and the broader post-Stonewall LGBT movement—since their founding in 1970. Also since these first events, LGBT advocates have debated how best to accomplish this goal. The inaugural events in New York and Los Angeles made a significant break from earlier gay and lesbian movement dem-

FIGURE 4.1 An eclectic group of participants pose together at New York City's Pride parade.

onstrations by presenting gay people as they are, celebrating rather than suppressing their divergence from the heteronormative mainstream. However, this bolder, more defiant visibility did not mean that gays and lesbians dropped all concerns about how their image would be perceived. Two overt displays of gay sexuality—one marcher's oversized jar of Vaseline in 1970 and the "cockapillar" of 1971, both featured in Los Angeles's parade—were flashpoints for LGBT advocates to debate the line between challenging culture and needlessly provoking offense.[6] Supporters of such displays argued that Pride must confront anti-gay culture at its heart; if heteronormativity renders gay sexuality unseen, undiscussed, and even unthinkable, then Pride should make gay sexuality undeniable. Opponents countered with an argument that sexual displays would only harden negative attitudes and thereby prove the dominant notion that gay sexuality is outside the bounds of respectable society.

This debate over how best to make LGBT people more visible extends far beyond Pride. Throughout the last fifty years of the LGBT rights movement, activists have argued over whether it is better to emphasize

LGBT difference from the heterosexual mainstream or to highlight the similarities between LGBT and straight people.[7] Most scholars have looked at this from the perspective of the activist leaders who design strategies and organize marches. Through this lens, researchers see that visibility is a distinct consideration for activists working to achieve movement goals. Sociologist Mary Bernstein, for instance, demonstrated that LGBT activists strategically choose how to present their identities.[8] In some campaigns they deploy identity for education (akin to my concept of "educational visibility"), emphasizing the ways LGBT people are similar in order to challenge the perception that they are too divergent from the mainstream to be accepted. In other campaigns they highlight LGBT difference, a strategy Bernstein calls "identity for critique" (similar to "defiant visibility"), in order to challenge heteronormative cultural ideas. The choice of which strategy to employ depends on a host of factors, including campaign goals, organizational structure, and political opportunities. Similarly, organizers mediated the image of the LGBT community as they worked out the often-mundane details to stage four national LGBT Marches on Washington.[9] For example, the inclusion of a public wedding ceremony for same-sex couples in the 1987 March drew criticism both from those who believed it portrayed gays and lesbians as too *similar* to heterosexuals and those who argued it too strongly highlighted their *difference*.[10] Given the incredibly public stage of the National Mall in Washington, DC, organizers knew that the Marches would bring new visibility to the LGBT community and therefore carefully debated over the best image to present.

Scholars of social movements tend to take the perspective of organizers rather than ordinary participants, thus presenting visibility as a top-down strategy that is explicitly debated by individual actors. This leaves participants in the role of passive recipients who enact the strategy set out by event organizers. While organizers' strategic decisions no doubt shape the visible image of LGBT people at public demonstrations, participants also play an important role as those putting themselves on display. Similarity and difference act as two poles around which to debate strategy. Queer theorist José Esteban Muñoz proposed a middle ground, called "disindentification," in which performers adopt mainstream norms as a way to transform them for their own purposes.[11] For example, same-sex marriage advocates who don traditional wedding dresses demand inclusion into this cultural ritual while simultaneously challenging its heteronormative basis. Since the ritual itself is premised on heteronormativity—only one woman wearing a dress per wedding— when two women present themselves as a couple to be married, this transforms traditional symbols for a contentious purpose. Similarly, Pride participants creatively show both similarity with and difference from the heterosexual mainstream as a way to bring greater visibility to their community.

At Pride in particular, visibility is not a top-down strategy. Since its early days, a feature of Pride has been to allow participants the freedom to choose how to represent themselves. Recall how Los Angeles organizers in 1972 resisted pressure from more conservative gay rights activists to impose rules on participant displays and instead put out guidelines to suggest, rather than dictate, how participants should look and behave at Pride. Today, Pride organizers in all of the cities I researched similarly took a hands-off approach to participant displays. They put out official guidelines specifying that marchers obey local laws regarding nudity and communicate only positive messages on floats, but otherwise left monitoring up to the police. Even with these minimal restrictions, participants were largely unaware that there were any formal limits on how they could present themselves. Instead, from the perspective of participants, making their identities visible at Pride was a matter of what felt right given the local cultural climate and what was possible given the resources available in their communities. In this way, their displays were forms of disindentification—by adopting and then transforming cultural symbols—that exist on a spectrum from similarity with the heteronormativity on one end and difference from it on the other.

Participants' displays of visibility coalesced into two distinct messages, defiant and educational visibility, that each trended toward one side of the debate over sexual displays. Defiant visibility is the message that queerness will not be toned down to fit with heteronormative standards. Pride participants show defiant visibility by clearly marking their identity as LGBT through hair and clothing styles, symbols like rainbow colors, and behaviors like same-sex affection. It targets culture in the world, aiming to upend the heteronormative code of meaning that obscures LGBT lives by labeling heterosexuality as the only natural form of romantic relationship. By emphasizing LGBT people's difference from their straight counterparts, defiant visibility, similar to Bernstein's "identity for critique," demonstrates an alternate sexual identity that challenges culture in the world. Of course, one way to flaunt queer difference is with sexual displays like the 1971 "cockapillar" in Los Angeles's parade or the group of Pride spectators in New York City's 2010 parade who were decked out in leather fetish gear. Just as in Pride's early years, some in the LGBT community argue that such displays go too far and end up doing more harm than good by provoking offense. With a target of culture in the world and an emphasis on queer difference, the message of defiant visibility trends toward bold, provocative displays.

Educational visibility, by contrast, trends toward conservative displays that, in turn, can result in excluding segments of the LGBT population. Like Bernstein's "identity for education," with educational visibility, Pride participants promote the compatibility of queerness with established cultural standards of respectability. Participants emphasize sameness with heterosexual society by showing that, just like straights, LGBT people fulfill key social roles. They play sports, attend school, serve as police officers and firefighters, and raise children. They are racially diverse and maintain connections with ethnic communities. Educational visibility is a message that targets both culture in the mind and culture in the world. Participants attempt to sway individuals to accept LGBT people into their communities while simultaneously offering new images of LGBT people that align with existing cultural values. To successfully change culture in the mind, this message needs to be sensitive to what skeptical individuals may find off-putting about queer sexuality and thus downplay overtly sexual displays and radical divergence from gender norms. Likewise, in its attempt to replace stereotypical images of LGBT people in the world as overly sexual or gender divergent, educational visibility must restrict displays that reinforce these stereotypes. While for some an emphasis on sameness is an easy matter of choosing a conservative outfit for the day or refraining from same-sex PDA, it requires suppressing important aspects of personal identity for others, such as transgender individuals for whom gender transgression is central to identity.[12] Thus, in order to be successful, a focus on educational visibility invites censorship of provocative displays, which, in turn, excludes some in the LGBT community.[13]

As participants at each parade tailored how they made themselves visible to their local environment, they revealed disparate approaches to the debate over provocative displays. It may seem that some parades emphasized defiant visibility with provocative displays, while others— perhaps those in more conservative regions—restricted such displays in favor of educational visibility. That is not what I found. Instead, participants at every parade from New York City to Fargo communicated both defiant and educational visibility in roughly equal measure. In each location, there were some who advocated defiant over educational visibility, and others who preferred the reverse. Still others thought both messages were valuable and should be presented side-by-side. Interestingly, whether the cultural climate was relatively accepting like in New York, or harsh like in Fargo, participants said that their preferred message was the one best suited to local challenges. For instance, Jakob in Fargo said that local culture needed to be "shaken up" with bold displays of the very gender-bending LGBT people that some residents wanted to pretend did not exist. Similarly, Monique in New York argued that cultural tolerance for gays and lesbians who mostly followed gender norms had the effect of making transgender and genderqueer individuals invisible, and that this should be challenged with visible displays at Pride.[14]

Though parades did not vary by *how much* they emphasized defiant versus educational visibility, they did vary in *how* they communicated these messages. Participants in relatively accepting cultural climates had more space to push the envelope with defiant visibility, while less welcoming local cultures were challenged by tame demonstrations of LGBT visibility such as the act of gay couples holding hands. With educational visibility, those in less tolerant cultural climates emphasized a conservative image that conveyed LGBT people's similarity to the mainstream. By contrast, in more tolerant places, the focus of educational visibility was on combatting stereotypes that limit LGBT people. With greater community resources, participants in New York and other big cities put on big, loud displays that dwarfed those of smaller cities. Similarly, those with more community resources communicated educational visibility with a greater diversity of marching contingents and spectators.

LGBT people in New York City today find a relatively accepting local cultural climate and a wealth of community resources. The massive LGBT Community Center exemplifies both the community's challenges and its opportunities. Located just a half mile from the historic Stonewall Inn, the site of the 1969 Stonewall riots, the Center occupies nearly a city block and offers a range of services, including health and wellness programs, family support, and community events. Its very existence and scale evince a local cultural climate that is accepting enough to allow such a visible presence of queer sexuality and gender. At the same time, the social and cultural marginalization of LGBT people is at the root of their need for the Center's services. As a group, the LGBT population has higher rates of substance abuse, depression, and other health concerns due at least in part to the added stress of concealing their identities or facing discrimination once they come out.[15] Adolescents are often rejected from families when they are open about their LGBT identity, prompting a need for community support, housing, and even suicide prevention services.[16] Pride participants told me that in their daily lives they felt comfortable being out as LGBT and did not experience open hostility, but they also were very aware of pockets of rejection. Monique, in particular, talked about rejection experienced by transgender youth in the Bronx who were kicked out of homes and discriminated against when applying for jobs and seeking social services. Despite remarkable visibility and acceptance in New York City, heteronormativity was still present, with both large and small consequences for LGBT people.

Along with cultural advances and remaining challenges, New York City's LGBT Community Center also represents the immense resources available to the local LGBT population. The Center finds ready financial sponsors in the city's business, non-profit, and civic sectors. With incredible diversity in the greater NYC population, community groups targeted to specific racial/ethnic groups, interests, and experiences often partner with the Center in their work.[17] Like the LGBT Community Center, Pride in New York City has myriad resources available to accomplish its mission, one part of which was to combat heteronormativity.

In New York City, where the cultural climate allows for some everyday signs of LGBT visibility, defiant visibility meant pushing further with brazen displays, including some that were overtly sexual. Available resources made it possible for NYC participants to make their displays of defiant visibility quite grand. In terms of sheer numbers, approximately one million LGBT people and allies made this show of LGBT visibility impossible to miss. Leading off the parade, a huge contingent of about one hundred leather-clad Dykes on Bikes flaunted their unmistakable defiance of the heteronormative prescription that women be delicate and passive. Local gay nightclubs sponsored decorated floats complete with costumed dancers and amplified music. Spectators had ready access to slogan t-shirts, rainbow clothing, and more outrageous costumes pieces like angel wings or leather pants with which to proclaim their LGBT identity. Though displays of overt sexuality were comparatively rare, there was certainly no shortage of participants wearing provocative clothing or dancing suggestively; neither a harsh cultural climate nor a lack of resources constrained them from choosing to communicate defiant visibility in this way.

Similarly, Pride participants drew from community resources to communicate educational visibility in a way that was tailored to their local cultural climates. In the diverse city of New York, LGBT marching contingents represented an impressive range of race- and ethnic-specific groups, including the Northeast Two-Spirit Society, African Ancestral Lesbians United for Social Change, the Indonesian group Satu Pelangi, and the Latino Pride Center.

FIGURE 4.2 Colombian group shows the diversity of the LGBT community in New York City's Pride parade.

Similarly, contingents portrayed LGBT people in a host of social roles, including civil servants (e.g., Gay Officers Action League, Gays and Lesbians in Foreign Affairs Agencies), athletes (e.g., Gotham Knights Rugby Football Club, NYC Gay Basketball League), and students from at least twenty high schools and colleges. New York City's relatively progressive culture meant that showcasing LGBT people in these roles did not mean putting strict limits on participants' self-expression. While gay athletic teams marched in sports jerseys in all but the smallest parades, a few of the male Gotham Knights of New York added flair to their outfits with extra-short shorts. LGBT participants showed that they fit into the larger NYC culture, and did so without adopting a strategy that excluded more radical expressions of queer sexuality.

Such an open forum for both defiant and educational visibility displays in New York City contrasted with the parade in Fargo, North Dakota. In this small Midwestern city, queerness was rarely even talked about, much less made visible. According to Pride participants, when queer people were discussed, they were described as stereotypical effeminate gay men or man-hating lesbians and thus as people considered foreign to the Fargo community. Though LGBT participants reported being out to most friends and families, they did not mark their identities in their everyday lives with things like non-normative clothing or rainbow symbols.

Like participants at other parades, Pride participants in Fargo tackled issues of invisibility and misunderstanding with two messages of visibility. In a show of defiant visibility, they announced their LGBT identities through dress and style, with many women wearing cargo shorts, t-shirts, and pulling their hair into ponytails, and many men sporting tighter fitting clothes like V-neck shirts. Unlike in New York City, though, Fargo's participants did not challenge heteronormativity with overt sexual displays or even more PG-rated same-sex PDA (public displays of affection). In fact, I saw little physical affection at all, despite a presumable number of same-sex couples in attendance. According to Jade, a bisexual woman in Fargo, this lack of PDA was not so much a strategic decision as it was a reflection of the small-town nature of the greater Fargo community. Since any displays at Pride would be retold in stories later, possibly to one's family, and would not be judged kindly, participants stuck to moderate demonstrations that challenged the heteronormative cultural code in the world without inciting personal backlash. Though Fargo participants conveyed defiant visibility, like the couple shown in figure 4.3, they did so with relatively tame displays.

As Jade indicated, participants were very aware of how their displays would be perceived in the less tolerant cultural climate of Fargo and they communicated educational visibility with a similar sensitivity to local reactions. This message was not just a matter of personal consequences, but of effectiveness. Since this message in part targets culture in the mind, successful displays of educational visibility need to convince skeptical individuals that LGBT people deserve full acceptance in society. In New York City, residents are used to seeing all manner of personal expressions and are unlikely to balk at the extra dash of flamboyance they see when the gay rugby team marches by. More likely, they would react with surprise to find that such a team exists, given the stereotype that gay men shy away from masculine pursuits like sports. In Fargo, though, cultural norms dictate more conservative clothing and style for everyone, while attitudes toward LGBT people are less accepting overall. Participants like Dee Ann wanted to change these attitudes by showing that transgender people like her are not so different from mainstream residents. To do this, she dressed in normatively feminine clothing and marched with a group holding signs that identified them as transgender. Though Dee Ann was comfortable participating in this way, younger participants Jade and Jakob felt constrained by the need to limit their personal expression at Pride. While they agreed that presenting a normative appearance was most likely to be effective in swaying attitudes, this aspect made Fargo Pride less attractive to them.

Fargo's small and fairly homogenous LGBT population also contributed to participants' tame visibility displays. Mass demonstrations have an impact by showing strength in numbers and disrupting the everyday.[18] Therefore, one way Pride parades communicate defiant visibility is by gathering a critical mass of people to display their LGBT identity. Even with participants travelling from up to one hundred miles away, Fargo's 350-participant parade was the smallest that I visited. In relative terms, this still created a visible queer space, but it did not have the traffic-stopping impact of New York's massive event. When the Dykes on Bikes kicked off Fargo's parade, it was comprised of just three women who rode their motorcycles up and down the parade route many times.

FIGURE 4.3 A lesbian couple shows defiant visibility as they ride together in Fargo's Pride parade. Photo courtesy of Jagnoor Singh.

Marching contingents' displays of defiant visibility were also more modest because without resources like thriving gay bars, there were no decorated floats or amplified music.[19] The community's lack of diversity affected both defiant and educational visibility. In addition to feeling constrained by the cultural climate, participants like Jade and Jakob who preferred more radical displays did not have the critical mass to, say, watch in a group wearing coordinated rainbow Speedos, as I saw young men do in San Diego. To communicate educational visibility, the local population had a limited pool of diversity from which to draw to showcase LGBT people in a variety of roles. While they did demonstrate that LGBT people are similar in many ways to their straight neighbors, this similarity was generic rather than composed of LGBT people with different racial/ethnic backgrounds, professional roles, and hobbies, as in New York.

At Pride, provocative displays, particularly those that are overtly sexual, are the flashpoint for diverging impulses to confront heteronormativity in the world, on the one hand, and to coax individual attitude change, on the other. From its inception, Pride has been about gays demonstrating *as gays*, putting their identities front and center to challenge their cultural invisibility. Creating such a visible queer presence, however, has raised the question of how to represent LGBT people on a public stage. As scholars of the LGBT movement have noted, activist leaders struggle at length to craft a visibility strategy that will advance LGBT cultural equality. These movement organizers debate whether to emphasize LGBT people's sameness with the heterosexual majority or their difference from it. Each strategy comes with attendant dangers: the exclusion of those less "respectable" members of LGBT community on the one hand, and the overly provocative displays on the other. Scholarship that takes an organizer perspective has considered how activist leaders weigh these dangers against movement goals to design a visibility strategy.

With Pride organizers taking a hands-off approach to participant displays, participants made their identities visible in the ways that best made sense to them rather than according to a top-down strategy imposed by leaders. The resulting displays coalesced into two messages: defiant visibility, which demanded that culture in the world change to make room for LGBT people's difference; and educational visibility, which sought to change both culture in the mind by persuading individuals that LGBT people are not so different after all and culture in the world by replacing stereotypical images of LGBT people with ones that are more compatible with heteronormativity. Despite quite dissimilar cultural climates, participants in New York City and Fargo alike found utility in both defiant and educational visibility, albeit in different forms and with the use of different resources. In each place, they sought to create more visibility for LGBT people. Rather than choosing one message, they communicated both side-by-side but tailored them to their local communities. Participants were wary of the tendencies toward provocative displays on the one hand, and exclusion on the other, but managed to largely avoid both by balancing the two messages.

Support

While walking among spectators at Atlanta's 2010 Pride parade, I met Sue and Bob, who were holding signs that read "I Love My Gay Son," and "I Love My Lesbian Daughter." When I talked to them, I learned that when each child came out as LGBT, they endured rejection from peers and struggled with the feeling that they no longer fit in their suburban community. Inspired to get active in the fight for LGBT equality, Sue and

Bob joined their local chapter of Parents and Friends of Lesbians and Gays (PFLAG) and Georgia Equality, a statewide LGBT rights group. They started attending Atlanta Pride every year, first marching with PFLAG and then, as they became less active with the group, participating on their own, armed with signs and buttons. They described their purpose as two-fold: to let LGBT people know that there were parents out there who accepted their children's queer sexuality without reservation, and to make a public statement of support for LGBT people.

Sue and Bob were joined by thousands of other spectators and marching contingents who all conveyed the message of public support at Atlanta Pride. PFLAG members from the greater Atlanta area marched together in one large contingent proclaiming family values of love, acceptance, and support. Contingents representing local Episcopal, Unitarian-Universalist, Lutheran, Jewish, and Baptist congregations marched with signs proclaiming God's unconditional love.[20] Both local businesses and national corporations were ubiquitous. Delta Airlines was named in all official parade communications as the event's presenter, and a large contingent of its employees led the parade just after the Dykes on Bikes. Renowned national and multinational companies like Coca-Cola, Home Depot, and Bud Light—along with smaller local businesses—participated with banners, marching contingents, and financial sponsorship.

While parents' demonstrations of support are enthusiastically welcomed at Pride, the involvement of mainstream institutional actors—businesses, politicians, and even churches—has been debated since Pride's founding in 1970. Skepticism stems from the fact that these groups may come to Pride with ulterior motives, hoping to sell products, gain votes, or recruit new members. Critics warn that unless their participation is kept in check, institutional actors will overrun Pride so that it becomes *only* a forum for their interests. For gay liberationists in the 1970s, the danger was even greater. According to gay liberation ideology, these actors, with firm footing in mainstream society, are part of the oppressive system that activists seek to dismantle and thus can only hurt the cause of gay liberation.

Gays and lesbians in the 1970s certainly did not have churches, major corporations, or politicians lining up to join their parade.[21] But they did grapple with whether to encourage participation from local gay businesses. In New York, organizers worried that, in their desire

FIGURE 4.4 The Bud Light sponsor contingent marches in Atlanta's Pride parade with messages of support. Photo courtesy of Stan Fong, Atlanta Pride Committee.

to attract customers, businesses would put on frivolous displays with go-go dancers and music. As we see today, they were not wrong; gay clubs sponsor floats with both salacious dancers and amplified music, though whether this is frivolous is a matter for debate. In Los Angeles, organizers faced the opposite pressure as business leaders pushed for a conservative representation of the gay and lesbian community in the parade. On both coasts, Pride committees faced the dilemma of whether to include gay businesses as important aspects of the community—they were, after all, one of the few places where gays and lesbians could gather openly—or to exclude them as detracting from Pride's purpose.

Despite these concerns, businesses have long participated in Pride both as marching contingents and financial sponsors. As parades steadily grew, so did the importance of businesses who provided the financial backing to help pay for them. In the 1990s, their involvement spiked as nationally recognized corporations sponsored Pride in New York City, San Francisco, and other large cities. Critics charge that with market motivations for participating in Pride, businesses misrepresent the LGBT population as more affluent, whiter, and more male than it actually is.[22] Indeed, organizers who pitch Pride sponsorship to businesses tout the high economic status of some LGBT people. Studies actually show that the LGBT population in the U.S. includes people at all economic levels and has higher rates of poverty and lower average incomes than the heterosexual population.[23] Despite this, some critics believe that the heavy involvement of businesses at many Pride parades further perpetuates the myth that LGBT people are better off than their straight counterparts.

The problem with this myth is three-fold. First, opponents of LGBT equality cite their supposed high economic status as evidence that LGBT people have already achieved cultural equality and do not need expanded legal rights like same-sex marriage or non-discrimination statutes.[24] Second, just as in the general population, those LGBT people with more money are disproportionately white and male.[25] In their drive to advertise goods and services, business participants will direct their messages to those LGBT people and allies with money, ignoring those without.[26] Third, businesses market a certain image of gays and lesbians (it is exceedingly rare to see an advertisement, even at Pride, that features or targets bisexuals or transgender people) as a distinct minority group that does not threaten heteronomative culture—that is, this image promotes LGBT sameness, not difference. As media scholar Katherine Sender argues, this stance puts LGBT people into a box that, while an improvement from invisibility and derision, is a barrier to full cultural equality.[27]

The myth of the affluent, white gay man is especially troubling with regard to lower-income LGBT people who, following broader social trends, are disproportionately non-white and female.[28] Additionally, due to intense social rejection and blatant discrimination (which is legal in most states), transgender people are four times more likely to be poor than a typical American.[29] Working-class and poor LGBT people stand to benefit most from increased legal protections like same-sex marriage (they also raise children at higher rates than affluent LGBT people), so if corporate involvement in Pride detracts from this need, as critics argue, they will suffer most. Similarly, business sponsors are unlikely to target LGBT people who do not have extra income, which may leave them feeling excluded from Pride. Finally, without the money to, say, buy fancy clothes and go on gay cruises, lower-income LGBT people are less able to fit into the image promoted by corporate advertising. Since they are often seen as diverging even more from heteronormative standards than do gays, lesbians, and bisexuals, transgender people in particular may suffer if LGBT people are accepted only on the condition that they fit into a nonthreatening box.

While by no means-off base, once again these critiques come from an organizer's rather than a participant's perspective. Critics put the onus on organizers to scale back business involvement because of its harmful effect on movement goals but rarely consider how participants interact with business sponsors. Lurking behind the censure is an assumption that spectators, especially, are passive consumers of Pride parades rather than active participants. One exception to this is research by Steven M. Kates and Russell W. Belk, who argue that Pride participants bought t-shirts and wore rainbow beads with the Bacardi Rum logo as a form of resistance to the heteronormative cultural code.[30] Similarly, as I contend in the previous section, businesses that sell LGBT-themed items serve as community resources that enable participants to make their identities visible (albeit those participants who can afford specialty clothing). Critiques also miss the ways that participants directly benefit from corporate sponsorship—namely, by being able to attend Pride parades free of charge. From this perspective, businesses offer much-appreciated financial and symbolic support for LGBT people through participation in Pride. As we evaluate the role of institutional actors in Pride, particularly businesses, we need to balance these two perspectives.

The message of public support fits the unique cultural challenges and opportunities faced by LGBT people in Atlanta. In the Bible Belt South, Christian religion—and more specifically, evangelical Protestantism—plays a dominant role in the regional culture. Christian symbols, music, news, and codes of meaning are embedded in everyday life, making up a major component of Southern culture in the world and of culture in the mind of Southerners.[31] Like the Mormon Church in Salt Lake City, major evangelical denominations such as the Southern Baptist Convention consider homosexuality sinful and believe that lifelong opposite-sex marriage is God's plan. This anti-LGBT cultural influence was embodied at Pride by six groups of counter-protesters spread throughout the parade route, far more than I observed at any other parade. These groups of five to ten people held signs that condemned homosexuality as sinful and shouted warnings to participants of their assured damnation. The largest group even used an amplified public address system to intersperse gospel music with preaching about the evils of homosexuality. While participants certainly did not encounter such strident condemnation in their daily lives, counter-protesters were a visible and extreme version of the region's harsh cultural climate.

As with most cities, Atlanta's local cultural climate is multifaceted. Though Bible Belt homophobia looms large, so does the city's pro-business drive and its urban multiculturalism.[32] During the civil rights era, Atlanta fashioned itself "the city too busy to hate," expressing a desire (even if it was not fully realized) to privilege economic growth over racial conflict and inequality.[33] People from all backgrounds moved to the city in the latter half of the twentieth century seeking economic opportunities and bringing with them diverse cultural traditions.[34] LGBT Southerners are among those who migrated to Atlanta, creating a thriving queer subculture, despite sometimes-violent opposition since the mid-twentieth century.[35] Like New York, there are pockets of Atlanta that are quite welcoming to LGBT people and others that are not as tolerant. The city's Midtown neighborhood, where Pride takes place, can even be described as a "gayborhood" with its LGBT bookstore, gay bars and clubs, and a visible LGBT population. Meanwhile, the climate towards LGBT people cools as one moves out from the city center to suburbs and rural areas, where many Pride participants live.

As a large metropolis, Atlanta is home to many resources that shape Pride's message of public support. Many major corporations with ample philanthropic budgets and household names have headquarters in the city, including Delta Airlines, Coca-Cola, and Chik Fil-A. Certainly not all are likely to support Pride—most notably Chik Fil-A, whose owner sparked controversy when he supported a number of staunchly anti-gay organizations—but the presence of so many corporations constitutes a source of potential funding and public support for Pride. Reflecting the importance of Christianity to the local cultural climate, there are over four thousand Christian churches in the Atlanta metro area. While

FIGURE 4.5 One of many groups of counter-protesters hold signs at Atlanta's Pride parade. Photo courtesy of Stan Fong, Atlanta Pride Committee.

the majority are evangelical Protestant and likely to oppose Pride, two hundred are affiliated with denominations that support LGBT rights, including the United Church of Christ, the Episcopal Church, and the Society of Friends (Quaker). By comparison, there are fourteen hundred Christian churches in the San Diego metro area, one hundred of which are part of LGBT-supportive denominations.[36] Finally, the Atlanta LGBT community is well established with a tradition of activism. Both in Midtown and elsewhere in the city, LGBT people have bars, clubs, a community center, and other spaces in which to congregate, organize, and have fun.

With a cultural climate and community resources shaped by the Bible Belt, quite a few church groups marched in Atlanta Pride. They represented many LGBT-friendly Protestant denominations, such as Episcopal and Quaker, as well as a Unitarian-Universalist and a Jewish congregation. Marchers with these groups separated themselves from evangelical churches that characterize the Bible Belt. For instance, one woman, marching with a large group of Baptists, held a sign that read "I am Southern, I am Baptist, [but] I am not a Southern Baptist," while another marcher's sign announced: "I am an Ordained Baptist Minister."[37] The implication of these signs is that being Baptist does not mean that one must condemn queer sexuality. By identifying themselves as Baptist and marching in Pride, these participants showed that Baptist faith, and more broadly Christian faith, may lead some to support LGBT people. Similarly, through their participation, Episcopalians, Quakers, and Jews showed that, in contrast to counter-protesters, religious faith may mean welcoming rather than rejecting LGBT people.

Motivated by the frequent condemnation of LGBT people by evangelical churches, many pro-LGBT congregations made a special effort to organize a marching contingent and travel to Pride in Atlanta. For two churches, St. Mark's United Methodist and the Lutheran Church of the Redeemer, Pride came to them and they responded by offering tangible support in the form of water stations and open buildings for participants to cool down in and use the restrooms. These two churches are located on Peachtree Street along the parade route, and according to one organizer, these water stations were a long-standing tradition. In the harsh climate of the 1970s when the parade was just becoming established, many participants marched with paper bags over their heads to mask their identities. Seeing this, members of these two churches offered water to marchers as they passed by. Though at the time their denominations condemned queer sexuality (and today they remain ambivalent), members of these congregations saw the struggle in front of them and responded in a way they felt their faith required.[38] They did not explicitly state that they backed the goals of Pride, but they publicly demonstrated that they were on the side of marchers rather than against them. The involvement of these churches in Pride is a reflection of the central place that religious institutions have both in Atlanta's cultural climate and in its stock of community resources.

Along with standing out for its heavy church involvement, Atlanta Pride put business sponsors in a prominent role. Nationally recognized corporate sponsors such as Wells Fargo, Sony, AT&T, and Bud Light were present at all the parades I studied—save the two smallest, Fargo and Burlington—but in Atlanta, they were especially visible through banners, large parade contingents, and logos on parade websites and publicity flyers. Atlanta Pride even included Delta Airlines as a presenting sponsor, placing the company's logo at the header of all Atlanta Pride materials and giving its marching contingent "pride" of place as the first group—after the Dykes on Bikes, of course. Local restaurants, gay bars and clubs, radio stations, gyms, and travel companies were also represented throughout the parade.

To a large extent, this considerable business involvement reflected organizers' strategic choices. Pride parades are expensive affairs, costing over $1 million in cities like Atlanta. Many Pride committees see corporate sponsorship as a way to offer the parade and other events without charge, while also gaining symbolic capital as nationally recognized corporations put their stamp of approval on the event.[39] In Atlanta, organizers' strategic decisions were aided by the city's vibrant business climate and the presence of many company's corporate headquarters. With many large corporations making their home in the city, organizers had no trouble finding potential sponsors.

Atlanta Pride participants saw these sponsorships as signs of public support from the business community. They recognized Delta Airlines, Coca-Cola, and Home Depot as Atlanta-based businesses and were glad to know that they would support such a visibly queer event. That said, participants were not ignorant to businesses' ulterior motives; they knew that businesses were there at least partially to market their brands, but most accepted these motives in exchange for the positive public statement and important financial resources that businesses bring to Pride. While participants at all parades had a generally positive view of corporate sponsors, in Atlanta, such sponsors found a particularly warm welcome. They provided a culturally respected voice in support of LGBT people that contrasted with the frequent condemnations from evangelical Christians at the heart of Bible Belt culture.

On the west coast, the slightly bigger San Diego Pride had similar community resources from which to draw, but was in a more LGBT-friendly cultural climate. Similar to Atlanta, San Diego is a large metropolis in which there is an established LGBT community with gay bars and restaurants, a community center, and many activist organizations. Pride organizers found ready financial partners in the many local businesses and large corporations in the area. As in Atlanta, access to financial and organizational community resources enabled the San Diego LGBT community to put on a grand parade through its own "gayborhood," the Hillcrest neighborhood.

In contrast to their counterparts in Atlanta, San Diego participants enjoyed relative acceptance from friends and neighbors in their daily lives. For instance, Desiree told me that she and her wife often went to work and to social events as a couple and were treated with respect. Outside these local environments, though, the couple was keenly aware that they did not enjoy the legal rights or cultural esteem that goes along with state-sanctioned marriage. As discussed in the last chapter, in 2010, public debates over gays in the military and same-sex marriage highlighted a cultural code of meaning that still regarded queerness as inferior to heterosexuality. Thus, while LGBT people in San Diego were concerned with the negative public debate on LGBT issues, the harmful cultural meanings did not seem to touch the daily lives of most.[40] Instead, their daily lives were marked by tolerance, if not full-fledged acceptance.

San Diego's more tolerant local climate led to there being less of an emphasis on communicating public support at Pride. Those institutional actors who marched with messages of support in other parades—churches, politicians, and businesses—conveyed a more celebratory message in San Diego than they did in Atlanta. As mainstream institutions, they still lent valuable symbolic capital by showing support for LGBT people through the act of participating at Pride. With their displays, though, many groups demonstrated that they did not just support queer sexuality, they celebrated it as well. A contingent of Quakers, for example, carried rainbow parasols that they occasionally incorporated into a simple dance routine. As an LGBT-friendly church, they demonstrated public support by marching, and with some extra festivity they actively took part in the fun. Similarly, the San Diego Public Defenders marched with a sign proclaiming they had been "Getting You Off Since 1988." With this sexually suggestive banner, the group joined LGBT participants in the celebration of queer sexuality. In a context where outright condemnation was rare, there was less of a need for institutional actors to stand up in support of LGBT people. What was needed, though, was the message that queer sexuality is not just something to be tolerated, but to be enthusiastically celebrated. In response, institutional actors marched *with* LGBT people at Pride in addition to marching *for* them.

Along with a difference in *how much* Pride participants emphasized public support, San Diego and Atlanta differed in *how* participants communicated this message. With a local climate heavily influenced by

FIGURE 4.6 A church member holds a playful sign in San Diego's Pride parade. Photo courtesy of Nathan Rupert.

evangelical Christianity, pro-LGBT churches publicized their support at Atlanta Pride. Their message spoke to the religious nature of queer sexuality's cultural condemnation in the Bible Belt. In San Diego, by contrast, public debate centered on whether queerness was "as good as" heterosexuality, but not whether it was a moral failing. As a result, religious groups were less prevalent in San Diego's Pride parade. In their place, many Democratic politicians organized marching contingents. California's state Democratic Party decorated a truck with campaign signs for governor, senate, state assembly, and even local school board candidates. Spread out through the parade, many of these hopeful candidates—along with politicians currently holding office—marched, waving rainbow flags and shaking hands with spectators.

These politicians advertised their public support of LGBT people in a place where the cultural climate was largely shaped by recent political fights over same-sex marriage and the military's exclusion of gays and lesbians. Though members (or aspiring members) of the government had the ability to influence legal policies, their participation was focused on sending a cultural message regarding the place of LGBT people in society rather than advocating for legal changes that ought to take place. Politicians refrained from explicit messages about LGBT legal rights, choosing instead to communicate the implicit (and vague) message that they were "on the side" of LGBT people. That is, they did not communicate explicit campaign promises of support for any specific legislation. Their participation reflected San Diego's stronger local code of tolerance, in which participating in Pride was not a political risk, particularly for Democratic politicians whose party has become increasingly known for its support of LGBT rights. Individual participants told me that they were happy these politicians made such a public statement in favor of LGBT issues and hoped that their voting record would reflect the same support. However, some were skeptical of politicians who participated in Pride, assuming that, like businesses, they had ulterior motives—in this case, to raise money and votes for upcoming elections.

San Diego Pride was a grand event that required significant financial backing. To meet this need, organizers turned to corporate sponsors to offset the cost. As in Atlanta, San Diego Pride organizers found plenty of nationally recognized corporations willing to partner. Bud Light, Cox Communications, and the travel website Orbitz were among the companies who were prominent financial sponsors. In exchange, their logos were included in official Pride materials and their contingents marched in the parade. These sponsors had a slightly less prominent role in San Diego than in Atlanta; there was, for instance, no corporation named as a presenting sponsor like Delta Airlines in Atlanta. According to one organizer, this was a deliberate decision in response to concerns about commercialization at Pride parades. While the San Diego Pride committee accepted business involvement as a "necessary evil" to cover the enormous costs of putting on Pride, they wanted corporations to be just one voice among many, rather than a dominating presence.[41] Echoing criticisms of Pride's commercialization, San Diego organizers worried that by giving corporate logos too much prominence, they would transform the parade from a place of protest to a marketplace. For their part, San Diego participants appreciated the financial and symbolic support of corporate sponsors. Talking to participants, both in formal interviews and casually during the parade, it was clear that they did not give much thought to business involvement. When pressed, most said that while they did not want businesses to play a bigger role, they saw sponsors as community partners.

Though they had similar community resources, LGBT people in San Diego had different cultural challenges than their counterparts in Atlanta. In the Bible Belt South of Atlanta, LGBT people struggled against an evangelical Christian worldview that defined queerness as sinful—a view that played a central role in shaping the local cultural climate. By contrast, in San Diego, the local culture was more accepting, but LGBT people fought in public debates against the notion that queerness is inferior to heterosexuality. Institutional actors in both communities, including businesses, churches, and politicians, showed public support for LGBT people by marching in the parade and, often, through financial sponsorship. Their message targeted culture in the world, contesting dominant meanings of queerness as sinful and inferior and a culture that condemned LGBT people by instead demonstrating their support.

Since Pride's early days in the 1970s, participants have debated the role of institutional actors as marching contingents and sponsors. Aside from some of the more radical gay liberationists, pro-gay churches have been universally embraced at Pride. Their involvement presents a powerful contrast to the faith-based condemnation of queerness that has long been part heteronormativity. In places like San Diego where religion has a weaker influence on a local climate that is more tolerant to LGBT people, politicians touted their cultural and political support for LGBT people by marching in Pride. Though they took a more skeptical view to politicians than churches, participants still counted it a win to have these prominent public figures align themselves with the LGBT community, rather than against them.

Local businesses and national corporations sponsored Pride financially and marched in parades. Their financial support in particular enabled parades to get bigger and bigger, while remaining free of cost to spectators. As LGBT acceptance increases nationwide, Pride organizers find more willing financial partners in local and national corporations than ever before. However, the participation of businesses raises concerns over whether commercialization corrupts Pride by shifting the focus of the event from social change to commercial exchange or by promoting a distorted image of LGBT people as affluent consumers who are doing just fine without full legal or cultural equality. Though aware of corporations' market motivations, participants still viewed them as valuable partners with the mainstream credibility needed to make a powerful statement in support of LGBT acceptance. Rather than creating an exclusive admission-only Pride event, which threatened to leave out working-class and poor LGBT people, participants credited businesses for footing the bill of Pride. From this perspective, businesses were positive additions to Pride, showing much needed public support through contingent displays and financial sponsorship.

That said, the level of commercialization in Atlanta in particular is a cause for concern. As early Pride organizers recognized, businesses have the financial resources and market motivations to put on bigger, louder, and more colorful displays than any other type of participant. This ability means their messages of support, delivered with the motive of selling goods and services, threatens to overpower other messages at Pride. With budgets that dwarf those of local gay businesses who were early Pride sponsors, corporations create professional displays that are even more flashy and attention-getting than early LGBT leaders could have imagined. These displays threaten to detract from those of more modest means, such as the ones created by churches, non-profit groups, and individual participants like Sue and Bob who held a simple sign declaring their love for their gay children. Commercial influence at Pride shows no signs of waning. As more and more corporations see public support for LGBT people as a smart business move, Pride organizers and participants will increasingly grapple with how to include the valuable contribution of businesses without letting them overtake those of individuals, community groups, churches, and non-profits.

Celebration

I only visited one Pride parade that did not begin with a contingent of Dykes on Bikes. Instead of this traditional opening contingent, a group of Samba drummers kicked off the parade in Burlington, Vermont, followed by four belly dancers. Like the lesbian motorcyclists, these drummers and belly dancers started off the parade on a festive note. As they marched down the pedestrian-only Church Street, crowds of spectators—who had been waiting for the parade to begin—let out a cheer. This celebratory tone carried through the rest of the parade. Next in the lineup, members of the University of Vermont's LGBTQA student group were decked in rainbows and cheering from the back of a pickup truck. Along the sidelines, spectators laughed and shouted approval as they watched each contingent of marchers go by. Even bystanders who happened to be out shopping or dining on this main street on a beautiful Saturday stopped to applaud as the parade passed by.

By beginning with the roaring engines of Dykes on Bikes or the energetic drumming of a Samba group, Pride parades mark themselves as celebrations from the outset. Similarly, participants throughout the parade celebrate their sexuality with playful signs, outfits, and chants. Pride parades are not somber vigils to remember the pain of oppression, nor are they angry protests designed to show strength against socially imposed marginalization. Pride parades do indeed recall oppression and display group strength, but they do so in the format of a grand celebration. Since the first Pride events in New York City and Los Angeles, those who participate have noted not just the way Pride makes queerness visible and showcases support, but also how it genuinely *celebrates* queer sexuality and gender. By doing so, it flips the heteronormative cultural code on its head, turning what is culturally condemned into a cause for celebration—hell, a reason to have a parade.

As fun as it is, Pride's festive tone is also the crux of a third long-running debate. Supporters and critics alike worry that too much focus on celebration will obscure Pride's serious purpose of changing the cultural meaning of queerness. There are two aspects to this. First, as with commercialization, excessive emphasis on celebration may distract participants—so that, instead of attending Pride to fight LGBT cultural inequality, they come merely to party. Second, similar to the concern over provocative visibility displays, lavish celebration could promote an image of a frivolous LGBT community that neither needs nor deserves legal rights and cultural inclusion. Once again, these criticisms focus on the planning decisions of the organizers rather than the experiences of

FIGURE 4.7 A couple marches with a simple sign to celebrate their queer sexuality in Vermont's Pride parade. Photo courtesy of David Garten.

the participants, leaving strategic decision-making in the hands of activist leaders. Additionally, the criticisms are based on an inside-out model of cultural change in which the focus is on how skeptic individuals receive Pride messages. If instead the celebration message targets culture in the world with an outside-in model, then we reach a more positive conclusion about its utility for social change.

Scholars of social movements stress the importance of participants' *intentionality* in considering what makes a protest.[42] Plenty of public acts may unintentionally challenge dominant culture. I grew up attending college football games during which students from the rival team would occasionally "moon" our side. Though the display of bare bottoms certainly challenged our culture's arbitrary insistence on wearing clothing in public, I do not think this was the message they intended; they were just having fun with a familiar and childish form of insult. Similarly, though, an event that may start out as a protest could transform into a benign public party as participants lose their activist intentions. St. Patrick's Day parades, for example, began as demonstrations of the important role that Irish immigrants played in American communities. Now, they appear for most participants to be a day to drink green beer and revel in a caricatured version of Irish identity.[43] Critics argue that participants have become so sidetracked by Pride's festive atmosphere, entertaining displays, and raucous after-parties, that the parade is more an excuse to have trivial fun that a protest for meaningful change.

However, just because a public act is fun does not mean that it is unintentional. Scholars note that protest participants often enjoy their experience.[44] It is this positive sentiment that attracts new activists and sustains them through long campaigns. For instance, when participants camped out in rainy, muddy conditions for six weeks on the grounds of the Washington Mall for the 1968 Poor People's Campaign, it was not all drudgery and sacrifice. They were making a serious statement about economic inequality, yes, but they also had the rare leisure time to socialize, play, and enjoy the many famous musicians who supported their protest with live concerts.[45] Moreover, protest itself can be fun as participants get the rare chance to flaunt en masse the demeaning social norms that are often part of the oppression they experience.[46] One side of this is the way that fun generates positive emotions, which in turn brings participants together as a community (as discussed in the next chapter). The other side, which I delve into here, is how having fun adds to, rather than detracts from, participants' commitment to social movement goals.

A related concern with Pride celebrations is that they may promote a damaging image of queerness as frivolous and of LGBT inequality as trivial. For instance, commentators like Cord Jefferson juxtapose popular Pride images of shirtless men dancing suggestively or leather-clad women revving motorcycles with iconic images from the civil rights movement that show activists protesting in full suits despite the summer heat.[47] Through their conservative dress and solemn bearing, Jefferson argues, civil rights activists conveyed the seriousness of their cause and demanded respectful attention. By contrast, iconic images of Pride parades often depict gleeful gay men covered in glitter and preening atop colorful floats, which is hardly the picture of oppression to tug at the heartstrings of the masses and convince skeptics to support greater acceptance.

But public demonstrations do not always target individuals with rational arguments aimed at persuasion. Activists may take more creative approaches, using dramatic displays to call attention to their cause, highlight existing cultural contradictions, and promote their vision of ideal society.[48] Sometimes these performances are tragic, as when anti-abortion activists hold up massive pictures of aborted fetuses in an attempt to recast the issue as one of victimhood rather than choice.[49] Other times, they are comic—such as when the anti-capitalist group the Diggers rode half-naked through San Francisco's Financial District in 1966, asking brokers to forget their work and join them. Through its playfulness, this demonstration made the point that there are other things in life aside from work, and that the capitalist drive to forever accumulate more wealth and possessions distracts us from enjoying life's true pleasures.

Though dramatic displays may cause more irritation than serious consideration from bystanders, we should consider that perhaps individuals' cultural attitudes in the mind are not the target of such protest message. Instead, protesters may target cultural codes of meaning in the world by embracing the primacy of individual choice or challenging the capitalist principle that wealth has inherent worth. When it comes to comedic displays, rather than detracting from serious protest, sometimes humor, joy, and celebration *are* the protest in dramatic form.

Pride's celebratory atmosphere is one of its defining features. The first events in 1970 set themselves apart from the preceding Annual Reminders of the homophile movement in part because marchers projected how much fun they had being their true gay selves. In Los Angeles, gay and lesbian leaders took the celebration a step further by staging a parade rather than a march, including vehicles and a variety of marching contingents. Though some argued that the format reduced Pride to a frivolous spectacle, throughout the early 1970s Pride events across the country established themselves as parades. Pride organizers found that the parade format worked both as a way to convey Pride's festive spirit and to accommodate the diverse range of gay and lesbian community members who wanted to participate.

However, gay and lesbian leaders were still wary that Pride might cross the line from productive festivity into meaningless frivolity. For some, this happened at San Francisco's 1974 Pride parade, when the majority of contingents displayed such carefree celebration that a reporter from the mainstream *San Francisco Chronicle* wondered whether the local gay and lesbian community even wanted society to change.[50] Without clear messages that tied celebration to gays' cultural marginalization, commentators both inside and outside the gay and lesbian community thought that this parade communicated only frivolity. That parade serves as a reminder that festivity, while an important component to Pride, can go too far and thus, obscure the demand for cultural change.

One reason that Pride participants were able to exhibit such carefree festivity in 1974 was that, at the time, San Francisco was the most hospitable place in the country for gays and lesbians. Despite intense cultural rejection at regional, state, and national levels, gays and lesbians had managed to create a safe haven in the city's Castro District.[51] It was this accepting climate that allowed them to display such carefree festivity at their Pride parade. Similarly, Burlington, Vermont in 2010 was arguably a contemporary version of an LGBT utopia. LGBT people enjoyed both legal rights, including same-sex marriage and protection from employment discrimination, and widespread cultural tolerance. Ever since Vermont passed the country's first law to recognize same-sex partnerships (in the form of civil unions) in 2000, business and civic leaders have promoted the state's welcoming culture to LGBT tourists, particularly those wishing to marry.[52] LGBT participants told me that local acceptance was such that walking down the street holding hands with a same-sex partner—an act that may draw violence in some cities—was basically a non-event that rarely drew so much as a raised eyebrow. Neighbors treated queerness with a nonchalance that conveyed their understanding of queerness as a valid, even unremarkable, human difference.

Still, LGBT people in Burlington saw plenty room for cultural change. Angela, a lesbian who worked with queer youth, described how young people still struggled to come out as LGBT. Even though they were eventually accepted, most still experienced the initial shock and disappointment of families and friends at discovering their sexuality or gender identity. Blake, quoted in the epigraph of chapter 3, said that he feels a marked hesitation, and even shame, at openly displaying his gay identity. He is acutely aware that this identity, even when tolerated, is not celebrated in the same way as heterosexuality. These experiences reveal the persistence of a heteronormative cultural code that, even when coupled with a strong code of tolerance, still privileges heterosexuality over queerness.

Burlington is the most populous city in the state, but with only forty-two thousand residents, it is still pretty small.[53] Few well-known corporations make their homes in Vermont, unless one counts the ice cream company Ben & Jerry's (which, if you are interested in fun, you definitely should). The city has a vibrant downtown district and two universities—the public University of Vermont and its tiny neighbor, Champlain College—but it is more of a small town than a big city. The active local LGBT community maintains a community center, a charitable foundation, and social and advocacy groups for LGBT families, people living with HIV/AIDS, and queer youth. With such a limited and sparse population, though, it is unable to sustain gay bars or other businesses. LGBT people in Burlington, therefore, have comparatively few community resources with which to put on their Pride parade. Though they find willing business, civic, and religious partners, they are modest in scale. Additionally, a small population means that LGBT people and allies lack the critical mass with which to stage regular large events.

With limited resources and a supportive cultural climate, Burlington Pride resembled a small town Fourth of July parade, albeit with a different color scheme and more of an edge. The mood was festive all around as marchers, spectators, and bystanders enjoyed the open celebration on a bright afternoon. After the Samba drummers and belly dancers announced the start of the procession, contingents like the New Cocks on the Block, a drag king performance troupe, and a group of men in rainbow tank tops rode on the back of a pick-up truck decorated with balloons and streamers. Spectators cheered as the men's group sprayed silly string and one group member, clad in gold hot pants and an elaborate headdress, danced to techno music blaring from a boombox. Along the parade route, spectators laughed together at the more entertaining displays and cheered as each colorful contingent passed. The atmosphere contrasted with that in Fargo, another small parade in which the limited population combined with a local culture that condemned queerness to inhibit participants' provocative displays. The fear that one's actions at Pride would quickly get back to disapproving family and neighbors resulted in tame displays in Fargo. In Burlington, though, the small population has a much more tolerant cultural climate so that participants felt free to celebrate their queer sexuality and gender openly.

As in San Diego, the tolerant cultural climate in Burlington led to a greater emphasis on celebration than support. While pro-gay churches marched in Burlington Pride with messages of support, they also celebrated queer sexuality with signs like the one by St. Paul's Episcopal Church reading "Come Out For Christ's Sake!" By urging LGBT people to be true to themselves, this sign communicated an extra level of comfort with queerness, showing that LGBT people will not just be welcome when and if they do come out, but that they will be celebrated for the positive impact that doing so will make.

According to participants, such celebration was needed in a place where, for all the tolerance, LGBT people felt their queerness was regarded as a disadvantage rather than a positive identity trait. Angela, who worked with LGBT youth, talked about how uplifting it was for them to be able to march down the street to cheers. Having recently come out as queer, many were still struggling with the lukewarm reception they received from family and friends. At Pride, the celebration of the crowd matched their own elation at their visible declaration of queerness. With the goal of changing the cultural code of meaning that regarded queerness as inferior to heterosexuality, Burlington retained its sense of purpose as a contentious protest. Even as its relatively tolerant cultural climate allowed for participants to celebrate in such a carefree way, the contrast between their displays at Pride and their more guarded everyday lives highlighted why Pride's contentious messages were needed. The limited resources of people, organizations, and businesses made for an intimate, homemade parade that contrasted with the grand affairs put on in bigger cities.

Critics worry that enthusiastic celebration communicates the lack of desire or need for social change. As I found, there is indeed greater emphasis on celebration at Pride when the local cultural climate is relatively friendly towards LGBT people. In the case of Burlington, Vermont, celebration did not cross the line into frivolity because it remained connected to the everyday challenge of LGBT participants to obtain not just tolerance, but unreserved acceptance. Perhaps with greater resources, bigger cities do cross this line to become frivolous displays. As Pride parades include elaborate floats, host flashy parties, and draw enormous crowds, participants may disconnect from their ordinary lives and go to Pride to escape their cultural challenges rather than to fight them.

Particularly in cities like New York that already enjoy relatively tolerant cultural climates, the combination of this tolerance with community resources may lead to the loss of purpose that critics fear.

There was certainly plenty opportunity to party during Pride in New York. In the week leading up to Sunday's big parade, there were three official parties hosted by Heritage of Pride—the committee that organizes the parade—along with numerous unofficial parties put on by gay bars and clubs. Like so many other elements of contemporary Pride, these elements have their roots in the early events of the 1970s. Some of the frustration felt by the 1969 Stonewall rioters came from a lack of safe places to socialize and one of the initial responses to the riots was to hold community dances that would allow gays and lesbians to get together and have fun. Since 1971, the second year of Pride, a week of workshops, political demonstrations, and social dances has preceded the parade in many cities. These events are a way for Pride to accommodate the diverse needs and interests of LGBT participants rather trying to fit everything into the parade itself. In 2010, the various Pride Week activities, including parties, offered LGBT people and allies the chance to participate in Pride in many ways and helped keep the parade focused on effecting cultural change.

As in San Diego, the harshest elements of New York City's cultural climate are a step removed from the personal lives of many LGBT people. While public debates about same-sex marriage at the state and national level reveal a heteronormative cultural code that regards queerness as inferior to heterosexuality, LGBT people in New York can often live their daily lives among accepting neighbors and coworkers. With a variety of parties to attend during Pride Week—and glitzy dancers, extravagant floats, and fabulous drag performances to watch during the parade, it is certainly understandable that some may attend Pride more for the party than the protest. If enough participants focus on the festivity while ignoring the contentious purpose, then Pride in New York could indeed be better described as a benign, even frivolous, community celebration.

Though there were undoubtedly some New York Pride participants who attended simply for the party, I only met one of them. In fact, I had to cut my interview with Jason short when it became clear that his recollection of the Pride parade was hazy after a weekend of intense partying.[54] Similar to Jason, Bill told me that while he attends Pride with

LGBT struggles in mind, many of his friends treat it simply as an occasion to have fun. By contrast, Bill and the other New York Pride participants I talked to conveyed the same sense of purpose as Burlington participants. For Kerrond, the carefree atmosphere that he enjoyed as part of Pride reminded him that, even in tolerant New York, in his daily life he felt more limited in the way he presented his sexuality. Though he did not dress up special for Pride, preferring to wear shorts and a t-shirt, he said that at Pride he got to laugh and cheer not *in spite* of his sexuality, but actually *because* of it.

Like in Burlington, the contrast between the lukewarm tolerance that participants felt in their daily lives and the outright festivity at Pride highlighted the significance of public celebration. As they paraded on city streets, participants were acutely aware that such revelry would be short-lived. Come Monday morning, social pressures would compel them into a more subdued stance on queer sexuality and gender in which it would be tolerated, but not celebrated. Though the extravagant parties and entertaining floats enticed a few participants to disregard remaining cultural struggles and treat Pride as merely an occasion to party, the majority promoted this celebration as a public statement against the very heteronormative code that made such celebration contentious.

This does not mean that Pride participants stayed away from both official and unofficial parties during Pride Week. Tony and Brian, both gay men in their twenties, told me that one of the things they look forward to at Pride every year is the supercharged atmosphere at their favorite gay clubs. On the Friday and Saturday before Sunday's parade, gay clubs pull out all the stops with go-go dancers, notable DJs, and drink specials. Floods of people in town from the suburbs, upstate, and even further away bring extra excitement and fresh faces to Tony and Brian's favorite clubs. However, as these participants explained, the parties were separate from the parade. Parties were at night in dark clubs with loud music, while the parade is out in the open on familiar streets. Behind the close doors of a club, there was nothing remarkable about having fun in a gay space, but out in public this experience transformed into a contentious statement. Being in the daylight on public streets brought purpose to the dancers, upbeat music, and elated feelings that Tony and Brian experienced because of the way they contrasted with their everyday lives.

As a result of this contrast, Tony and Brian approached Sunday's parade with an intention to effect change.

Criticisms of Pride celebrations can be broken down as concern for the message that Pride communicates "out there" to the public at large and critique of the effect "in here" as participants experience the parade with or without the intention to change society. Commentators see a connection between the two sides as a lack of intentionality "in here" leads to a frivolous message "out there." I found a connection between "out there" and "in here," but rather than detract from Pride's contentious messages, this connection enabled even the grandest parade to retain its significance. Participants in Burlington and New York, both cities with quite tolerant cultural climates, felt a difference between the way they were able to revel in queerness at Pride and the reserved tolerance of their daily lives. As they experienced this contrast "in here," they purposefully communicated the message "out there" that queerness is cause for celebration.

Heteronormativity is behind both the lukewarm reception of queerness in participants' daily lives and their intentional celebration at Pride. The reason that LGBT people are at best accepted, but not congratulated, when they come out is that queerness is still defined as a second-rate sexual and gender identity. A strong code of tolerance in both Burlington and New York allowed many to feel comfortable being open about their queerness, but it did not encourage celebration. Similarly, it is the heteronormative cultural presumption that heterosexuality is natural that drives public debate over whether LGBT people can be *as good* parents or spouses as heterosexuals. Pride participants combatted this cultural code of meaning in the world with the message that queerness is an identity that should be celebrated. This message was particularly useful in the relatively tolerant Burlington and New York, where participants did not regularly deal with the harsher side of heteronormativity that flat out condemns queer sexuality and gender. A friendlier cultural climate allowed participants to emphasize celebration more than their counterparts in places like Atlanta, but it also motivated them to push beyond tolerance to full acceptance.

Abundant community resources in New York led to extravagant parties put on both by the official Pride organizing committee and by gay bars and clubs. During the parade, contingents had a fabulous time dancing on floats and preening as they marched down the street. With so much fun to be had, it would be understandable if participants chose to simply escape into the revelry rather than approach the parade with serious intentions for social change. While some participants did take this route, I found that the majority did not. Some may, like Tony and Brian, party at gay clubs on Friday and Saturday night and then go to the parade on Sunday hoping to effect change. Or, like Bill and Kerrond, they may contribute to the public celebration specifically because they want to bring about similar appreciation for queerness in the larger culture. A wealth of community resources in combination with a more tolerant cultural climate does carry the potential for Pride to devolve into pure frivolity, but I did not see this happening in 2010.

Conclusion

Like a St. Patrick's Day parade, a Fourth of July celebration, or a march on Washington, Pride is a unitary phenomenon, a community event with a recognizable form and meaning. In form, Pride is a parade that declares its association with the LGBT community through cultural symbols like the rainbow flag. In meaning, Pride targets cultural change with the messages of visibility, support, and celebration. But like any cultural ritual, each time it is enacted, participants adapt it to their own needs and capabilities. In the small, conservative city of Fargo, North Dakota, 350 people put on a simple, twenty-minute procession downtown—while in New York City, one million LGBT people and allies gathered for a five-hour grand production including floats, celebrity grand marshals, and contingents as diverse as the city itself. Both events communicated visibility, support, and celebration but delivered these messages differently according to local cultural climates and community resources. In essence, each city did Pride a little differently.

In exploring variations among Pride parades, this chapter yields two conclusions. First, participants in each city adapted Pride to fit with local contexts and resources. These factors influence both *how* and *how much* participants communicate visibility, support, and celebration through their parades. With greater acceptance of LGBT people in cities like New York, San Diego, and Burlington, participants emphasized the message of celebration over support. A relatively strong code of tolerance in these cities meant that LGBT people lived mostly open and unmolested in their daily lives, but this tolerance stopped short of being a full embrace of queerness. Participants thus confronted the lingering heteronormative code of meaning by celebrating queer sexuality and gender. By contrast, in the less LGBT-friendly climates of Atlanta, Salt Lake City, and Fargo, participants emphasized support for LGBT people. Lower tolerance meant that in these cities, participants focused more on confronting the harsher condemnation of queerness by showing that churches, businesses, and even politicians stand on the side of the LGBT community. Cultural climate also influenced how participants communicated visibility, support, and celebration. In each city, participants pushed the envelope on heteronormative cultural meanings, but in cities with greater tolerance, they could push further with provocative displays of sexuality or gender defiance.

Just as local cultural climate allows participants to display more or less divergence from heteronormative standards, community resources of money, people, and organizations determine the size and diversity of parade displays. In the bigger cities of New York, San Diego, and Atlanta, Pride advertised the diversity of the LGBT community in showing educational visibility through marching contingents representing various racial and ethnic groups, interests, and affinities. Pride parades in bigger cities found ready sponsorship partners in local small businesses and large corporations, which enabled grander displays of visibility, support, and celebration. Where a small parade like Burlington communicated celebration with homemade signs and festively decorated pick-up trucks, contingents in New York marshaled their greater resources to celebrate sexuality on professionally produced floats. In each city, participants drew on available resources to communicate messages that challenged the heteronormative code of meaning.

Second, variations among Pride parades reveal the ways that each community responds to long-running debates over provocative displays, involvement of institutional actors (especially businesses), and festivity. Pride planners first articulated these debates in the 1970s as they worked to establish Pride as an annual community event. At that time, infighting between gay power, gay pride, and gay rights activists—as well as between gay men and lesbians—produced conflicts over the event's format, the involvement of businesses, and the guidelines for provocative displays. As they worked through these practical problems, planners also grappled with abstract questions about movement strategy. Today, participants continue to engage with debates of representation, commercialization, and festivity. Instead of top-down strategic discussions among organizers, we see varied responses to these issues according to everyday experiences of participants. When deciding what to wear to Pride, for instance, transgender women like Dee Ann in Fargo choose outfits that conform with gender norms, after considering neighbors' perception that queer people do not fit into normal, "good" society. With greater tolerance and more community resources in New York, contingents like the Gotham Knights Rugby team show the diversity of the LGBT community while confronting the stereotype that gay men do not play masculine sports. Whether each parade encouraged modesty, embraced the involvement of businesses and politicians, or threw extravagant parties all depended on local cultural constraints and on the resources available to the LGBT community and its allies. Though no parades that I studied fulfilled critics' worst predictions that Pride would (or already has) become a frivolous corporate spectacle, those with more resources came closest to it.

Looking ahead, perhaps there may come a time when LGBT people and allies in progressive communities no longer struggle against a cultural code that marks queerness as inferior to heterosexuality. In fact, some argue that this time has already come.[55] In big cities where a gay-friendly climate combines with sufficient resources to put on a well-produced, flashy parade that is funded by major corporations, it is possible that Pride would cease to be a cultural protest and instead become one of many celebratory parades. In this book's conclusion, I consider this possibility, among others, for the future of Pride. For now, we turn to explore the effects of Pride—both on those who participate and on the solidarity of community that those participants build.

5

"We Are Family"

Building Community at Pride

For a day on Sunday, everyone's covered in rainbows and glitter. I got covered in glitter. I did not leave my apartment wearing glitter, but I had glitter all over me when I left. So it's good in that way. It kind of marks everybody in a way that we aren't marked typically. You can obviously choose to do that; you can choose to make yourself look the way gay people look hypothetically. But you can also not . . . But especially when you're on the train going there and half of your train is covered in rainbows, you think, "Wow that's a lot of gay people."
—Morgan, a spectator at the 2010 Pride parade in
New York City

Morgan is a lesbian in her early twenties living in New York City. In the bustling city, she is accustomed to going about her day among strangers. She commutes on the subway and learns little about fellow riders; she certainly does not learn their sexual orientation or gender identity. Unlike race or gender, sexual identity is physically invisible, so it must be purposefully declared. The day of the city's Pride parade was different for Morgan as fellow LGBT people made themselves visible with rainbows and glitter. She went from feeling like an outsider in a heteronormative world to seeing others like her nearly everywhere she turned. The same symbols that Pride participants used to communicate visibility to the greater society also made them visible to one another, which in turn helped participants feel closer to one another as a community.

In this book's introduction, I talked about how the collective joy exhibited at Pride turns both outward, as participants creatively challenge negative meanings applied to queerness, and inward as participants grow closer together by sharing positive emotions. This principle extends to Pride's messages of visibility, support, and celebration. At the same time scores of New York subway riders were turning the tables on LGBT invisibility in the culture at large, they were also letting Morgan know that she was not alone in her queer identity. As public statements, Pride's messages challenge the heteronormative cultural code by telling the world that queer sexuality and gender will no longer be hidden or apologized for. Turned inward, Pride participants receive the same messages, creating a fun and supportive atmosphere that is a needed antidote to the often-harsh cultural climates LGBT people experience every day. Indeed, the same heteronormative cultural code that underpins LGBT cultural inequality also makes it difficult for LGBT people to come together in their own community. This chapter focuses on the ways in which Pride fosters community solidarity among LGBT people and their allies amid demographic, cultural, and diversity barriers that keep them apart.

Bringing together diverse gays and lesbians has been a goal of Pride from the beginning. Without many public venues in which to gather, gays and lesbians were fragmented into groups according to gender, race, class, and affinity. Scholars and activists alike contend that in order to effectively push for social change, protesters need to share a common bond so that they can act together as a coherent group.[1] Thus, when the 1969 Stonewall riots ignited a new spark of activism in gays and lesbians across the country, one important order of business was to form a community out of this diverse group of people.[2] Gay and lesbian leaders invited artists, churchgoers, drag queens, business people, and militant activists to march together on public streets. Participants were elated as they openly declared their gay identity, a feeling that was more intense because it was shared. As the phenomenon grew in the 1970s, leaders struggled with infighting among the many facets of the gay and lesbian community, each with their own demands about what changes Pride should seek, who should be included, and how their community should be portrayed to the world. Early planners settled on a parade format with each contingent making their own displays as a way to both include diverse groups and to foster an upbeat, fun event that would unite gays and lesbians into a coherent community.

Though LGBT people can now gather in a host of public spaces, they still face distinct demographic, cultural, and diversity barriers to community solidarity. As less than 4% of the overall population and with few (and decreasing) neighborhoods, LGBT people need to actively work just to be in the same physical space. This demographic barrier means fewer daily interactions through which LGBT people can form connections with one another. Cultural barriers that make it difficult for many to come out as LGBT combine with demographics to inhibit the LGBT community. Queer people often "pass" as straight to avoid negative treatment, either all the time or only in certain situations, making it difficult to identify one another. Finally, though LGBT people are similar in one respect, queerness, they come from different racial, ethnic, and class backgrounds and represent different genders and identities. Such diversity of experience and social location makes it difficult to form community around one aspect of identity.

In the previous two chapters, I described how Pride parades reach outward and contest cultural codes of meaning by showing visibility, support, and celebration. This was and continues to be a large part of the purpose of Pride. As a public event, open to all and staged on city streets, it demands attention and its primary audience is the general public. However, as the first planners and participants recognized, Pride also carries enormous potential to bring LGBT people together and build community. This chapter charts the ways in which the messages of Pride focus inward to foster social bonding among LGBT people and straight allies.

Demographic Barriers

Shane is a young gay man living in Burlington, Vermont. He enjoys performing in drag occasionally, particularly during the city's annual Winter Drag Ball. Along with Pride, it is the big LGBT community event of the year. As Shane described, though Burlington is remarkably accepting, simple demographics mean that he is often the only gay person in the room. He is comfortable being open about his sexuality with straight friends and neighbors but hesitates to show them his gender variant side, worrying that they would not accept this aspect of his queer identity.[3] The region's small LGBT population is spread out and only gathers together en masse for these two annual events. During the rest of the year, there are simply not enough LGBT people to sustain a gay bar where community members can regularly gather. Though there are a number of community service and political groups like the RU12 Community Center and Outright Vermont, these did not offer the casual socializing opportunities that Shane was looking for. As he told me, one gets involved in these groups to work, not to play.

Sociologists recognize the importance of geographic space to facilitate the work and play that builds community resources, including group solidarity, to use in social movement activism. Isolated and socially marginalized neighborhoods can become "free spaces" where residents have the autonomy to imagine new possibilities for their worlds.[4] In the case of the civil rights movement, the geographic segregation of African Americans reinforced their social inequality but it also allowed them to develop resources that they mobilized to challenge this inequality. Because African Americans were segregated into poor neighborhoods, they created their own social institutions—such as the black church and community leaders—that enabled them to organize for social change.[5] Feminists, who could not draw on women-only neighborhoods (though some radical feminists did establish women's communes), built cultural institutions such as community centers and feminist bookstores in which to gather free from patriarchal power. In small consciousness-raising groups, many were able to experience their femininity as a source of joy and power, not subordination, for the first time. The interpersonal connections, awareness of inequality, and sense of feminist community that these institutions facilitated were especially important to sustaining the women's movement during the more conservative 1980s.[6]

LGBT people also need to build community solidarity and resources without geographically isolated neighborhoods that can serve as "free spaces," as they did for African Americans during the civil rights movement. Unlike women, though, LGBT people do not make up 50% of the population and thus must first find each other if they are to form a community. In the U.S., the few existing "gayborhoods"—neighborhoods that are strongly identified with LGBT community such as San Francisco's Castro district or Chicago's Boystown—have served as refuges of cultural freedom for those with the ability to move there.[7] It is in these few-and-far-between neighborhoods that LGBT people have developed many of the service groups, businesses, community centers that serve as resources for activism. However, the majority of the LGBT population—people like Shane in Burlington—does not live in or near a gayborhood.

Of any city in my study, the Burlington, Vermont metropolitan area has the highest concentration of same-sex couples: 1.4% of all households, totaling 220 couples.[8] By comparison, in 2010, there were 6,016 opposite-couple households, outnumbering same-sex couples by 27 to 1. It is unclear how many LGBT versus straight single people live in the city, but without compelling evidence to the contrary, it is fair to assume that LGBT singles are similarly outnumbered. LGBT people in Burlington thus face the simple demographic challenge of finding one another amid an overwhelmingly heterosexual population. In fact, even in the few U.S. neighborhoods with high concentrations of LGBT people, same-sex couples comprise at most 15% of the population, and evidence suggests that LGBT people are leaving these neighborhoods.[9] Thus in Burlington, as in the rest of the country, LGBT people are a small and spread out population who must find, meet, and build relationships with other LGBT people in order to form a community.

As Shane and other participants indicated, Burlington Pride was one of two big annual events that drew LGBT people together in one physical space. Similarly in Fargo, Salt Lake City, and even the bigger cities of Atlanta, San Diego, and New York, Pride was the biggest gathering of the year for the LGBT community. Though I did not measure the ratio of LGBT to straight people at each parade, it is safe to say it was dramatically higher on Pride Day than any other day of the year.

FIGURE 5.1 A large crowd of Pride participants carries a rainbow flag in Salt Lake City. This parade drew over twenty thousand marchers and spectators. Photo courtesy of Jay Jacobsen.

At Pride, LGBT people get the rare opportunity to be surrounded by others who share their queer gender and sexual identity. Queer people are visible to each other simply by gathering together en masse. Many participants found that alone to be an emotionally powerful part of Pride. Ted, an older gay man in San Diego, recalled the feeling of seeing crowds of gays and lesbians at his first Pride parade:

> It was in 1977 in San Francisco and I was just amazed. I was stunned to see so many gays. I was like, oh my god, it was a feeling like coming home—almost yeah—so my first one was . . . it meant a lot.

Even after thirty-five years attending Pride parades, Ted feels a thrill to step onto the street and be among so many other LGBT people. Similarly, Deb and Lori, lesbians I met in Salt Lake City, each drove over four hours to attend Pride, citing the large gathering of fellow LGBTs as a major draw. These participants and others described feelings of joy from the simple gathering of so many LGBT people in one place.[10]

Beyond the emotional experience, bringing LGBT people and allies together gave participants the opportunity to have fun with one another. For Court, a gay man in New York City, going to Pride means having the chance to interact with other gay people.

> On a day-to-day basis, I don't really interact with many gay people. I'm not saying I'm in the closet in any form or fashion, I'm totally out, but I generally don't have many gay friends . . . So it's really great to have those events every year where you're able to see other people or meet other people who might be going through same things . . . or some similar experience. Just that you have the common language with them already. That always makes the situation for me much more comfortable and I like that. People who have to deal with some of the same issues I have to deal with . . . whether or not it's there or justifiable, I really appreciate that in and of itself.

Court explained that he feels a connection with others simply because they are gay, and that at Pride he is able to interact with many more LGBT people than in his daily life.[11] Interestingly, he did not mention having trouble finding other LGBT people outside of Pride. If he were sufficiently motivated, he knew he could socialize with LGBT people often. But at Pride, the sheer volume and density of LGBT people made interaction easy.

Though Pride parades in my study varied widely by size, at each one I observed ample interaction among both marchers and spectators. Marchers socialized with those in their own contingents as well as others while lining up to march. Spectators talked with each other before, during, and after the parades. New York was the only parade where interaction was somewhat restricted because police placed physical barriers between spectators and marchers on the parade route. This limited spectators' movement, as I learned when, in trying to get from Fifth Avenue to where the route turned into Greenwich Village, I had to take numerous detours. At other parades, the movement of spectators was free, allowing people to interact all along the parade route.

Many Pride planners in the early 1970s favored a parade format for its potential to draw greater numbers than a protest march. While marches carve out a role only for those who actively walk in the procession, parades include both marching contingents and spectators. This allows people to participate in varying capacities and attracts a broad spectrum of LGBT people and allies. Participants like Ashley, a straight ally in Atlanta, could attend Pride on a whim while visiting friends without any prior arrangement or special knowledge of the event. Or Chase, a drag queen in Salt Lake City, could come to Pride in a dress, make-up, and heels and walk around seeing friends and meeting new people. In New York City, Tony, a young gay man who wanted a greater level of involvement, could volunteer to help with parade set-up and clean-up. Meanwhile in Burlington, Angela, a lesbian who mentors LGBT youth, could march with her youth group. Participants can come to the event through various channels and choose the type of involvement that best suits them.

As a parade, Pride attracts participants because it is fun and entertaining. Pride planners had this emotional draw in mind, too, when they advocated the parade format in the early 1970s. They wanted to attract not just the committed activists, but also those gays and lesbians who had shied away from contentious action. Today, participants like Shane in Burlington attend Pride for the chance to connect with fellow LGBT people in a fun atmosphere. Though he knows he can meet other queer people in the many political action and community service groups in Burlington,

FIGURE 5.2 A gay man and two lesbians meet on the street at San Diego's Pride parade and pose together. Photo courtesy of Nathan Rupert.

he told me that he is not the "activist type." Shane supports the work that groups like Outright Vermont, an organization that helps at-risk LGBT youth, do to create a more inclusive society but he is not personally interested in doing the work required to be part of them. At Pride, Shane gets to wear a skirt, see creative floats, and socialize. In doing so, he also has a chance to participate in an event that he sees as changing society for the better, but one that he would not attend if it were not so fun.

Jonah, a gay man in San Diego, described the infectious good mood of Pride by comparing it to the heavier emotions one may feel at a political protest:

> You just can't not see a smile at a Pride parade. As to where like somebody might just be so riled up and stuff at some political affair. You know, they forget to smile.

Now, political protests certainly can be fun, but as Jonah reveals, people do not perceive them as such. Pride is overtly a celebration with marchers dancing on floats to upbeat music, cheering spectators, and festive, colorful clothes. Such a public celebration communicates that queerness is a positive identity. Turned outward to culture in the world, Pride is a contentious message that challenges heteronormativity. Turned inward to participants themselves, Pride celebrations make people happy by creating a rare space where it is explicitly a good thing to be queer. This atmosphere attracts people, particularly those not already drawn to activism, in a way that a more somber protest march cannot. Once there, participants have the opportunity to simply enjoy themselves, getting to know one another outside the regular pressures they feel in society, where heteronormativity reigns.

LGBT Americans live most of their daily lives as the odd person out when it comes to sexual and gender identity. Only 3.5% of Americans identify as lesbian, gay, bisexual, or transgender—a small percentage of the population.[12] And unlike many racial and ethnic minority groups, LGBT people do not cluster very much geographically. Their numbers and geography are demographic barriers to LGBT people's ability to form community. As Pride planners of the 1970s envisioned, Pride's parade format attracts more people than would be possible with a protest march. Once there, participants feel community simply through the unique experience of being among so many fellow LGBTs and allies, and they grow community further by interacting with others and forming relationships. Pride's messages of visibility and celebration turn inward to create a fun gathering full of LGBT people and straight allies that people of all sorts want to attend.

Cultural Barriers

Kevin is nineteen years old, lives in rural North Dakota, and came out as gay to close friends and family a year before I met him at the 2010 Fargo-Moorhead Pride parade. In his small town, he does not know of anyone else who is LGBT; but then, other queer people do not know about him either, as he keeps his sexuality secret to all but those closest to him. He wants to be "out" to more people, he told me, but fears social ostracism and even outright hostility from acquaintances. Growing up, queerness had rarely been the subject of conversation but when it was, the speakers were negative, calling it anywhere from sinful to simply not compatible with solid, Midwestern values. More recently, in high school, male class-mates constantly called each other "gay" or "fag," driving home for Kevin the fact that those in his hometown held his sexuality in low esteem.[13] So Kevin made the hour-long drive to Fargo at the urging of his cousin who wanted him to have the chance to be around other gay people.

Though certainly not unique, Kevin's experience is more extreme than that of many LGBT people. In places like San Diego and New York, LGBT acceptance is more forthcoming and rejection, when it happens, is less stark than in rural North Dakota. Even in Atlanta and Salt Lake City, bigger and more diverse populations mean that LGBT people can often find pockets of inclusion without making an hour-long drive. However, there are few, if any, places where LGBT people have achieved full cultural equality with heterosexuals. Though expressed differently across the country and coupled with a strengthening code of tolerance, prevailing heteronormativity constructs queerness as inferior, which in-hibits LGBT people's ability to be fully open about their sexuality and gender identity. In places like Fargo, LGBT people feel inhibited to even come out publicly as queer regardless of how otherwise "normal" they are in the way they dress or act. In more LGBT-friendly places like New York City, LGBT people may be welcomed by friends and neighbors as they affirm their identities, but find less acceptance to fully express their queerness by say, wearing clothing of the opposite sex. The everyday effect of this for LGBT people is to feel cultural pressure to affirm a straight identity first, and second, if they are "out" as LGBT, to downplay their sexual or gender difference in personal interactions.

On an emotional level, having a stigmatized identity produces shame, which the social psychologist Thomas Scheff considers a social emo-tion that is the opposite of pride.[14] Both shame and pride result from looking at oneself through the lens of dominant cultural codes of mean-ing. Many heterosexuals therefore feel pride as they see their identities celebrated in images of happy couples and models of masculinity and femininity that fit the way they express their genders.[15] Queer people, in contrast, feel corresponding shame at their exclusion and devaluation.[16] Social emotions, in turn, inspire us to either share our pride with others or hide from them in shame.[17] Behavior produces emotion as well—so that when displaying ourselves in public, we feel pride and when hiding, we feel shame.[18] Thus, heteronormativity promotes shame for LGBT people in two ways: by stigmatizing queer identity itself as inferior and by pressuring LGBT people to hide their queerness from others. Shame and hiding lead to social isolation, making it difficult for LGBT people to come together as a community.

Social movements play a role in transforming personal emotions like shame into pride. Just as geographic neighborhoods can act as "free spaces" in which marginalized people find a degree of autonomy to develop community resources, movements also offer emotional free spaces where participants can express emotions that run counter to dominant cultural norms.[19] In these spaces, participants actively reframe beliefs about their identities—for instance, that being queer is a moral failure—according to a new set of empowering beliefs generated by the group.[20] Activist groups create their own emotion cultures with a set of expectations about how members should feel about shared identities like queerness and how they should express these feelings.[21] In feminist consciousness-raising groups of the 1970s, for instance, group norms encouraged women to celebrate feminine traits like nurturing as a source of strength rather than a sign of weakness. By creating space and then providing a new set of norms, social movements facilitate the transformation of negative, isolating emotions into ones that empower and bring people together.

The heteronormative cultural code adds a cultural challenge to the LGBT population's demographic one. LGBT people like Kevin must overcome shame to come out as queer in order to look for others like them. Though stronger tolerance in some places certainly lessens the cultural challenge to coming out and expressing one's LGBT identity, it has not erased it. Thus, LGBT people are not only few and far between, but they also face a cultural barrier to declare and freely display their identity. Pride parades create a space that is free not only of the demographic barrier to LGBT community, but of the cultural barrier as well. By flipping cultural messages of heteronormativity, Pride promotes an emotion culture that transforms shame of LGBT identity into pride and thereby encourages community.

Free Expression

Defiant visibility, support, and celebration came together at the Pride parades I visited to promote participants' free personal expression.[22] Similar to tension management holidays such as Halloween or New Year's Eve, at Pride, the normal rules of society are suspended.[23] LGBT people and straight allies alike are free to play with expressions of queerness, having fun with what usually incurs social sanctions. As I overheard one San Diego participant tell his friend, Pride was his opportunity to "fag out" by playing up his more stereotypical attributes, like wearing the tight, low V-neck t-shirt that prompted the conversation with his friend. Advertising queer identity at Pride by showing affection for a same-sex partner or wearing a stereotypical outfit marks one's membership in the majority rather than in the margins. Pride is a rare space where one is encouraged to have fun being queer—even by proxy, if one is a straight ally—making the occasion one of collective joy.[24]

Like the New York participant shown in figure 5.3, many participants took the opportunity to try out new ways to express themselves. Shane in Burlington, for example, dressed in more feminine attire than he normally does, in order to express the genderqueer part of his gay identity.[25] In his everyday life, he is out as gay but wears masculine clothing so as not to radically defy heteronormative culture. At Pride, he felt there was enough acceptance and celebration of gender and sexual variance that he could show this part of his identity. Similarly, although Kevin in Fargo was far from the gay-friendly cultural climate of Burlington, Vermont, he found Pride to be a place where he could freely express his gay identity as well. By attending Fargo Pride, Kevin said,

> I wanted—it was kind of like [I am a] closet case everywhere, so the parade was the only place that I could be out publicly.

Though he did not visibly mark his gay identity with even a rainbow bead necklace, the visibility, support, and celebration shown by others made him feel free to simply tell other participants that he is gay.

Depending on one's context, risky personal expression could be simply publicly identifying as gay, as it was for Kevin, or it could be dressing in a skirt to show one's feminine side, like Shane did. By suspending the heter-

FIGURE 5.3 A New York Pride participant shows off his creative outfit (and love for Canada).

onormative restrictions of dominant culture, Pride allowed participants to freely express aspects of their identity that they could not safely show in their everyday lives. In contrast to the heavy feeling of shame that comes from hiding queerness in everyday life, Pride facilitated lightness with an emotion culture that encouraged participants to have fun being queer.

Even straight allies were able to express themselves more freely at Pride than in their everyday lives, similarly pushing against heteronormative restrictions. Sarita in Burlington, for instance, said her brother who is "a really straight guy" loved attending Pride because he "got to wear a dress." In San Diego, Jonah's "older heterosexual" father rode his motorcycle with a gay men's biker group. In a study of straight people in an age of expanding tolerance, sociologist James Joseph Dean noted the new importance for them to assert a heterosexual identity since this could no longer be assumed.[26] While a sign of progress, such need to declare one's heterosexuality may conversely strengthen the heteronormative code of meaning that privileges heterosexuality over queerness. When straight people join in the flaunting of heteronormativity at Pride, then, they too challenge this code in the world while at the same time enjoying a rare break from its restrictions.

A long-running debate at Pride parades is whether to set limits on participants' expressions. This debate is principally about how Pride parades represent LGBT people outward to the larger public. On one side, some argue that Pride should limit provocative displays and present an image of LGBT people that ordinary citizens will judge positively. On the other side, people argue that Pride should encourage all displays, even the most provocative ones, in order to challenge the heteronormative cultural code that defines queerness as objectionable. When turned inward, the debate over free expression was about how limiting participants' displays may create a more or less welcoming environment for all. Since the early days, many people have opposed limits of expression at Pride events, so as not to exclude more marginalized LGBT people. The Annual Reminders of the late 1960s, for instance, required marchers to dress following gender norms with women in dresses and men in shirts and ties. This dress code meant that drag queens, with their male bodies and feminine attire, were excluded from the demonstration. Pride established itself as a more open demonstration by imposing no limits on participants' dress or behavior and thus welcoming all gays and lesbians.

Contemporary participants mentioned a different downside to unrestricted free expression. They worried that too many radical, especially sexual, displays of LGBT identity would discourage straight allies from participating in Pride. While allies like Sarita's brother or Jonah's father may relish the chance to be "gay for a day" at Pride, many others may be turned off by provocative displays. Ted, a gay man in San Diego, noticed that gay participants toned down their sexual displays in recent years, making the parade more inviting to straight participants:

Pride is not just for gays and I am kind of glad about that this year, believe it or not. Maybe it's because I'm older now [and] becoming a little more prude, it wasn't so sexual. The first parades I used to go to were real, real sexual—a lot of men gyrating and stuff like that. But this year you didn't see a whole lot of that. It was more toned down. I feel like if you tone it down, it's more accessible to more people and it was like opening arms to everyone.

To Ted, overt sexual displays mark Pride as an event exclusively for LGBT people and communicate to straight allies that they are not welcome. This view is understandable considering that heteronormative culture makes even the most benign displays of public same-sex affection a rare sight. While many LGBT people (and some straight allies) find this free expression liberating, straight allies may see it as a mark of in-group behavior, signaling an exclusive event to which they are not invited.

For their part, straight allies who I talked to said that while sexual displays were not their favorite part of Pride, they understood that this was a rare public space in which the normal rules of society were suspended and so they expected to see same-sex affection, scantily clad dancers, and the like. However, many straight allies conveyed a sense that Pride was not "for" them. It was an event to which they were invited as guests but not full participants because they were not fully part of the LGBT community. Danielle in Fargo, for instance, said that she marched in the parade as part of a contingent promoting a political candidate and—while she loved the experience—as a straight ally, she "can't think of another context where [she] would have felt comfortable walking." Similarly, LGBT participants said that most of their straight friends would not feel comfortable attending on their own without an LGBT person.

When they organized the parade in the 1970s, Pride planners did not consider straight allies. They thought a few straight people might attend as spectators, either out of support or curiosity, but they did not dream that straight allies would ever play a major part in the event. It is a triumph of LGBT activism that so many straight people are allies to the community. But at Pride parades in 2010, LGBT participants were still on the fence about the extent to which straight allies are truly a part of it. I did not talk to anyone who wanted to discourage straight allies from participating in Pride, but they also did not want to place any rules on how participants expressed themselves in order to bring more straights to the parade.[27] Most participants, both LGBT and straight, saw Pride as an event for the LGBT community and regarded straight allies as active supporters but not full members. The place of straight allies at Pride and in the LGBT community more broadly will be an interesting issue to consider as the Pride phenomenon continues to grow.

Pride in Self and Community

Pride parades, as the name suggests, promote the feeling of pride both in oneself and in one's community. Once again Pride's messages turn both outward and inward. As public statements, defiant and educational visibility, support, and celebration tell the world that being queer is nothing to be ashamed of but rather an identity to revel in. As inward statements, the messages of Pride tell LGBT people that they are okay as they are and give them a chance to celebrate being queer. The desired effect is to give many a feeling of pride in their identities.

The participants pictured declared their pride with self-affirming shirts. The emotion culture of Pride encouraged such explicit statements of self-worth. Jonah, a gay man from San Diego, described the effect of Pride's affirming atmosphere:

> Every year, there's one day, one day a year, where my entire community mobilizes together and is truly proud and confident about all of ourselves. You know, and I think that's very powerful for us to have a day of Pride and being GLBT.

Jonah talked about the contrast in the emotional atmosphere at Pride and that of his everyday life. Coming from the more LGBT-friendly San Diego, Jonah did not describe his daily life as one of constant denigration. Most people with whom he interacted were perfectly accepting of his gay identity. But at Pride the atmosphere went from acceptance to full-blown celebration, where his gay identity was a source of personal pride. Being gay at Pride was a good thing, a reason to dress up, gather with others, and have fun.

FIGURE 5.4 Participants march wearing shirts affirming their self-worth as unique and amazing in San Diego's Pride parade. Photo courtesy of Nathan Rupert.

For Dee Ann, a transgender woman in Fargo, the message of educational visibility gave her a feeling of self-worth.

> When I see my community come together . . . It just wells up inside, you know, like the feelings people get when they hear the "Star-Spangled Banner" or they see rockets exploding. I see that I have other people just like me and [that] there's nothing wrong with me.

Educational visibility is about publicizing the multifaceted lives of LGBT people. Its goal is for those who see Pride to identify with participants and come to a fuller understanding of queer sexuality and gender. When

Dee Ann attends Pride in Fargo, she gets to see others who are trans-gender, gay, or bisexual and face similar misunderstanding in their communities. By identifying with fellow participants, the feeling of shame from being maligned in society turns into a feeling of pride in a celebrated common identity.

Dee Ann and Jonah both described a boost in their personal self-esteem from attending Pride. Echoing the insights of the social psychologist Thomas Scheff, they said that this increased pride drew them closer to their fellow LGBT people because their sense of pride came from being part of a group that they saw celebrated and supported. As Scheff explains, pride is a social emotion that is the opposite of shame; we feel pride when our personal characteristics are culturally valued and shame when they are scorned.[28] Dee Ann likened the experience of seeing LGBT people come together to that of a patriot hearing the anthem of her country. Like a national anthem, the sight of so many people celebrating queerness made Dee Ann feel that she was part of something that was culturally honored. Feeling such pride, Dee Ann was excited to share it with others.

When people experience emotions in a group, they feed off one another and the emotions get stronger. The sociological term for this is "collective effervescence." Emile Durkheim, one of the founders of the discipline, coined the term to describe the ecstasy witnessed at religious ceremonies.[29] Such an intense experience energizes its participants, giving them a boost of confidence that they carry with them after the interaction has passed.[30] It also binds them together as they remember the good time they had as a group. Not only does Pride generate individual feelings of pride that motivate people to draw closer to others, but with collective effervescence, it turns these individual emotions into group ones that further unite participants in community.

Once again, straight allies were partially but not fully included in this community formation. Straight allies do not directly experience the cultural stigma against queer sexuality and gender and thus do not get the same emotional boost from being in a rare gathering that celebrates their identity. Pride specifically makes visible, supports, and celebrates LGBT identity, so when turned inward toward participants themselves, straight allies may feel happy and join in the collective effervescence of parades, but they do not receive messages of self-worth about their own identities.[31]

Straight participants are, nonetheless, applauded for being allies to LGBT people and for voicing their support at Pride. Margaret, for instance, has a gay son and marched with her PFLAG (Parents and Friends of Lesbians and Gays) chapter in the Atlanta parade. She said the first time she marched she felt like a celebrity because so many LGBT participants approached her to thank her for her support and told her they wished their parents were like her. This year, she said,

> I told my daughter that it was the closest thing to a religious experience without actually having one. Just the love and the—it just seemed like we belonged to the community. And they embraced us as much as we'd embraced them.

When he coined the term "collective effervescence," Durkheim theorized it to express the divine quality of religious experience. Margaret similarly identified the atmosphere at Pride as being close to a religious experience because the collective joy lifted her beyond her individual emotions. This joint experience with LGBT participants made Margaret feet like she belonged to the LGBT community—not as one who shares in LGBT people's cultural inequality, but as one who is part of the visibility, support, and celebration of LGBT identity at Pride. Other straight allies that I talked to felt similarly welcomed and included in the community formed at Pride, though as supporters rather than full members.

Interestingly, though the level of cultural acceptance for LGBT people varied among parade sites in my study, participants from Fargo to Burlington spoke passionately about their emotional coming together at Pride. Whether they were generally accepted in their daily lives, like Jonah in San Diego, or faced ignorance and even rejection, like Kevin in Fargo, participants experienced Pride as an oasis where LGBT identity was a source of particular pride that bonded them with others. Straight allies, too, felt welcomed and celebrated at each parade they attended.

The heteronormative cultural code that regards queerness as deviant means LGBT people are deemed culturally unequal to their straight counterparts. It is this meaning system that Pride seeks to change by targeting the both cultural codes themselves and the individual cultural attitudes that uphold cultural meanings. This outward struggle for change also has an inward dimension. Though moderated by a code of tolerance, heteronormativity still makes it hard for individuals to come out and be visible as LGBT, which in turn makes it difficult to form a community that can work together to challenge their inequality. In the early days of Pride, community leaders saw that coming together and celebrating LGBT identity as a group had a liberating effect on individual gays and lesbians and made them feel closer to others. At Pride parades today we see this same effect. By creating an environment where queerness is visible, supported, and celebrated, LGBT people feel free to join in by expressing themselves openly. This free expression, in turn, bonds them together with an experience of collective effervescence as they feel pride in their own identities and their connection to a community of LGBT people. Straight allies, meanwhile, are invited to join in the love fest, as one participant called it, and while most did not feel they were full members of the LGBT community, they had a connection with this group that strengthened their own commitment to cultural equality.

Diversity as Barriers

Monique and Ralph are two LGBT New Yorkers with many differences to separate them. Monique is an African American transgender woman who works with homeless LGBT youth in the Bronx. Ralph is a white gay man living in Manhattan who marched in the first Pride parade in 1970. These two individuals are separated by race, class, gender, and their identities within the broad umbrella of LGBT community. Though Monique recognizes that she as a transgender woman and Ralph as a gay man are often grouped together politically, she sees this as an unequal partnership. While gays and lesbians have made incredible gains with increased cultural acceptance and political rights, transgender people are struggling against intense cultural ignorance and disdain with few explicit political rights. Added to that, on a daily basis she sees the way racial, class, and sexual inequality intersect to restrict opportunities for those not born into privilege. For his part, while Ralph is aware that as a relatively affluent white gay man he has benefited most from growing cultural acceptance, he still believes that queerness is a distinct identity that unites him with people like Monique.

As a cursory description of Monique and Ralph indicates, what we call the LGBT community includes a broad diversity of people. Despite a common stereotype that imagines LGBT people as white, affluent, male, and gay (not bisexual or transgender), researchers actually find slightly *higher* percentages of LGBT identification among non-whites, those with lower incomes, and those with less education.[32] They are still teasing out the sociological reasons for these figures—for instance, LGBT people tend to have lower incomes because they routinely face employment discrimination—but they do tell us that the LGBT population is marked by the same types of diversity as the general population. Given this diversity, the same barriers to solidarity that exist in the larger population, such as inequality and geographic segregation, also affect LGBT people. Simply put, a shared queer identity is not necessarily enough to bring people as socially different as Monique and Ralph together.

Moreover, not all racial, class, and gender groups understand sexuality and gender in the same way. Our dominant conceptualization of queerness as a distinct identity about which one should be open and proud—that is, the definition that Pride promotes—was developed predominantly by white male activists to fit their self-understandings. For many LGBT people of color, coming out as queer in this way connotes rejecting their racial or ethnic communities in favor of LGBT community. For this reason, many in the African-American community, for instance, prefer the term "same-gender loving" to "gay" or "queer" to describe a sexual identity that remains connected to African-American identity and community.[33]

Finally, many distinct identities are grouped together under the LGBT initialism. As Monique indicates, transgender individuals, whose gender identity does not match their biological sex, do not necessarily have anything in common with gays and lesbians who are attracted to their own sex. Though they have a shared history of cultural stigmatization for their divergence from heteronormativity, gender identity and sexuality are increasingly understood as variations with distinct cultural and legal implications. Additionally, those with other types of gender and sexual differences are alternately included and excluded from the LGBT umbrella as community centers, political advocacy organizations, and LGBT events like Pride attempt to define their target population. For example, many groups debate whether to explicitly include those who are intersex, with both female and male biological sex characteristics, by adding an "I" to the LGBT intitialism.

Given these barriers between LGBT people by race, class, gender, and identity, many question whether sexual and gender variation constitutes a salient basis for group identity. Scholars of social movements and culture debate whether individuals can create a basis of unity amid their differences. On the one hand, some argue that groups construct collective identities, like LGBT identity, so that they feel close to one another and can work together.[34] As this chapter illustrates, Pride is a venue for LGBT people to come together, despite the demographic and cultural barriers that separate them in their everyday lives. By bringing LGBT people and allies together in one place and turning the messages of visibility, support, and celebration inward, Pride creates a unique queer space with a positive emotion culture that encourages solidarity among those who attend.

On the other hand, some individuals will always be closer to the group norm than others, making conflict inevitable and threatening the semblance of group unity. Though Pride aspires to welcome all, it is not immune to the power imbalances by race, class, gender, and identity that shape the world at large. With greater social power, white gay men have long had a disproportionate influence on both the practical planning of Pride and the more abstract task of defining LGBT identity. Seeking an event more explicitly focused on their segment of the community, splinter groups in some cities have created Black Gay Pride, Dyke March, and Trans March events. Though not always antagonistic toward Pride, these events expose the tensions between LGBT people and lead some to question the feasibility of Pride event that truly includes all.

Since the founding of Pride in the early 1970s, community leaders envisioned the event as a gathering of all facets of the gay and lesbian community, but they also recognized the need for each group to represent themselves as they chose. A parade format with multiple contingents—instead of one unit marching as a single block—facilitates both unity and diversity. That way, gay power activists of the Gay Liberation Front could communicate their demand to "Smash Imperialism" alongside business-oriented gays who promoted a mainstream image of the gay community. Though their debates over representation, commercialization, and frivolity continue today, so does the diverse LGBT community's yearly gathering for Pride. Sociologists Amin Ghaziani and Delia Baldassarri argue that instead of complete unity or fragmentation, groups may develop a middle ground in which cultural ideas like LGBT identity may serve as anchors that bring us together while simultaneously providing the forum for us to air our differences.[35] Along with intangible ideas, diverse groups may also engage in tangible practices that temporarily unite them without erasing their differences.[36] Echoing Pride planners' early theme of "unity in diversity," Pride today is a bridging practice that brings diverse LGBT people together once a year in a forum that allows them to express their different ways of being queer.

Identity Diversity

In the years since Pride parades were established, bisexuals and transgender people have joined gays and lesbians to make up the LGBT community. Both these identities are a bit different from homosexuality, which complicates community formation as all groups try to find common ground. Bisexuality means having a sexual attraction toward both women and men. Transgender is not about sexual orientation at all but about gender identity, one's internal sense of being woman or man regardless of biological sex. Like gays and lesbians, bisexuals and transgender people violate the heteronormative cultural code, but these groups face greater ignorance both inside and outside LGBT community.[37]

According to a recent survey, though bisexuals make up a bigger portion of the LGBT community than any of the other three groups (lesbians, gay men, and transgender), only 28% are out to family and friends.[38] By contrast, 77% of gay men and 71% of lesbians say that most or all of the important people in their lives know their sexual orientation. One reason for this difference is that many bisexuals form long-term partnerships with people of the opposite sex, so they can "pass" as straight.[39] With queer sexuality devalued, bisexuals in this situation feel cultural pressure to affirm a straight identity.[40] Ignorance and lack of acceptance within the LGBT community is another reason for bisexual invisibility. Lesbians and gay men accuse bisexuals of "really" being either gay or straight, thus denying both their self-identification as bisexual and their attraction to men and women alike.[41]

I noticed a conspicuous lack of visibility of bisexuals at Pride parades. While lesbian, gay, and transgender participants declared their identities with signs and t-shirts, I did not see any participant explicitly identify as bisexual. Likewise, I did not observe a specifically bisexual marching contingent in any parade.[42] While it has become commonplace for community and advocacy organizations to include "bisexual" in their names, self-identified bisexuals were not visible. Jade, from Fargo, was the only self-identified bisexual participant I interviewed. She attributed the lack of bisexual visibility at Pride to a general lack of acceptance of bisexuals in the gay and lesbian community in Fargo. After dating women for a time, she said she was called a "traitor" by another lesbian when she began dating a man. Jade described an all too common situation where both she and her accuser felt betrayed.[43] To Jade, she was simply following her heart, which is the very thing that gays and lesbians strive for themselves. Her accuser similarly felt betrayed by someone who, like her, had long resisted the cultural pressure to date men. Though only one instance, this situation illustrates a difficult barrier to fully including bisexuals in LGBT community. From their lack of visibility at the Pride parades that I observed, it appears that plenty of work still needs to be done on this front.

Transgender is the latest group to be regularly included in LGBT community.[44] At times this inclusion is fraught because while lesbians, gays, and bisexuals fight for cultural acceptance of their sexuality, transgender individuals fight for acceptance of their non-normative gender. Culturally, transgender individuals face greater ignorance, hostility, and discrimination as they try to live their lives according to the gender they feel themselves to be, not the gender they were assigned at birth. Politically, the two groups have different priorities. Same-sex marriage, for instance, is a leading priority for most gay, lesbian, and bisexual activists but one that does not affect as many transgender individuals.[45] Instead, transgender activists prioritize ending workplace discrimination, getting health insurance to cover gender reassignment treatments, and making sure that transgender individuals can legally change their names and gender designations on official documents. In addition to these different priorities, tensions between LGB activists and transgender people is exacerbated because it is often easier to pass measures that protect sexual orientation but leave out gender identity.[46] Understandably, many transgender individuals feel that lesbians, gays, and bisexuals are willing to "throw them under the bus" to get their own legal protections.

Despite these tensions, transgender is included in LGBT community (in theory if not always in practice) because sexual orientation and gender are intertwined in Western culture. The heteronormative cultural code prescribes not just that men and women should be attracted to one another, but also that two (and only two) genders are tied to biological sex differences and reinforced by looks and behavior.[47] In practice, many gays, lesbians, and bisexuals break gender norms in their personal expressions with things as simple as shorter haircuts for women or tight jeans for men, and a number of transgender individuals also identify as gay or bisexual. On a grander scale, drag—adopting clothing and mannerisms normative for the other gender for theatrical performance—has a long history in gay culture and drag queens and kings (men performing as women and women performing as men, respectively) were quite visible at Pride parades.[48] In fact, the conceptual separation of sexual orientation and gender, and thus LGBs and transgender people, is a new development of the last forty years; when Pride parades began in 1970, transgender did not exist as a category distinct from gay and lesbian. Thus, though including transgender in LGBT community is not always smooth or politically expedient, the considerable overlap in the cultural struggles of lesbians, gays, bisexuals, and transgender means that these groups can find common cause.

The uneasy inclusion of transgender individuals was evident at the Pride parades that I studied. All six parades billed themselves as "LGBT" indicating at least official inclusion, but from my observations and interviews with participants, it was clear that transgender people were not fully part of the celebration. Though all parades included at least one marching contingent from the transgender community, six participants said that transgender people were not as visible as they should be. Winston, a young gay man in Fargo, described tensions between transgender individuals and LGB people, both in Pride and elsewhere, as arising from political battles:

> I have noticed at Pride parades and festivals that transgender people are always kind of grouped together. I kind of feel like that's just running with the pack, safety in numbers, and I do wish we could incorporate transgender more with everything else as gender equality and gender

identity issues. I think that's something that a lot of the community
tries to push away.

INTERVIEWER: *Why do they push it away, from your perspective?*

Because especially with trying to pass bills, a bill's going to be easier to
pass if it's LGB. The moment you put the "T" on it, it's like, now this
is getting kind of weird, I don't want a guy who comes in a dress to
work—which is complete BS if I may say. We're all part of . . . they
talk about how we shouldn't incorporate transgender in because
the moment they transition they're probably going to ditch the
community.

To Winston, transgender individuals stick with each other at Pride
because they do not feel fully welcomed into the community by lesbians,
gays, and bisexuals. He detected suspicion, on their part, that transgender people are "really" part of the community. Much like Jade, a bisexual
woman who was told she was a "traitor" when she dated a man, Winston
suspected that transgender people are sometimes viewed as only temporary members of LGBT community. Moreover, he cited the political
expediency of excluding gender identity from rights legislation as a
motivation to exclude transgender individuals from LGB community.
Similarly, Monique, a transgender woman in New York, said that com-
promises in the political arena translated at Pride to a focus on political
and cultural equality for lesbians, gays, and bisexuals but not for transgender people.

Dee Ann, a transgender woman in Fargo, had a more positive view of
Pride. She saw it as an important venue to educate straight people, and
also lesbians, gays, and bisexuals about transgender issues. For many
years, she worked with others to organize a transgender contingent in
Fargo Pride so they could educate LGB and straight people alike.

All of my floats have had an educational theme to them. Last year I
actually did the rainbow umbrella on a cart with all kinds of different
cards hanging down from them—talking about transvestites, trans-
sexuals, drag queens. So all of these were on it, plus the whole thing
was against a background of a pink and white and blue flags. So it
showed, you know, the "T" pride there.

INTERVIEWER: *When you say you want to educate, are you primarily trying to educate other people who go to the parade or members of the greater Fargo community?*

Actually both because I've found that the LGB community doesn't really know what the "T" is and they need a little bit more education about where the "T" fits into the whole thing. There's a lot of confusion within the general public that could use the transgender, transvestite, transsexual—what are all these trans, trans, trans? They just think it's a drag queen at the show, you know, on the weekend, whatever. So I want to bring an element of education to my activism so people actually see and learn.

Dee Ann described promoting educational visibility both outward to the greater Fargo community and inward to her fellow LGBTs. While Winston and Monique took a more skeptical view, saying that LGB people excluded transgender individuals out of suspicion and political expediency, Dee Ann thought it was plain ignorance about how transgender concerns intersect with those of lesbians, gays, and bisexuals.

In many cities, including New York, Atlanta, and Salt Lake City, transgender people organize separate "Trans Pride" marches to bring better visibility to their community and, in some cases, to protest their marginalization at the larger Pride parades. These events are new, having been held for at most six years in New York City. Unlike Pride parades, Trans Pride events take the form of a march as a few dozen people walk in a block, holding signs and chanting.

In both Atlanta and Salt Lake City, organizers worked with Pride planning committees and included Trans Pride marches as part of the official slate of Pride week activities. For Pride planners in these cities, helping to coordinate Trans Pride was a way to reach out to transgender people and signal their inclusion in the larger LGBT community. As a smaller segment of the community facing greater inequalities, one Atlanta organizer told me that it was important to have a separate march to bring greater attention to transgender issues. Rather than working against the larger Pride, Trans Pride events in Atlanta and Salt Lake City supplemented the big parade by providing an event specifically for transgender individuals. New York's Trans Day of Action was a bit dif-

FIGURE 5.5 Participants in Atlanta's Trans Pride march on the Friday before Sunday's Pride parade. Photo courtesy of Stan Fong, Atlanta Pride Committee.

ferent from these events, as it was separately organized and a bit more critical of the bigger Pride parade. Though not explicitly antagonistic, event materials refer to transgender individuals' invisibility within the larger LGBT community. Held on the Friday before Sunday's Pride parade, the event aimed to bring attention to the lives transgender people of color and the issues affecting them.

A cultural bridging practice is a ritual action that temporarily unifies people across their differences.[49] Pride does indeed bring lesbians, gays, bisexuals, and transgender people together in the same physical space, partially bridging their differences, but it does not (yet) offer an equal forum for all. Through Trans Pride events and contingents within Pride parades, transgender people did have some opportunity to make themselves visible and educate LGBs. However, bisexuals and transgender people and concerns were underrepresented at Pride. While all Pride parades included bisexuals and transgender people in official naming and with trans-specific contingents, inclusion appeared only skin deep. I did not see that Pride parades made significant steps toward overcoming existing tensions between bisexuals and lesbians and gays or between transgender individuals and LGB people. When it comes to identity diversity, then, Pride still has a ways to go before fully serving as a bridge between different segments of the LGBT community.

Race, Class, and Gender Diversity

LGBT people come in every race, ethnicity, social class, and gender, and the same barriers to racial and ethnic integration that exist in the broad population exist among LGBT people. These divisions also mean that different segments of the LGBT population have developed different understandings of queer identity. The dominant understanding used in much LGBT activism, in Pride parades, and in this book, defines sexual orientation and gender identity as separate dimensions of one's personal identity that mark one as divergent from the heterosexual majority. As I describe in the first part of this book, the Stonewall riots ushered in a spirit of activism in which gays and lesbians proclaimed not just their acceptance of, but their pride in gay identity. This ethos is embodied in Pride parades.

However, this definition of gay identity (and later queer identity, with the inclusion of bisexuality and transgender into an umbrella term) was developed by those with the racial, class, and gender privilege to separate sexual orientation from a web of intersecting oppressions.[50] Lesbian feminists, for instance, point out that lesbians' lower economic status reflects their experience of workplace discrimination both as women and as gays. Similarly, working-class and LGBT people of color experience their sexual and gender difference as bound up with their class, racial, and ethnic identities. For the white, middle-class gay men who have long led the LGBT movement, freedom from other types of inequality has meant the ability to define queerness as a distinct identity around which to come together and be proud. For others, joining the community organized around this gay identity can mean rejecting racial and class-based identities, something that they may have neither the ability nor the desire to do. By gathering diverse people together in a common space, Pride can act as a bridging practice that facilitates solidarity across differences without requiring that participants fully resolve their divisions.

I did not observe divisions by race, class, or gender among participants at Pride; in fact, from my vantage point Pride brought people together across the lines which usually divide them. Spectators of different races and genders mingled with one another as they watched the parade, and the majority of contingents included diverse marchers. Particularly in the bigger parades, participants displayed their queer and racial/ethnic identities with contingents like the LGBTQ South Asians in Atlanta or African Ancestral Lesbians United for Change in New York. These groups conveyed educational visibility outward to mainstream society, but this message also turned inward to participants themselves. Many said they learned just how many different people identify as LGBT by seeing the parade. Participants commented positively on how Pride was a unique time for them to celebrate with such a wide array of LGBT people and allies. In this way, Pride served as a bridging practice as diverse LGBT people and allies came together in a common action, but had the space within this action to show their unique identities.

While these observations point toward the conclusion that Pride reduces diversity barriers to LGBT community similar to the way that it diminishes demographic and cultural barriers, a counterargument comes from what I did not observe. Those who feel left out by the way queer identity is defined at Pride likely do not attend the event. For a practice like Pride to bridge the differences between diverse people, they must first participate in the practice. Monique in New York, for one, said that she would just as soon have stayed home on Pride Day because she felt the parade was more representative of the white gay male experience that of her own as a black transgender woman. She only attended, she said, because she wanted to raise support within the LGBT community for her work with LGBT youth living on the street. Though she thought that New York Pride's organizers could do a better job reaching out to people of color and transgender individuals like her, Monique did not feel that her exclusion was intentional. Instead, it reflected the fact that those with privilege design the most floats, make up the majority of marching contingents, and thus have the biggest hand in making Pride what it is. Similar to Monique, countless others likely do not go to Pride because its version of visibility, support, and celebration of queerness does not reflect their own understandings of sexuality and gender identity in their own lives. That is, Monique's experience reveals that, for some at least, Pride does not serve to bridge differences so much as it invites marginalized queers to participate.

One clue to persisting racial divisions in the LGBT community is the existence of alternative Black Pride and Latino Pride events in a number of major cities, including Atlanta and New York City. Like Trans Pride marches, these events highlight a specific segment of the LGBT population that has often been excluded from community organizing. However, Black and Latino Pride events operate at more of a distance from Pride, with separate organization and often at a different time of year. Despite this separation, these events generally take a parade form and look very similar to Pride. Their main difference from Pride seems to be the racial make-up of leadership and participants while otherwise displaying the same visibility, support, and celebration as Pride.

Though not explicitly antagonistic to Pride, these events show that not everyone feels equally included in the big parade. Rather than demanding fuller inclusion in Pride, some black and Latino LGBTs organize separate events at which to come together and bring attention to issues important to their communities. In Atlanta, I noted a dearth of African American–specific contingents in the Pride parade. When asked, participants pointed to the city's Black Pride event as the reason for lower participation of African Americans. In New York City, the Harlem neighborhood hosts a community festival to promote pride among same-gender loving people and to highlight their connection to the neighborhood.[51] According to a Harlem Pride organizer, the big parade is both physically and metaphorically far away from LGBT Harlem residents' daily lives; just as they must travel to a new area of the city to participate, so they must also distance themselves from the racially inflected culture embodied in their neighborhood. Harlem Pride creates a space where residents can be LGBT while remaining grounded in their home community. Thus, while Pride aspires to include all LGBT people and to bridge the differences between them, some find alternate events more meaningful to them.

Without obvious visible signs, I could not tell whether there was diversity by social class at the Pride parades I visited. This is one aspect of diversity that was not made visible either outwardly to the general public or inwardly to the LGBT community. When asked about it, participants pointed to the fact that all parades are free to attend and based on that, they believed there were not barriers to participation by economic level. However, as the group OccuPride critiques, the involvement of corporate sponsors at Pride parades promotes an image of the LGBT community as affluent consumers untouched by economic inequality.[52]

Like race and class, the same divisions of social status and cultural codes that separate men and women in the world at large affect and are even heightened for LGBT men and women. Just as in the early 1970s, gay men and lesbians can socialize romantically and platonically in separate spheres. In the 1970s and '80s, lesbian feminists even maintained that they had no real connection to gay men. The true identity of lesbians, they held, is to embrace the feminine culturally, emotionally, and sexually, thus rejecting straight and gay men alike.[53] Though lesbian feminism is past its heyday, LGBT women and men continue to work through their often-separate social spaces and political goals. Additionally, though things have improved since the 1970s, affluent white men continue to enjoy higher social status than others in the LGBT community, which makes them more able to contribute to and run major activist organizations.

Participants said that Pride parades brought queer men and women together despite separation in their everyday lives. Dee Ann in Fargo saw women and men bridge gaps at Pride:

> I think Pride is an opportunity for us all to come together and put those differences aside. I see gay men dancing with lesbians and I see all of the hugging and touching and caressing and all of the good side of what we really are, and that's wonderful.

I observed many interactions between men and women at Pride parades, though not to the extent characterized by Dee Ann. Most typically spectators were in single-gender groups of three or four but in close proximity to many others and with some interaction.

In the early 1970s, lesbians struggled to share in the organizing of Pride parades and make it an event truly for women and men equally. As evidenced by the continued existence of Dyke Marches in many cities, some lesbians still feel that men dominate Pride parades. And like those lesbians who were part of Pride in its early years, many of those who organize Dyke Marches do so specifically because they believe Pride is overly festive and commercialized. Flashy commercial floats, they argue, detract from the serious issues of discrimination and institutional oppression and exclude those radical, working-class, and non-white queers who are not targeted by commercial sponsors.[54] With their stripped down march format, Dyke Marches look more like the first Pride march in New York City—a protest march with a few festive elements.

It is true that some of the flashiest, loudest floats featured male dancers and were sponsored by clubs that cater to gay men. Still, I did observe plenty of female-dominated contingents as well. Each parade, save Burlington, was led by a contingent of Dykes on Bikes. In San Diego, the hundred or so Dykes were followed by roughly fifty men riding motorcycles. Parades included contingents of feminist organizations like Planned Parenthood and NARAL Pro-Choice America. In terms of both educational and defiant visibility, by my reading, both lesbians and gay men were well represented. Additionally, like Trans Pride events, Dyke Marches were included in the official line-up of Pride Week events publicized by Pride committees. Instead of competing with Pride, in most cities these events provided another forum to include diverse LGBT people.

Taken together, Pride parades do take some steps toward building LGBT community across diversity barriers of identity, race, class, and gender, but these steps are small. LGBT people bridge differences by participating in Pride as marchers in distinct contingents and as spectators. With the goal of showing LGBT people as they "really are," educational visibility turns inward to show participants the diversity of their own LGBT community. Bringing people together across these divides, Pride also gives participants the opportunity to interact with each other and form new connections. However, Pride parades did not go far in surmounting the divisions of race, class, gender, and identity. Just as they are in society at large, bisexuals and transgender people were less visible at Pride than their gay and lesbian counterparts. Similarly, those with less racial, class, and gender privilege in society did not always feel that Pride fully belonged to them. While those who attended Pride felt welcomed, others either stayed home or attended alternate Trans, Dyke, Black, and Latino Pride events that better spoke to their understandings of queer identity.

Divisions within the LGBT community by identity, race, class, and gender run deep, but for the most part they are not acute. While diversity is a resource to LGBT activism, it is also a barrier to community solidarity. In some ways Pride creates a space for diverse LGBT people to come together across the lines that divide them; people as different as Monique and Ralph were in the same physical space and participated in the same fun event. As an event organized around a particular understanding of queer identity, though, Pride suited those whose social privilege allowed them to share in this formulation. In 2010, this mostly included white lesbians, but bisexuals, transgender people, working-class LGBTs, and LGBT people of color were left out to varying degrees. Planning committees of each parade in my study made efforts to reach out to underrepresented segments of the LGBT community, they could not (nor did they seem willing to) turn Pride into an event that worked for everyone. Pride is an event that is driven by participants and thus reflects their understandings of queer identity. When it came to diversity, Pride was unable to overcome many of the divisions that separate LGBT people in their everyday lives.

Conclusion

Forty years ago when community leaders staged the first Pride parades, they recognized that they needed to unite gays and lesbians in order to make a strong public demand for change. The gay and lesbian community encompassed many different segments that did not always get along. The 1969 Stonewall riots and the Pride events in New York, Chicago, and Los Angeles one year later showed the potential for unifying this disparate people into a cohesive community. Through the early 1970s, Pride planners settled on a parade format as the best way to accommodate diverse members and to produce the positive emotional experience that brought people together.

Today LGBT people have many venues at which to come together, including Pride parades in 116 cities in the U.S. and over thirty countries across the world. Lesbians, gays, bisexuals, and transgender people have worked together to expand legal rights and dampen cultural hostility toward their sexual and gender difference. But they still face demographic, cultural, and diversity barriers to forming true community. Demographically, LGBT people are spread throughout the population rather than living together in dense neighborhoods, so they need venues to gather in the same physical space. Culturally, the codes of meaning that stigmatize queerness make it hard for many to be out as LGBT, so they need spaces where their identity is a positive feature. Finally, just as their diversity made community a challenge in the 1970s, LGBT people today vary by identity, race, class, and gender and they struggle to unite across their differences.

Pride parades communicate visibility, support, and celebration. As outward public statements, these challenge cultural invisibility, condemnation, and indifference both in the world and in the mind, but as inward messages to the participants, they make parades fun and supportive environments to enjoy queerness. When they don rainbows and glitter, march (or dance) in festive contingents, and cheer on their favorite parade displays, participants feed off each other's revelry and experience collective effervescence. This shared emotional experience brings them together so that they feel they are one community. For the day, at least, Pride parades remove the barriers of demography, culture, and diversity.

Pride's positive emotion culture and resulting collective effervescence builds community, but not everyone shares equally in the happy togetherness. Though bisexuals and transgender people are part of the now LGBT community in name, they are not entirely included in practice. For a few participants, Pride was an opportunity to educate not just mainstream society, but also their fellow LGBTs about transgender lives. For many though, bisexual and transgender invisibility were perpetuated at Pride and these two groups did not feel fully included in the community that was built at Pride. Likewise, Pride's ability to bring people together could not fully overcome the deep divisions by race, class, and to some extent gender that exist within the LGBT population. Pride is organized around a particular conceptualization of queer identity that fits the experiences of some (those with racial, class, and gender privilege) more than others. In response, some communities organize separate Black, Latino, Dyke, or Trans Pride events to better represent their identities. While Pride succeeded in providing some with the opportunity to learn about the diversity of the LGBT community and bridge differences, continued challenges with inclusion suggest that that there are limits to its ability to unite all with a queer identity.

Conclusion

The Future of Pride

Pride Day 2010 in Burlington was gorgeous. It was a sunny Saturday in July with the temperature right around seventy-five degrees Fahrenheit. Like most Saturdays, especially the ones with such great summer weather, the pedestrian-only Church Street was buzzing with activity. Restaurant patios were full with the lunch rush, stores had their doors open to welcome shoppers, and street-side kiosks selling coffee and quick meals did a bustling business. To mark that the Pride parade was about to pass, bars and restaurants advertised drink specials and hung rainbow flags. As the noon step-off time approached, the street got more crowded and many of the new arrivals were visibly LGBT with rainbow bead necklaces, gay-themed t-shirts, and hair and clothing styles associated with queerness.

Unlike many of the parades in my study, the streets of Burlington on Pride Day did not belong to participants alone. They were shared with shoppers, diners, and Vermonters just out for a stroll on a picturesque Saturday. When the parade went by, these bystanders joined with those who had come to Church Street for Pride with cheers and applause. After it passed, the diners went back to their meals and the shoppers to their spending. Watching the whole scene, I got the sense that for most bystanders the Pride parade was an entertaining diversion on a central city street where diversions are common. In an area with a remarkably LGBT-friendly cultural climate, Pride was a momentary acknowledgement of one of the city's cultural groups.

Burlington Pride in 2010 was a far cry from those first trepidatious marches in New York and Los Angeles. When Pat Rocco, Steven F. Dansky, and their thousands of fellow marchers stepped off on June 28, 1970 in the first Pride marches, this simple act of public celebration could very well have sparked violent backlash.[1] Gays and lesbians at the time

were culturally understood as sinful, mentally ill, criminal, and sometimes all three. These meanings were enshrined in institutional policies
and state laws. All major religious denominations in the U.S.—whether
Protestant, Catholic, or Jewish—condemned homosexuality as morally
wrong.[2] The American Psychological Association, the leading institutional authority on mental health, considered homosexuality to be a
curable mental defect.[3] And for all intents and purposes, being gay was
illegal in the United States. Sodomy, defined in practice if not always in
theory as homosexual sex, was illegal in most states, gays and lesbians
could be fired at will if their sexuality was public, and the idea of same-
sex marriage was laughable for its implausibility.[4] This cultural, institutional, and legal climate gave gays and lesbians plenty to fight against.
Christopher Street Liberation marches, which evolved into Pride, were
a bold step to challenge the culture that underpinned their harsh treatment in society.

Though LGBT people in Burlington enjoy much more social acceptance than those early pioneers, Burlington Pride participants told
me that LGBT people face cultural challenges even in this place that
seemed to me at least (coming as I was from North Carolina) to be a
veritable LGBT utopia. Angela led a group of LGBT youth in the parade
and told me of the emotional lift that they get from marching. Coming
out as LGBT is still a difficult process for them, she said, and when they
marched they received cheers. For many it was the first time that their
LGBT identity was a cause for celebration and it made them feel empow-
ered. Likewise for Blake, even though he had only ever attended Pride
in two very LGBT-friendly places—Burlington, Vermont and Provinc-
etown, Massachusetts—he still felt that, while everyone might want to
be Irish on St. Patrick's Day, "you have to be pretty brave to be gay on
Pride Day." That need for courage to visibly identify as LGBT (even just
for the day, if one is a straight ally who may be mistaken for gay) speaks
of a cultural climate still tinged with heteronormativity. To be straight
and appropriately masculine or feminine is still the gold standard, even
in Burlington, and that cultural code then interprets queer sexuality and
gender as second class.

Burlington is not a utopia of LGBT cultural equality and so Burlington Pride is a contentious protest event. With one of the friendliest
cultural climates for LGBT people in the U.S., however, Burlington gives

us a glimpse of what Pride could become if we continue on the trajectory toward full cultural equality. In that glimpse we see a benign public celebration of a valued cultural group. The city's residents come together to honor LGBT people's contributions to society, to remember their past struggles, and to have (excuse me) a gay old time. LGBT people enjoy their day in the sun and the chance to connect with their fellow queers. In this vision, all contestation at Pride—the messages that challenge the heteronormative cultural code that stigmatizes queerness—is gone because there is nothing left to contest. Pride may still communicate visibility, support, and celebration, but like a Fourth of July Parade's commemoration of freedom and independence, these are dominant and thus uncontentious cultural messages. Pride participants in Burlington and elsewhere still have a way to go until this vision becomes a reality. But in Burlington Pride's community-wide feel and in the way bystanders joined in to cheer on the parade as it passed, we can see what Pride may become if and when the U.S. achieves LGBT cultural equality.

To conclude this book, I look to the future of Pride, asking if it will ever become the benign community celebration for which Burlington Pride gives us just a peek. To do this I summarize how my research contributes to our understanding of social movements and cultural change. Then I speculate on how Pride may evolve in a future where LGBT people enjoy cultural equality.

Pride Is a Cultural Protest

In this book's introduction, I argued that social movements attempt to change individual behavior on a large scale. Whether they wish to save the environment, improve labor conditions, or end the practice of abortion, activists work together to change the laws, institutions, and cultural codes that underpin people's actions. To do this, social movements each have an ultimate goal, devise strategies to achieve that goal, and stage collective action tactics in line with these strategies. Like other identity movements, the LGBT movement's ultimate goal is cultural equality for a social group (LGBT people) that is defined by a shared sense of self on a socially meaningful characteristic, in this case queer sexuality and gender.[5] Cultural equality for LGBT people would mean that cultural codes of meaning in the world and individual attitudes in the mind do not regard queerness as inferior to heterosexuality and gender norma-tivity. It is these codes and attitudes that motivate mistreatment of LGBT people on an interpersonal level and that underpin discriminatory laws on an institutional level.

Heteronormativity stands in the way of LGBT cultural equality. This is a cultural code that holds up women and men as two opposite and complementary genders that naturally experience sexual desire for the other.[6] In a heteronormative culture like the U.S. (and pretty much all cultures, for that matter), LGBT people are defined as different and infe-rior because they are not attracted to the opposite gender or they do not express femininity or masculinity to match their biological sex. In the U.S. and other Western countries, heteronormativity is moderated by an increasingly strong cultural code of tolerance that renders explicit anti-LGBT behavior less socially acceptable. LGBT people today can find many places where they may live openly and are embraced by family and friends. Progress has been so swift, in fact, that some sociologists argue we are now in a "post-closeted" or "post-gay" era—such that sexual ori-entation is not such a big deal as in the past.[7] In this view, the hetero-normative cultural code is rapidly crumbling, if not already dismantled. Though I am hopeful that such an era is in our future, the experiences of participants—like Blake in Burlington, who has "to be pretty brave to be gay on Pride Day," and Kevin, who drove for an hour to attend Pride in Fargo for the chance to be open about his homosexuality—convince me that heteronormativity is still alive and well. Activists continue to work not just for increased tolerance, but for an end to the heteronorma-tive cultural code that necessitates this tolerance. As sociologist Suzanna Danuta Walters argues, cultural equality reaches beyond tolerance to unqualified inclusion.[8] Or, as this study of Pride reveals, LGBT advo-cates not only push for support but for full-throated celebration of queer sexuality and gender.

Social movement researchers have long since noted that many ac-tivists, including those working in the LGBT movement, seek cultural equality as a goal. Where debate has arisen is in analysis of the strategies that activists devise to achieve cultural equality and the discrete tactics that make up a strategic campaign. Most movement scholars propose a strong role for the state as the target of movements' strategies and tac-tics. Just as all roads once led to Rome, in the social movement literature, it is often the case that all activism leads to the state. This orientation certainly has merit. As theorists argue, the modern state exercises quite a bit of control over our lives, while empirical researchers observe that many social movements do indeed work to change state laws and stage protests that target the state.[9] Pride shows, however, that there is a whole realm of social movement activity that exists outside the framework of state-centered strategies and tactics.

I am not alone in claiming that social movements pursue strategies that bypass state action or that they stage tactics with targets other than the state. Theorists of new social movements argue that in Western postindustrial societies such as the United States, culture exerts power over individuals independently of the state.[10] Similarly, with their multi-institutional politics framework sociologists Elizabeth Armstrong and Mary Bernstein say that many institutions, including but not limited to the state, hold social power. At the level of tactics, Verta Taylor and colleagues propose a definition of social movement tactic as a collective action with three dimensions: contestation of the social order, whether it is embodied in the state, a tangible institution, or culture; intentionality of participants, and a collective identity that binds participants as a cohesive group.[11] Each of these theories urges us to look beyond state-focused strategies and tactics to find meaningful social movement activity.

My study of Pride builds on—rather than challenges—the work of these scholars. Their studies revealed how in some campaigns activist organizers make the strategic decision to target culture, whereas mine highlights the role of ordinary participants.[12] Pride is distinctive for the way that it is driven by its participants. Though paid and volunteer members of planning committees work year-round to secure funding, negotiate permitting, and organize the myriad logistics involved in a large public event, they take more a role of event planners than activist organizers. Instead of designing and implementing clear messages in line with a comprehensive strategy, as activist organizers would do, event planners provide a framework within which participants can act. Within these basic guidelines for participant behavior, it is the marchers and spectators that craft Pride's messages of visibility, support, and celebration. In doing so, they draw from the cultural challenges that they experience in their daily lives. As LGBT people feel invisible when viewing dominant images of family, for instance, they combat this at Pride by publicly showing themselves as parents and spouses. Scholars have showed us that activists implement strategies and tactics that target cultural change. My study builds on this insight by demonstrating one case in which targeting culture arises out of participants' grounded experiences rather than leaders' strategic choices. Pride targets culture because that is the realm in which its participants most acutely experience social inequality.

Since the start, Pride has been a cultural protest, primarily targeting culture with messages that contest dominant meanings. Pride began as a commemoration of the 1969 Stonewall riots, when local gay residents joined with patrons to fight back against a routine police raid against a gay bar called the Stonewall Inn. Even as they were happening, the riots grew in importance from a much needed collective resistance to police harassment to a fight against gays' cultural oppression.[13] Though some marchers did have the narrower issue of police harassment on their minds, most participants in the first marches in New York and Los Angeles demonstrated against the hostile culture that police represented. A mass demonstration in defiance of cultural norms also satisfied a growing dissatisfaction with more modest, image-conscious homophile tactics. The early marchers that I talked to told me how good it felt, and how meaningful, to walk proudly on the streets and declare their sexuality to the public.

In 1970, Pride, as these marches would soon be called, targeted culture as opposed to the state or an institution because this target fit marchers' grievances with the society at large and with their own movement for change. In the succeeding years, Pride continued to target culture as planners found that the abstract, cultural message that "gay is good" combined with a festive atmosphere enacting this message attracted more and more people every year. Though some wanted Pride to address specific political issues, community leaders agreed that bringing together mass numbers of gays and lesbians was a primary aim of Pride and to do this they needed to stick with a broad cultural focus. Planning committees thus did not issue official lists of demands for their marches, instead creating a format in which each contingent could offer its own messages. For instance, members of the Metropolitan Community Church, a Christian organization created specifically for gays and lesbians, could ride on a float and sing hymns to promote their message that God loves and welcomes gay people. At the same time, Gay Liberation Front activists could hold signs calling to "smash imperialism" by overturning the intertwined political, economic, and cultural system that marginalized people according to their sexuality, race, gender, and more. These messages need not be consistent in their specifics, but they conformed to the broad cultural message of Pride that homosexuality should be celebrated as a positive human variation.

Echoing the insights of other scholars, infighting over practical issues like whether to include business contingents facilitated important discussions among community leaders over the abstract issues of representation, commercialization, and frivolity—discussions that continue today.[14] During this time Pride crystallized its form as a parade with many contingents and a festive air rather than a more dour protest march. The reason, again, was that a parade was able to unite diverse gays and lesbians by allowing each contingent to put its own spin on Pride within a single procession. Thus, Pride as a cultural protest continued to fit the concerns of most gays and lesbians. They wanted cultural change and a united community and Pride was a fun event that worked towards both of these goals.

Once established as an annual parade with a cultural message, Pride grew through the years without substantially altering its form.[15] Though they varied greatly in size and regional cultural climate, each of the six parades that I studied in 2010 was an annual event that targeted culture with its messages of change. As a cultural protest, Pride is in a realm of social movement activity that has often been overlooked by social movement scholars as they focus on state-directed activism. Cultural protest may be part of a coordinated campaign alongside state-targeted tactics, or activists may use it as a separate strategy to try to directly change culture. In the campaign for marriage equality, for instance, many of the same activists who organized and participated in public same-sex weddings in San Francisco in 2004 also took part in future state-targeted protests.[16] In this book on Pride, I have shown how cultural protest can take place apart from other movement activity. That is, it is not a part of a state-focused strategy like the one for marriage equality. The strategy of Pride is to directly challenge cultural meanings and attitudes in order to ultimately improve how individuals treat LGBT people in society. Activists with groups like the Human Rights Campaign that pursue state-focused strategies did march in the parades I studied, but their work was largely separate from that of Pride. With this study of Pride, I have built on the work of those who assert that movement strategies and tactics may target culture directly by showing one phenomenon that pursues cultural change with little coordination to other movement efforts. Moreover, I show that the particularly cultural focus of Pride developed not because activist leaders directed the strategy, but because participants were free to craft messages that tackled the struggles they face in their daily lives.

This book's tour through the history and current work of Pride also shows how activists mix fun and protest. Similar to Leila Rupp and Verta Taylor's work on drag performances, my work shows that a collective event does not have to be either fun entertainment or serious protest—sometimes it is both.[17] The fun of Pride serves a purpose. First, as planners in the 1970s realized, a fun parade brings out more people than an angry march. Second, at Pride fun is a message in itself; when LGBT people and allies get together to revel in queerness rather than lament it, they make a cultural statement that queerness is a quality to be celebrated. Finally, fun unites people. As Pride's messages turn inward, the event is defined by a positive emotion culture so that participants feed off one another's joyful emotions and feel connected by their collective effervescence. I do not know if this mix of fun and protest is a particular feature of cultural protests or if it is possible in all types of movement tactics; I certainly have enjoyed myself when marching in protest of state actions too. It does seem though that since culture is in itself an intangible force both in the world and in the mind, protesting it may allow for more creativity and greater freedom to break from one's own entrenched mindset, and that is where the fun begins.

Looking ahead to the future, I think that Pride will continue as an annual parade for years to come regardless of the status of LGBT cultural or political equality. Pride has grown steadily in number and size of parades since its founding in 1970, even as social conditions for LGBT people in the U.S. have improved substantially. Since it operates largely apart from state- and institution-focused LGBT movement activity, Pride could continue even as state laws and institutional policies change. In 2011, for example, New York Pride was held two days after the state legislature approved, and the governor signed, a bill legalizing same-sex marriage. By all accounts, the atmosphere was more festive than ever. Similarly, in 2015, LGBT people and allies celebrated nationwide marriage equality two days after the U.S. Supreme Court declared all statewide same-sex marriage bans unconstitutional. Parades have continued in essentially the same form even as the LGBT movement wins these historic victories. Though LGBT activists have achieved one measure of legal equality, they are still working toward cultural equality.

More doubtful is whether Pride would continue even if visibility, support, and celebration of queerness were entrenched in dominant culture; that is, even if LGBT people achieve cultural equality with straights. Currently, Pride's fun atmosphere and ability to unite partially comes from the contrast with LGBT people's everyday lives. Participants told me they felt a sense of freedom in their identities while at Pride that they just did not get every other day of the year. This freedom and pride, in turn, generates collective effervescence that helps participants forge bonds with each other that solidify their collective identity as LGBT. Success for an identity movement can present what sociologist Joshua Gamson calls a "queer dilemma": the very oppression that necessitates activism is what creates the conditions for diverse individuals to unite around a common identity.[18] When a group then achieves cultural equality, the identity that brought them together—be it their sexuality, ethnicity, or another quality that marginalized them in society—is no longer central to the way they experience the world. Amin Ghaziani argues that gays and lesbians in LGBT-friendly cities are already retreating from sexual orientation as a core identity.[19] Some non-white LGBTs understand queer sexuality differently than white LGBTs, blending queer identity with their ethnic and racial identities rather than separating sexuality from other ways in which they are socially marginalized (see chapter 5). Thus, the question for Pride is whether in a world where they are culturally equal, LGBT people will still find it meaningful to come together and celebrate their queerness.

I argue that Pride likely will continue if and when LGBT people achieve cultural equality but it will evolve into a benign community celebration with broad appeal. Just as we all (at least during our twenties) drink green beer on St. Patrick's Day, perhaps one day, we will all enjoy rainbow martinis and be "gay for the day" on Pride Day. The broader acceptance of queerness in society will indeed make it less important for LGBT people to openly declare their identities as they parade down public streets, but this acceptance will also mean that straight allies feel more comfortable playing with gender and sexuality as they parade themselves. Just as veteran participants like Ted in San Diego reported seeing increasing participation of straight allies, we can expect this trend to continue as more straight people like Sarita's brother in Burlington or Jonah's dad in San Diego adopt queer-identified styles for the day while at Pride.

Pride may also continue to serve a special role in uniting LGBT people around a common history and identity. As described in the previous chapter, LGBT people, representing a small and geographically diffuse segment of the population, face demographic barriers to creating community. These are only likely to grow as they inch closer to full cultural equality and as fewer LGBTs move to queer-identified "gayborhoods" like the Castro in San Francisco to escape cultural marginalization elsewhere.[20] As it already does, Pride will culturally anchor LGBT people by commemorating queer history, most notably the Stonewall riots of 1969, and by keeping queer identity alive as participants perform queerness with rainbows, drag shows, and Dykes on Bikes in this annual ritual.[21] Though no longer brought together by shared experiences of oppression, LGBT people may still unite around the common history and identity that is embodied in Pride.

Pride's Models for Cultural Change

To better understand what it means to protest culture, it is helpful to separate the concept into two parts. On the one hand, there is culture in the mind: each individual's internal attitudes, values, and worldviews with which they interpret social phenomena.[22] Through socialization we internalize culture so that it becomes part of the way that we think. On the other hand, there is culture in the world: explicit language, symbols, and codes of meaning that carry with them a collective interpretation of phenomena.[23] These are the external tools that we use to communicate with one another. Both types of culture guide individual behavior, one from the inside by motivating some actions over others and the other from the outside by making certain actions justifiable and others unacceptable.

While staging cultural protest tactics such as Pride, activists communicate messages targeting culture in the mind or culture in the world. These messages are then part of a model for cultural change. In an "inside-out" model, messages seek to change individual attitudes (culture in the mind).[24] If successful, a change in attitudes will lead to better individual treatment of a marginalized group, which, when adopted by enough people, will change the collectively held cultural symbols and codes of meaning used by all members of society. On the other side, an "outside-in" model starts with messages directed at culture in the world.[25] Rather than work on individual attitudes, these messages attempt to change the cultural codes that individuals use to justify their actions. When culture in the world defines queerness as a sexual orientation or gender identity of equal value as heterosexuality, for example, then individuals will feel social pressure to first act as if this is so, and then adopt a corresponding attitude. With the inside-out model, activists seek to persuade individuals to change how they view an issue like queerness, while with the outside-in model, they bypass individuals and work on the collective meanings of that issue.

Pride parades adopt both outside-in and inside-out models for cultural change. All messages—defiant and educational visibility, support, and celebration—target culture in the world by offering new meanings for queer sexuality and gender to replace dominant negative ones. Defiant visibility, in particular, is very much a message that is *not* directed at individual attitude change. Defiant visibility says that LGBT people refuse to be silent, to hide their sexuality, or to change to accommodate a culture that is uncomfortable with queerness. It does so by offering images of LGBT people in ways that overtly defy established norms of acceptable behavior. When delivered as scantily clad men dancing on a float or short-haired women wearing leather and riding motorcycles, this message can in fact harden individual attitudes against LGBT people. Throughout Pride's history, participants have debated the wisdom of sexual displays for this reason. As part of an outside-in model for cultural change, clear displays of queer sexuality make sense because their intent is not to persuade individuals but to change the cultural understanding of what is acceptable public behavior.[26] Celebration and support likewise aim to change culture in the world even at the expense of individual attitude change.

Educational visibility was the one message of Pride parades that also targets culture in the mind, seeking to change the individual attitudes that motivate behavior. Participants communicated this message by showing that LGBT people are "just like" their straight counterparts. They are friends, neighbors, family members, and churchgoers. Directed at individuals with negative attitudes, this message was responsive to common prejudices about LGBT people. With educational visibility, participants challenged stereotypes with images of LGBT people who conform to dominant cultural values like family and civic duty. Just as the other three messages may sacrifice a change in individual attitudes in order to make a public statement about how culture in the world should change, however, educational visibility may sacrifice changes to collectively held codes of meaning in order to influence individual attitudes. While images of "respectable" LGBT people may persuade those who know only stereotypes and boogeyman images of LGBT people, it may sacrifice what, for some, is a needed critique of heteronormativity in the world.

Just as Pride's overall targeting of culture stems from participants' grounded experiences of invisibility and intolerance, its messages target culture in the world and culture in the mind according to the challenges that participants face in their daily lives. Participants respond to daily ignorance and skepticism from family members, neighbors, and coworkers about their queer sexuality and gender by attempting to show what LGBT people are "really like" with educational visibility. This is not a top-down strategy devised by activist leaders, but a response to participants' daily frustrations. Similarly, marchers and spectators contest the way queerness is so often denigrated as inferior in public debates by celebrating all that makes being queer special. Participants target culture in the world with messages defiant visibility, support, and celebration in order to contest the effects of the heteronormative culture code of meaning in their lives.

Considering the distinction between outside-in and inside-out models for social change adds a layer of complexity to the way that we think about cultural protest. Since participants largely drive the message of Pride, these were models, rather than top-down, planned out strategies. Future research may explore how activists design outside-in or inside-out strategies in a more proactive way. Mary Bernstein, for instance, found that political opportunities, opposition, and inclusiveness of activists to diverse supporters affected whether they tried to change broad cultural meanings about homosexuality or individual's attitudes about gays and lesbians.[27] Combining these insights with my call to explore movement activity exclusively in the cultural arena, researchers may look to how activists decide to pursue cultural change either from the outside-in or the inside-out.

Another question for future research is the effectiveness of mass demonstrations to target culture in the world or culture in the mind. My research on Pride parades does suggest mass cultural protests have a better chance to affect culture in the world than culture in the mind. There are two reasons for this. First, targeting culture in the mind requires a high degree of organizational message control. With this target, protests attempt to speak to individual bystanders with the message of educational visibility, but their good impression of LGBT people may easily be ruined by one errant sexual display. Every participant's actions are subject to interpretation and are likely to be attributed to the group as a whole. Creating a positive impression for skeptical members of the public thus requires every participant to be fully on board with this scheme. Second, any identity group that stages a cultural protest is already subject to negative cultural attitudes and cultural codes. With little opportunity to explain the meaning of displays, individuals with negative perceptions are likely to interpret demonstrative action in line with their current attitudes. Put plainly, a parade probably will not change anyone's mind. It can, though, change the conversation and the meanings associated with particular groups.

Along with my skepticism about the effectiveness of targeting culture in the mind, my finding that Pride's messages mainly target culture in the world lead me to conclude that Pride's future will be driven by dominant cultural codes about queerness, not by trends in individual attitudes. Again, Burlington hints at what Pride could become. With a strong cultural code of tolerance, Burlington-area residents by and large hold favorable attitudes about LGBT people and this translates to a cultural climate that is generally LGBT-friendly.[28] However, the heteronormative cultural code remains so that despite this positive air, Burlington participants felt that their queerness was merely tolerated. With Pride, they went a step further and pushed against heteronormativity by celebrating queerness, supporting it, and making it visible. With a majority of messages targeting culture in the world, Pride has a job to do as long as the heteronormative cultural code of meaning still positions LGBT people as inferior.

In addition to contesting culture with outward messages, with a hostile culture in the world, Pride also serves a role in creating community with positive messages to the LGBT community. In my study, Pride parades were oases in which participants' queer identities were truly accepted and celebrated. This special atmosphere enabled them to form bonds and feel together as a community. Thus, I believe that Pride parades will continue as cultural protests as long as culture in the world includes a heteronormative code of meaning that renders queer sexuality and gender inferior. Moreover, I do not see Pride parades keeping their contentious edge if and when their primary target is culture in the mind. Tactics that involve meaningful one-on-one interaction would likely be much more effective than Pride parades at reaching individuals with negative attitudes.

Pride Variation

Pride is unique among mass demonstrations not just because it targets culture, but also because it is institutionalized.[29] Pride started over forty years ago and evolved into a phenomenon with events all over the country and world. There is an International Association of Pride Organizers that works to tie individual Pride events together by encouraging collaboration, holding educational conferences, and choosing an annual theme.[30] Aside from these organizational ties, the coherence of Pride parades as a common phenomenon comes mainly from drawing on the collective memory of Stonewall and invoking the theme of pride in LGBT identity. By contrast, mass demonstrations studied by social movement scholars are typically singular events or a short wave of protests that end when activists succeed, try new tactics, or move on to new campaigns.[31] The cohesion of Pride parades means that unlike most mass demonstrations, each community draws on a unitary phenomenon with many symbols (like rainbows) and traditions (like Dykes on Bikes to lead the parade) when putting on a Pride event.

Parades vary widely in size, grandeur, and local context. In the summer and fall of 2010, when I did my field work for this book, I first travelled to Salt Lake City where the medium-size parade was a brief intermission from the city's usual conservative, straight-laced vibe. Later, in San Diego, the funky Hillcrest neighborhood hosted Pride with house parties and drink specials as thousands of LGBT people and allies put on a flashy and colorful parade. In the fall when the summer heat finally died down, Atlanta's Pride gathered a mix of business, churches, and the famous Pride Band to march up the commercial Peachtree Street and into the crowded Midtown neighborhood. Pride parades in New York City, Burlington, and Fargo similarly had their own unique flavor as participants marshaled their community's resources to put on events adapted to their cultural climates.

Among the myriad differences between Pride parades, I found a few patterns. First (and perhaps most obviously), communities with more resources of people, money, and organizations put on flashier events with decorated floats and amplified music. With a greater need for financial backing and a bigger crowd for those wishing to advertise, these larger parades also had prominent business sponsors like Delta Airlines, Coca-Cola, and Home Depot. Second, the diversity of participants at Pride reflected the local populations. The larger and more diverse populations in New York, San Diego, and Atlanta brought out participants with more racial, ethnic, and affinity groups than the smaller populations in Salt Lake City, Burlington, and Fargo. Third, the contingents who marched to show support for LGBT people varied along with community resources and local climate. Churches were particularly prominent in the Bible Belt South of Atlanta, in Mormon Salt Lake City, and in the smaller cities of Fargo and Burlington. Though they did participate, I saw comparatively fewer churches in San Diego and New York. Similarly, many politicians marched in the left-leaning and culturally more LGBT-friendly cities of Burlington, San Diego, and New York, but I saw only two politicians in Atlanta and Fargo and none in Salt Lake City. Fourth, each parade adapted how they communicated Pride's messages of defiant and educational visibility, support, and celebration to their local cultural climates. That is, parades pushed their local cultures only so far. Though they still contested cultural meanings of queerness, in less-LGBT friendly areas, participants chose more modest expressions in deference to local norms.

The clearest pattern of variation among Pride parades was in participants' emphasis on messages of support versus celebration. Both messages combat cultural disapproval of queerness, but support is geared toward a harsher, fire-and-brimstone version while celebration tackles a milder sentiment. In the more LGBT-friendly areas of New York, San Diego, and Burlington, participants emphasized the celebration message, whereas in less LGBT-friendly areas, they focused more on communicating public support for LGBT people. Parades adapted messages to their local environments. In harsher cultural climates, Pride parades pushed for tolerance by showing that queer identity is cause for support, not opposition. By contrast, in more accepting areas, Pride parades could push beyond mere tolerance by unabashedly celebrating queer identity.

This finding is a clue to how Pride parades may change in the future. With increasing acceptance of queer sexuality and gender, we may expect Pride parades across the country to become more like those in the already more LGBT-friendly areas. That is, if American culture keeps on its current trajectory towards understanding queerness as a natural human variation, then celebration will become an even more central message of Pride parades. The message of public support would drop out of Pride entirely because culture at large would support the existence of LGBT people. Though both support and celebration challenge the heteronormative cultural code, the message of support may also lend weight to a code of tolerance. While this code brings a welcome change from climates that encourage harsh condemnation of queerness, it stops short of fully embracing queer sexuality and gender. In a more welcoming future, Pride parades would emphasize celebration over support in order to challenge the culture to not only tolerate but to value queer identity. That is, Pride would make clear that a cultural code of tolerance is not enough and would squarely attack the heteronormative cultural code that deems queerness unworthy of celebration. Finally, further progression towards cultural equality would render such celebration of queerness an utterly non-contentious act. At that point, Pride parades would become benign community celebrations rather than contentious protests.

Bumps in the Road

I have laid out a vision in which Pride parades gradually shift from contentious cultural protests to benign community celebrations. In this scheme the driving factor of the change is the dominant heteronormative cultural code of meaning and attendant meanings and attitudes about queerness. As those become more accepting, Pride parades would become less contentious and their role in LGBT community formation would shift. However, two long-running issues—commercialization and frivolity—threaten this trajectory.[32] Since the early years of Pride, organizers and participants have debated the role of business sponsors and the balance between carefree festivity and serious-minded protest. The concern is that while commercialization and a fun atmosphere play important roles, when taken too far, they erode Pride's sense of purpose as a social movement protest. If Pride participants stop attending the event to effect social change and instead participate in order to get free stuff from sponsors or to have a fun party, then even if such a public celebration went against dominant culture it could not accurately be called a protest tactic.[33]

Businesses have always participated in Pride parades. First it was local gay bars that contributed money and organized some of the first Pride floats, and then more and more national corporations became sponsors with the hopes of tapping into the LGBT market. Businesses provide needed financial support to Pride parades and by participating with banners and marching contingents, they show public support for LGBT people. But with the money to put on bigger and flashier displays, businesses can drown out other voices.[34] In Salt Lake City, for instance, Bud Light joined the parade with a tractor-trailer and marchers wearing beer bottle, wheat, and hops costumes. Similarly, the Delta Airlines contingent in Atlanta consisted of a Mini Cooper with the company's logo followed by marchers in flight attendant uniforms who handed out rainbow scarves to spectators. It is hard for churches, high school gay-straight alliances, and activist groups with homemade signs and streamers decorating their pickup trucks to compete with such high production value in order to communicate their messages of support.

Annual infighting over the practical details of how many sponsors to include have been the focal points for this larger debate over commercialization.[35] Throughout Pride's history, community leaders have rightly feared that too much business involvement could alter the purpose of the event from a protest to a marketplace. In doing so, it would alter participants' motivations for attending and present a distorted image of LGBT people as more affluent than they actually are. Looking at parades like that in Atlanta, where Pride is officially presented by Delta Airlines, some believe that this already the case.[36] Though I saw cause for concern over corporate sponsorship, I also saw many genuine displays of contentious support, visibility, and celebration at the Pride parades I studied. However, overcommercialization is a possibility for the future of Pride. Even if Pride's messages remain contentious, if future participants attend solely to receive free goodies from business sponsors and to be entertained by their glitzy floats with choreographed dancers, then Pride would no longer be an intentional protest. Similarly, with the power to drown out individual participants and groups that represent lower-income LGBT people and issues, overcommercialization would result in a much narrower vision of LGBT equality.

A second danger is that Pride could become just too much fun so that the festive atmosphere obscures Pride's greater purpose from both participants and the greater public. Pride's fun atmosphere is one of the things that make it special. At Pride, queer identity is a source of fun; it means playing with gender roles by putting a spot of makeup on a masculine face, or cheering on a gay men's chorus for their rendition of Deniece Williams's "Let's Hear it For the Boy." As an outward statement to mainstream society, the public display of hundreds, often thousands of LGBT people and allies celebrating queer identity challenges the dominant cultural code of meaning that regards queerness as a source of shame. As an inward statement to LGBT people and allies, this collective revelry gives many LGBT people a space to feel pride in their identities and then to feel closer to one another as a community. Like business involvement, though, too much festivity can distract from the true purpose of Pride, which is to bring about cultural equality so that such celebrations of queer identity are not such isolated and notable events.

Throughout their history, Pride parades have struggled to keep a sense of purpose amid the fun. San Francisco's 1974 parade projected such festivity that any calls for cultural change were lost on reporters from the city's major daily newspaper, the *Chronicle*.[37] Similarly, many of today's parades, particularly those in more LGBT-friendly areas like Burlington, San Diego, and New York, include so many cheering spectators and carefree, dancing contingents that an outsider may wonder what oppression such happy people face. However, it is a mistake to view celebration as evidence of equality; as I have argued in this book, the message of celebration does not target individual attitudes in the mind but rather cultural codes in the world that interpret queerness as unworthy of celebration. For participants, though, Pride's vibrant revelry can be a reason in itself to attend. In fact, in the beginning, Pride organizers favored a parade format because they knew festivity and fun would bring out more people than a solemn and angry protest. In making this choice, though, they built in a dual motive for participants, both to protest inequality and to have fun. In 2010, I only met a handful of participants who attended Pride solely to have fun, but in the future, Pride could cease to be a true protest if this number increased so that for the majority Pride was no more than a good party.

Parading toward Equality

I have described many scenes throughout this book. There were the three leather-clad lesbians in Fargo who kicked off the parade with a roar of their motorcycles and the DC Cowboys who did a line dance on a float in Salt Lake City wearing short cut-off jeans, cowboy boots, and little else. There was the symbolic smashing of a cardboard closet after Boston's 1971 march and the man who marched with an oversize jar of Vaseline to celebrate homosexuality in Los Angeles's 1970 parade. There were parents, church members, and politicians who affirmed the worth and dignity of queer sexuality and gender with printed signs and vocal chants while drag queens, "bears," and groups of gay and lesbian students who embodied this message as they strutted, danced, and cheered, in all their fabulous glory.

Each of these scenes illustrates the spirit of Pride: a playful challenge to the heteronormative cultural code that renders LGBT people culturally unequal to their straight counterparts. This spirit was central to the innovation of the first marches in 1970. Instead of angry or solemn state-directed protest demonstrations, Christopher Street Liberation Day in

New York and Christopher Street West in Los Angeles were festive declarations of gay identity. For the first time, gays and lesbians gathered en masse to protest a culture that alternately thought of them as sinful, mentally ill, and criminal—and they did it with style. Wearing bell-bottoms and linking arms, they marched the streets of New York with smiles on their faces to show that "gay is good." In Los Angeles they put on a parade, again showing through their decorated cars carrying shirtless "Groovy Guys" and the drag queen "Imperial Court" that being gay is a source of pride and good cheer.

The playful spirit of Pride continues on today in the scene that opens this book. When confronted with evangelical counter-protesters railing against the evils of homosexuality, Atlanta's Pride Band turned up the volume on their fabulousness and belted out the chorus of Lady Gaga's "Poker Face." Like their forebears in 1970, Atlanta participants did not protest with explicit arguments or lists of demands; instead, they defied their detractors with humor while refusing to compromise their queer identities. Participants showed that they are happy with themselves and do not intend to change. They demanded that culture change instead.

For over forty years, Pride participants have been parading toward equality. With humor and self-assurance, they have challenged cultural codes of meaning and individual attitudes that demean LGBT people. As long as American culture and the individual minds of Americans continue to view queerness as inferior, Pride parades will protest by offering messages of visibility, support, and celebration. When they reach the end of that long road and finally achieve equality, perhaps LGBT people and their allies will celebrate with a parade.

APPENDIX A

Studying Pride

Sometimes I feel silly calling my research "ethnography"—especially when talking to my graduate-school colleague who worked in a poultry plant and lived in a trailer for six months for her dissertation research. Ethnography requires immersing oneself in one's field site in order to understand the whole system of meanings and influences (or variables, to the quantitatively minded) affecting a group or a phenomenon. Since the group or phenomenon under study is usually stable, researchers can spend months and even years in the field. By living and working with laborers in the poultry industry, for instance, my colleague had the chance to see how they interacted with each other, with their employers, and talk with them over many months about their lives. The phenomenon I studied, by contrast, only lasted five to ten hours. Once each Pride parade ended, participants packed up and left, and cleaning crews erased all physical traces of the event.

In the short span of a one-day event, I attempted to uncover all the rich detail that the typical ethnographer takes months to discover. I used the same tools any ethnographer uses: field observations, formal and informal interviews, and background studies of each parade's origins and current goals. Guided by my research questions, I sought to discover what participants communicated about queer sexuality and gender whether they marched in the parades or cheered from the sidelines. Ethnography was the best research method to uncover these cultural meanings; but with the short time span, it meant a few extra challenges.

SELECTION OF CASES

My first challenge was to select which six parades to include in my study. Though this is not a representative sample in a statistical sense, it did need to reflect the diversity of Pride parades in the U.S. I began by collecting information on each of these parades. Working from a list of Pride parades on a gay tourism website, a research assistant of mine visited parade websites and emailed organizers to obtain estimates of 2008 parade sizes (defined as number of marchers and spectators), year of parade's founding, and date of 2009 parade. We added to this list by searching gay periodicals and websites to make sure the data set included all parades in the country. I define a Pride parade as an event that uses the name "Pride," is aligned with the LGBT community, and includes collective locomotion. In 2009, there were 110 Pride parades held in 43 states and the District of Columbia.

With a full list of Pride parades, I systematically selected six parades to comprise my sample. I separated parades into quintiles by size and selected one event from each group. I added the parade in New York City as my sixth research site because it is both the largest Pride event in the country and it carries symbolic importance as the site of the Stonewall riots. To choose between parades in the same quintile, I considered region of the country, demographics, and measures of LGBT-friendliness. Geographically, I chose parade sites in each of four Census regions and from separate divisions within these regions. Since there are nine Census divisions and I was only able to attend six parades, I did not attend a parade in the East North Central, West South Central, or East South Central divisions.

Demographically, I matched parade data with census data by the Metropolitan Statistical Area (MSA) in which parades were held. I used the percentage of white population as a representation of racial and ethnic diversity and chose parades in cities with high, middle, and low diversity. I also looked for variation by the median income in each city. I used measures of individual-level cultural attitudes and relationship recognition statutes to represent gay-friendliness. Data on cultural attitudes come from the 2010 General Social Survey and are separated by Census division. A second proxy for LGBT-friendliness is the presence of state laws recognizing same-sex relationships. Passage of these laws requires both public support and muted opposition. Such laws represent steps toward legal equality, which may then make the cultural climate friendlier to LGBT people. Finally, as a practical matter, I chose parades with different dates. Table A.1 lists the parade sites I chose with their size and information on geography, demography, and gay-friendliness.

TABLE A.1. Parade Sites

Site	Date 2010	Size 2010	Region	% White[i]	Median Income	% Homosexuality is not wrong at all[ii]	Relationship Recognition
Fargo/ Morehead, ND	August 15	350	W. North Central	92.3	$24,290	45.3	None
Burlington, VT	July 25	1,500	New England	93.6	$26,897	75.1	Legal Marriage
Salt Lake City, UT	June 6	20,000	Mountain	77.8	$25,492	40.9	None
Atlanta, GA	October 10	60,000	South Atlantic	54.9	$29,030	38.3	None
San Diego, CA	July 18	150,000	Pacific	51.6	$25,329	55.1	State Civil Union*
New York, NY	June 27	1 million	Middle Atlantic	51.3	$29,913	51.4	Domestic Partnership*

* As of 2010. In 2011, New York State passed marriage equality and now issues marriage licenses to same-sex couples. In 2013, the Supreme Court declined to overturn a lower court's ruling on Proposition 8, effectively allowing same-sex marriage in California. In 2015, the Supreme Court declared all same-sex marriage bans unconstitutional, meaning that same-sex couples can now marry in all fifty states.
[i] U.S. Census 2010a.
[ii] Smith, et al. 2011.

The parades in my study represent a wide diversity on all variables and mirror the diversity of the population of Pride events. Parades were distributed throughout the country such that the two closest parades, Burlington, Vermont and New York City, were separated by 350 miles and vastly different in size. The MSAs in which parades are located vary from 51.3% white population in New York City to 93.6% white population in Burlington. The make-up of non-white population is different as well. African Americans are the largest minority group in Atlanta, and Latinos are the largest group in San Diego. These groups both make up substantial proportions of the population in New York City. Parades vary by median income in their host MSA, though there is slightly less diversity in the parades chosen, compared to all parades. For the population of all MSAs that host parades, the median annual income ranges from $16,000 to $39,000, but the range in my sample is from $24,000 to $30,000. However, over half of all Pride parades are in MSAs that have median incomes within this range.

Parades were located in diverse cultural landscapes—from the more LGBT-friendly cultural climate of Burlington, Vermont, where three quarters of residents believe homosexuality is not wrong at all and the state grants marriage licenses to gay couples, to the less LGBT-friendly climates of Salt Lake City and Atlanta, where there is no legal relationship recognition for same-sex couples and majority disapproval of homosexuality. Unfortunately, the latter two are not the most unfriendly regions; residents of East and West South Central regions (the Deep South, Texas, and Oklahoma) have even higher rates of disapproval. Though there were fourteen parades in these regions, none fit the criteria needed on other variables.

FIELD OBSERVATION

My second challenge was to get a complete picture of each event with only limited time to make observations. Before the first parade in June 2010, I spent months preparing by talking with parade organizers in various cities, delving into the history of each parade, and researching its current cultural climate. I added to this my personal knowledge of and familiarity with these events through years of participation as both a marcher and spectator. Before starting this project, I had attended Pride events in six cities across the country and one in Asunción, Paraguay while serving as a Peace Corps volunteer. Combining this personal experience with professional preparation, I started data collection with a thorough knowledge of what to look for in light of my research questions.

Once on site, I arrived at each parade one to two hours before the scheduled start time (depending on size) and observed the preparations made by parade contingents and organizers and watched spectators interact as they gathered for the parade. I spoke informally with both marchers and spectators about their perceptions of the events. During the parades, I walked back and forth along the route to watch the parade and observe spectators as various contingents passed by. When there were counter-protesters, I observed interactions between the two sides. I paid particular attention to parade contingents that received especially positive reactions from spectators; there were none that received negative reactions. I noted the signs participants carried, the shirts they wore, and the slogans they chanted. I took detailed audio field notes during events and summarized them with theoretical notes after events concluded.

In addition to the simple challenge of having limited time, another challenge was to establish a position from which to observe the event.[1] With many months at a field site, ethnographers can typically develop their observational position over time as they get to know their research participants. An ethnographer may begin as an outsider who does not know the cultural customs and history of the research site and then gradually gain an insider's perspective as she becomes accepted by participants.

With only a few hours, I did not have time to establish relationships with anyone that I met. However, given my experience with Pride parades and my membership in the LGBT community, I am able to approach Pride as an insider. I dressed casually in polo shirts and shorts, typical of the more conservatively dressed parade participants. A number of features of my personal appearance—my short, spiked hair, nose ring, and visible tattoos—mark me as "family" to fellow LGBT people.[2] This observational position as an insider helped me in my work, as I was able to easily build rapport with participants and parade volunteers. In one instance in New York, a female volunteer in a very crowded area allowed me access to a table on which to stand and observe the start of the parade, remarking that "there aren't many cute soft butch girls like you around!" While I blended in with my personal appearance and familiarity, I also set myself apart from Pride participants through my behavior. Most participants staked out positions along the parade route with groups of friends and interacted with those in their immediate vicinity. I limited my contact with any one person or group, instead walking along the parade route making observations and taking pictures.

PARTICIPANT INTERVIEWS

My third challenge was to recruit and interview a diverse sample of Pride participants. Like establishing an observational position, recruitment and interviewing typically relies on developing relationships over time. Ethnographers seek to interview not just those who are most interested and available, but also those who may be reticent to interact with an outsider. For my study I employed research assistants to canvass crowds and recruit potential interview subjects. I define Pride participants as those

who attended Pride parades in supportive roles as a marcher, spectator, sponsor, or volunteer. Starting one to two hours before each parade,
research assistants dispersed through the crowds; I placed one or two in
parade line-up areas to approach marchers and others at various points
along the parade route. Once parades started, the assistants interviewing
marchers moved to other areas and continued to solicit interviews and
contact information from spectators.

Research assistants sampled participants by quota according to perceived gender, age, and race/ethnicity. I set a 50/50 gender quota for
each parade, and research assistants strove for diversity by gender presentation, approaching some participants who presented themselves
normatively and others who did not. By age, I achieved variation with a
quota of two-thirds perceived under 40 years of age and one-third over
40. All respondents were over age 18. I set race/ethnicity quotas relative to the non-white population in each hosting MSA. In Atlanta, San
Diego, and New York, research assistants approached participants they
perceived to be non-white for one-third to one-half of all interviews,
while at the remaining parades they followed an informal quota by approaching non-white individuals according to their relative presence
in the crowds. Finally, I instructed research assistants to approach participants that were diverse in terms of their stereotypically "flamboyant"
behavior and the formal and informal groups with which they socialized. This is a nonprobability sample—meaning that respondents were
chosen by walking through the crowd and soliciting brief information—
and as such, results cannot be generalized to the population of Pride
parade-goers.

Research assistants conducted brief on-site structured interviews
with participants asking about their experience with Pride parades and
demographics. The main purpose of these interviews was to solicit contact information for semi-structured interviews via phone. Between
one and six months after each parade, I conducted a total of fifty semi-
structured interviews with Pride participants. In the case of two parade
sites, Burlington and Fargo, participants were also recruited via local
email lists since the initial sample was comparatively small. All participants attended Pride parades in one of the six cities in 2010 as either a
marcher, spectator, volunteer, or sponsor. Given initial quota sampling,
participants were diverse in terms of gender, sexual identity, and role

in the parade. Table A.2 summarizes these characteristics of interview respondents.

Semi-structured interviews lasted between twelve and forty minutes, during which participants described their experiences at their respective Pride events and their perceptions of Pride parades in general. I asked interview respondents to compare Pride parades to other mass demonstrations like political marches and St. Patrick's Day parades in order to place Pride in the spectrum of collective public displays. The interviews sought to capture participants' understandings of the purpose and meaning of Pride parades and their evaluations of their respective events. I asked them about the local cultural climate for LGBT people and the role of Pride parade in the community. Finally, I asked respondents for their impressions of the racial/ethnic, gender, and class diversity at their Pride parades.

TABLE A.2. Characteristics of Interview Respondents, N=50

Variable	N (%)
City	
Fargo, ND	10 (20%)
Burlington, VT	6 (12%)
Salt Lake City, UT	11 (22%)
Atlanta, GA	6 (12%)
San Diego, CA	8 (16%)
New York, NY	9 (18%)
Gender	
Woman	23 (46%)
Man	27 (54%)
LGBT identity	
Lesbian, gay, or bisexual	32 (64%)
Transgender or drag*	4 (8%)
Straight	14 (28%)
Role in parade	
Marcher	14 (28%)
Spectator	30 (60%)
Volunteer or Sponsor	6 (12%)

* Two respondents identified as transgender women; two were gay men who dressed in drag and considered this a significant part of their personal identities

ANALYSIS

My fourth challenge was to accurately understand Pride without the opportunity to refine research questions in light of new insights. One of the major strengths of ethnography compared to other sociological research methods is that it offers the ability to respond to what one learns on site. Fortunately, though I developed new questions and insights at each parade, my observational goals did not change substantially between them. I interviewed participants while completing parade visits and for three months after these were finished. Using the "swarm strategy," I was also able to rely on the perspectives of my research assistants to check my assumptions about the meanings of Pride.[3]

Once semi-structured interviews were complete, I transcribed and analyzed them to find common themes using MAXQDA qualitative software. I started by sorting responses according to whether they addressed external or internal dimensions of Pride. External dimensions were those that spoke to Pride as a public statement for those outside of the LGBT population (see chapters 3 and 4) and internal dimensions were those that related to this community (see chapter 5). I grouped responses within the external dimension according to common themes such as the target of action and the means to achieve external goals. Within the internal dimension, I sorted responses further into three groups—demographic, cultural, and diversity barriers. After isolating common themes from interviewer data, I compared these to my detailed observations to see if participants' perceptions matched my own. Finally, I analyzed whether common themes followed an "inside-out" or "outside-in" strategy of cultural change by identifying the intended audience for these messages. When participants referenced the goal of changing individual minds, this was an inside out model; when their message was to change cultural codes of meaning, this was outside in.

LIMITATIONS

Like any study, mine is not without its limitations, and a few deserve mention here. I present a view of Pride that is quite positive, which may be exaggerated given my methodological choices. First, I recruited interviewees at Pride parades so I drew from a pool of people with positive impressions of the event. While some participants were critical of aspects of Pride, their attendance indicates they still found value in the event. Second, I further narrowed my sample by interviewing participants after the event itself. Interview subjects willing to give their contact information may be more interested in promoting visibility, for example, than those who do not. Third, while my previous experience as a marcher and spectator at Pride parades strengthened my ability to understand the messages and symbols that were conveyed, it also meant that I approached this research as a fan rather than a critic.

APPENDIX B

Descriptions of 1970 Pride Participants

All participants interviewed for chapter 1 were active in the gay and lesbian communities of New York and Los Angeles at the time of the first Pride events in 1970. All but one (Tommi Mecca) marched in these first events. Below is a brief description of each person I interviewed for this chapter. All names are real and used by permission except when noted.

LOS ANGELES

Pat Rocco. Male, white. Gay filmmaker and performer in Los Angeles from the early 1960s through the 1980s. Rocco was prominent in the gay community and had a large social network and strong ties to other community leaders. Fans of his performances formed the Society of Pat Rocco Enlightened Enthusiasts (SPREE), a social club to honor his work. With Morris Kight, Troy Perry, and Bob Humphries, Rocco organized the first Pride parade in Los Angeles in 1970. He was later president of the Pride planning committee in 1973 and was involved for many years afterward.

Ruth Weiss (pseudonym). Female, white. Lesbian feminist activist who lived both in New York and Los Angeles. Weiss moved from New York to Los Angeles in May 1970 and marched in the Christopher Street West (CSW) Pride parade with the local chapter of the Gay Liberation Front (GLF). She was outspoken about homophobia within the women's liberation group National Organization for Women (NOW) and sexism within male-dominated gay liberation groups. Weiss attended many Pride events in both cities.

Del Whan. Female, white. Analysis is based on a memoir and personal communication about her experience at the first Los Angeles Pride parade. Whan had similar experiences with NOW as Weiss. She was part of the Los Angeles Pride planning committee for many years. She also founded a gay and lesbian student group at the University of Southern California in 1971.

NEW YORK

Martha Shelley. Female, white. She helped organize the first Pride march in New York in 1970 and gave a speech at the end. Shelley got involved through her membership in the lesbian group Daughters of Bilitis. She has been cited in many books and articles about the Stonewall era of gay rights activism.

Stephen F. Dansky. Male, white. He marched in the Christopher Street Liberation Day (CSLD) Pride event in New York with fellow members of GLF. Dansky also participated in protests for civil rights, the women's movement, and the Poor People's movement.

Roberto Camp. Male, Mexican-American. He also marched with GLF in CSLD. Throughout the 1970s, Camp moved back and forth between Berkeley, California and New York City.

Nikos Diaman. Male, white. He marched with GLF in CSLD. Diaman described "passing through" New York on his way to Paris in 1970.

Paul Guzzardo. Male, white. He marched in CSLD. Guzzardo was involved with various gay activist groups in late 1960s and 1970s. He lived in New York City throughout this time.

Perry Brass. Male, white. Brass was present at the GLF meeting when Pride was first discussed in early 1970. He marched with this group in CSLD. Brass founded the Gay Men's Health Project Clinic, the first clinic for gay men, in New York in 1972. He has written gay poetry and fiction since the early 1970s.

Ralph Cohen (pseudonym). Male, white. Cohen marched in the first CSLD. He founded a GLF chapter at college in Buffalo, New York and participated in protest actions in New York City during summers. Cohen organizes a contingent of participants from the 1970 CSLD to march in New York's Pride every year.

PHILADELPHIA

Tommi Mecca. Male, white. He marched in CSLD in 1971 and organized the first Pride march in Philadelphia in 1972.

The Spread of Pride from 1975 to 2010

From 1975 to 2010, when I conducted my study of LGBT Pride, the number of American cities hosting a parade grew steadily from 11 to 110. As of this writing in 2015, the number is up to 116. This does not count Pride parades outside the U.S., which are held in thirty countries around the world. Between 1975 and 2010, the American LGBT movement certainly had its ups and downs. In the 1970s, there were early successes gaining cultural acceptance and passing gay rights ordinances, then backlash as Anita Bryant led a national campaign to repeal these newly enacted laws.[1] The 1980s saw further cultural and legal backlash as the Christian Right gained political power and pushed their agenda against gay rights, women's rights, and what they saw as a trend toward secularism in the public sphere.[2] This was also when AIDS swept through the gay community, claiming the lives of thousands, shifting LGBT movement priorities, and fueling the fire of cultural backlash against LGBT people.[3] In the 1990s, the tide came back for the cultural acceptance of LGBTs with increased positive media visibility, including TV shows like *Will and Grace* and out celebrities like comedian Ellen Degeneres and Olympic diver Greg Louganis.[4] At the same time, the Defense of Marriage Act was signed into law in 1996, prohibiting federal recognition of same-sex marriages, and a host of states passed constitutional amendments to the same effect. The cultural and political fight over same-sex marriage continued in the 2000s, with more constitutional amendments against marriage, a few states passing laws to grant licenses to same-sex couples, and overall the issue—prompting many to think about LGBT people to an extent they had not before.[5]

Through all the ups and downs of the LGBT movement in these thirty-five years, Pride grew at a remarkably steady pace. The graph in figure C.1 shows this even growth.[6]

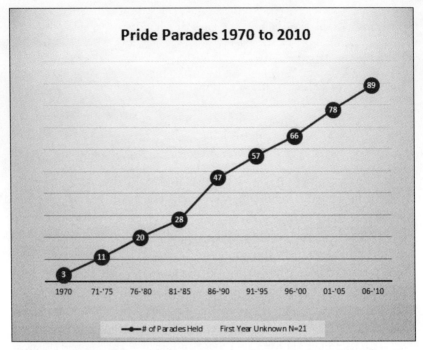

FIGURE C.1 Number of Pride parades held in the U.S. every five years from 1970 to 2010.

Except for the period from 1986 to 1990, where there was a spike in new parades, an average of two new parades were founded in the U.S. each year.[7]

Along with simply growing at a consistent pace, Pride parades spread evenly throughout the country and to cities big and small. Figure C.2 shows how the Pride phenomenon spread geographically, growing evenly in each region of the country.

As illustrated in the figures, Pride parades were never isolated to one particular area of the country. While they cluster in major population centers, they are not clustered by political or cultural dimensions. By 1980, half of the parades were held in either the South or the Midwest, in major cities like Houston and in smaller places such as Des Moines, Iowa. In the early 1980s, two parades in this study, Salt Lake City, Utah and Burlington, Vermont, got their start in very different areas of the country. By 1990, there were Pride parades in half the states, plus one in

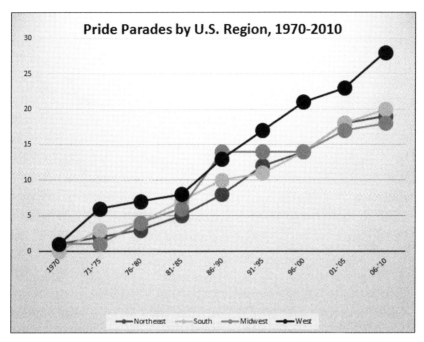

FIGURE C.2 Number of Pride parades held in each region of the U.S. every five years from 1970 to 2010.

the District of Columbia. Pride continued to spread through 2001, when Fargo, North Dakota first held a parade, and on through to 2010. Parades are held in forty-three states and the District of Columbia. Those states without a parade host Pride festivals—one- or two-day events with booths and entertainment that do not include a collective locomotion component.

One final graph illustrates the way Pride spread evenly from its beginning until 2010. Just as Pride never clustered in one region of the country, nor was it restricted to only large cities, figure C.3 shows the growth of Pride parades separated by the size of their host cities.[8]

After the first parades were founded in the 1970s in large metropolitan areas, there was a steady growth of parades cities of all sizes. It is true that Pride parades are held in urban centers, but the common perception that they happen only in major cities like New York and San Francisco that have vibrant gay neighborhoods is not correct. I found

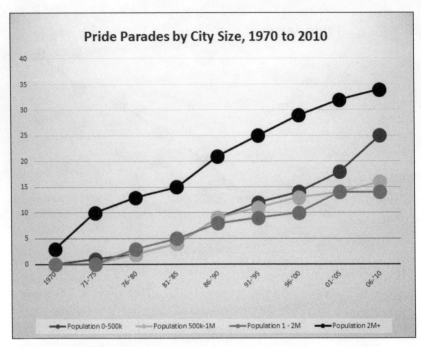

FIGURE C.3 Number of Pride parades held in the U.S. every five years from 1970 to 2010 by city population.

that all metropolitan areas with populations over two million (save Detroit) hosted Pride parades.[9] However, these account for only one-third of all parades. Since 1976, parades have been founded in roughly equal proportions across all sizes of cities. The biggest growth has been in the smallest and largest city groups, each accounting for 30% of new parades. Most recently, from 2001 to 2010, half of all parades were founded in the smallest cities, those with populations below five hundred thousand. Moreover, of the twenty-one parades with unknown starting years, roughly one-half are held in cities with fewer than five hundred thousand residents. Despite common perception, then, Pride parades are not a strictly metropolitan phenomenon.

Between 1975 and 2010, Pride spread to cities big and small in all regions of the U.S. (and to many cities elsewhere in the world). By 1979, ten years after its inception, there were Pride parades in at least eighteen U.S. cities. Ten years later that number more than doubled so that by the twentieth anniversary of Pride in 1989, there were at least forty-two parades held in cities across the U.S. LGBT Americans continued to establish parades in new cities through the 1990s, 2000s, and by 2010, the phenomenon showed no signs of stopping. Despite the ups and downs of the LGBT movement since 1970, the Pride phenomenon has grown and diffused steadily throughout its history.

NOTES

INTRODUCTION

1 Sociologists Amin Ghaziani (2011; 2014b) and James Joseph Dean (2014) describe a new "post-gay" or "post-closeted" era, marked by the de-emphasis on sexuality as a core identity and easing of social pressure to hide one's queer sexuality. See also McCormack 2012; Seidman 2002.

2 Ghaziani 2014b.

3 Durso and Gates 2012; Kann et al. 2011. Though LGBT people comprise less than 5% of the population, 40% of homeless youth identify as lesbian, gay, bisexual, or transgender (Durso and Gates 2012). LGBT youth are four times more likely to attempt suicide as their straight peers (Kann et al. 2011).

4 Newport and Himelfarb 2013; Poushter 2014.

5 Doan, Loehr, and Miller 2014.

6 Ingraham 2003. In 2004, same-sex couples in San Francisco made their weddings into a cultural protest as they publicly celebrated their unions en masse (Taylor et al. 2009).

7 Butler 1990; Warner 1993.

8 Butler 1990; Warner 1993.

9 This is especially true in Western states where women are legally autonomous from men and laws do not prohibit homosexuality.

10 Dean 2014.

11 Sedgwick 1990; Warner 1993. As sociologist Suzanna Danuta Walters (2014) points out, tolerance is a stance one takes toward something undesirable and thus falls far short of full acceptance. When heteronormativity and tolerance coexist, then, LGBT people may live openly and be treated with respect, while still experiencing their queerness as deviance from the heterosexual norm.

12 Though Ginger identifies as a man, it is customary to use feminine pronouns for queens in full drag.

13 Kameny coined this phrase in 1968, and it was quickly adopted by the National Conference of the Homophile Movement as its motto (Adam 1995; Kameny 2014). Inspired by civil rights activists' slogan, "Black is Beautiful," the phrase challenged the entrenched cultural notion that homosexuality is inferior to heterosexuality by declaring gay a positive identity (Armstrong 2002; Kameny 2014).

14 McAdam, Tarrow, and Tilly (2001) make this claim most stridently. It is also evident in political process theory's focus on political opportunities, which defines these opportunities as openings for state action (Taylor 2010).

249

15 Major lines of critique come from new social movement theorists (Melucci 1985; Pichardo 1997) and multi-institutionalists (Armstrong and Bernstein 2008). Empirically, some research on the LGBT movement as well as cultural and radical feminism has demonstrated ways that activists challenge cultural attitudes and meanings. I discuss these critiques and empirical studies in more detail later.

16 Throughout the book, I use data on Pride parades that I collected in 2008 from parade websites and Pride organizers and updated in 2015. Parades' sizes (as measured by the number of participants) are reported according to organizers' best estimates. Population data come from the 2010 American Community Survey 5-year estimates (U.S. Census Bureau 2010a). I define a "Pride parade" as any event that uses the name "Pride," intends to promote acceptance of LGBT people, is open to the public, is organized by a non-profit group, and includes collective locomotion. An additional eighty-four cities host Pride festivals, which are held on public or private grounds and open to the public. Three amusement parks— Disneyworld in Orlando, Florida, Knott's Berry Farm in Buena Park, California, and Dollywood in Pigeon Forge, Tennesseee—host Pride events that fall outside my definition because their organizing groups are for-profit. See appendix A for further information.

17 Armstrong and Crage 2006; Carter 2004; Duberman 1993.

18 InterPride 2009.

19 Brickell 2000; Browne 2007; Johnston 2005; Kates and Belk 2001; Kenney 2001.

20 Browne 2007.

21 Kates and Belk 2001. I use the terms "gay" and "queer" slightly differently throughout this book. "Gay" refers to men and women who identify their primary attraction to members of their own sex (the "L" and "G" of LGBT). "Queer" includes gay and bisexual men and women as well as transgender people whose physical sex is incongruent with their internal sense of gender ("L," "G," "B," and "T"). Queer is thus a broader term than gay.

22 Brown-Saracino and Ghaziani 2009.

23 Joseph 2010.

24 I use the term "political" here in a narrow sense, referring to any activity related to official governance by the state. Many scholars use the term to mean any activity oriented toward public affairs about which people disagree, whether it involves the government or not (see Armstrong and Bernstein 2008; Whittier 1995). For this activity I use the broader term "contentious." The difference is a semantic one about how to refer to serious, change-oriented action that is not directed at the state; it is not meant to be a substantive distinction between instrumental and expressive action.

25 See also Valocchi 2010.

26 Bernstein 2005.

27 My definition of cultural inequality is quite broad, in that I refer to any inequality among individuals in society that can be traced to cultural meanings. This stands in contrast to the term "economic inequality," which is the disproportionate distri-

bution of material resources. Fraser (1995) called the former goal "recognition" and the latter "redistribution." Beyond this broad definition, there is much debate among activists and scholars about what changes are required to achieve true cultural equality. For some, like radical feminists and gay liberationists discussed later, current cultural meanings—and the institutions that embody them—need to be completely overhauled (Armstrong 2002; Willis 1984). For others, like liberal feminists and homophile activists, equality is possible with more modest changes (Armstrong 2002; Ferree and Hess 1985).

28 Certainly, activists challenge cultural meanings and attempt to sway public attitudes as part of strategies directed at state action; see Benford and Snow 2000; Bernstein 1997; Earl 2004. Here I highlight the basic strategic choice between pursuing changes in the state and pursuing direct cultural change without state action.

29 Ferree and Hess 1985. While both liberal and radical feminists shared the goal of cultural equality as I have broadly defined it (a society in which one's gender is not the basis for unequal treatment), they differed in their visions of what such equality would look like. Radical feminists believed that the heteronormative system of sex and gender needed an overhaul for women to be truly equal, while liberal feminists thought equality was possible without such radical change (Ferree and Hess 1985; Willis 1984).

30 Ferree and Hess 1985.

31 According to radical feminists, the state was thoroughly patriarchal. It was built by men to serve men's domination, and thus could not be a force for women's equality (Ferree and Hess 1985).

32 McAdam, Tarrow, and Tilly 2001; Tilly 1978, 2008.

33 McAdam, Tarrow, and Tilly 2001; Tilly 1978, 2008.

34 Armstrong and Bernstein 2008; Melucci 1985; Pichardo 1997.

35 Armstrong and Bernstein 2008.

36 Benford and Hunt 1992; Tilly 2008.

37 Activists will often tailor their actions in attempts to gain media attention (Sobieraj 2011).

38 For more on social movement framing, see Benford and Snow 2000.

39 Bernstein 1997.

40 Mazzulo 2012; see GoTopless 2016 for more information on this organization.

41 Taylor et al. 2009.

42 The state and culture are not mutually exclusive targets. "Go Topless," for instance, targets both state laws and their cultural bases. The point here is that the state need not be the primary target of a social movement tactic.

43 Ferree and Hess 1985.

44 ACT UP engaged in this cultural tactic alongside its state-directed action, through which the group sought increased government funding for AIDS. ACT UP tackled both the cultural stigmatization of homosexuality and the concrete policies that were encouraged by this stigma (Gamson 1989).

45 State-directed collective actions also employ drama and play, but with a concrete, identifiable target, they are easily recognized as protests (Shepard 2011; Sobieraj 2011).

46 Rupp and Taylor 2003; Taylor and Van Dyke 2004; Taylor et al. 2009.

47 Rupp and Taylor 2003.

48 The bra-burning myth actually came from the 1968 Miss America protest referenced earlier, when feminists put many items, including bras, into trashcans.

49 McPhail and Wohlstein (1986) argue that there are various levels of coordination in any instance of collective locomotion, from strangers milling in a crowd to highly organized state processions. Verta Taylor's addition here is that the organization of a protest comes from the collective identity of its participants (Rupp and Taylor 2003; Taylor and Van Dyke 2004; Taylor et al. 2009).

50 Morris and Staggenborg 2004.

51 Piven and Cloward 1977.

52 Becker 1982; Swidler 1986.

53 Alexander and Smith 1993; Melucci 1985; Swidler 1995.

54 Herrell 1996.

55 Tilly 1975; Weber 1978.

56 Vaisey 2008.

57 Eliasoph and Lichterman 2003; Swidler 1986; Vaisey 2008.

58 This description of how culture affects action is by no means uncontested. Following Stephen Vaisey (2008; 2009), I present a dual-process model of culture that is both an internalized motivator and external justification for action. This model combines two often-conflicting theories for culture's effect on individual act. Drawing on Max Weber (1978), Talcott Parsons (1937) argued that culture is internalized as a set of values that then motivate us to act in particular ways. Many now dispute this with evidence that individual behavior is rarely consistent enough to be regulated by internal values. Instead, scholars such as Ann Swidler (1986) suggest that we act first (often in irrational ways), then use cultural symbols and meanings as a "toolkit" to make sense of our actions.

59 Bachrach 2011; Vaisey 2009.

60 Bachrach 2011; Gamson 1998. This conceptualization of culture in the world is different from Robert Wuthnow and Marsha Witten's (1988) "explicit culture" or Jennifer A. Johnston-Hanks and colleagues' (2011) "materials," which refer to observable products such as works of art or group rituals. Culture in the world includes group-level shared meanings that Wuthnow and Witten call "implicit" because they cannot be directly observed, but must instead be inferred from behaviors and expressions.

61 An example of the distinction between culture in the mind and culture in the world is "public opinion" versus Emile Durkheim's ([1912] 1995) "collective representation." As it is conceptualized by survey researchers, public opinion is the aggregation of discrete pieces of information held in individuals' minds, describing consensus not as a socially negotiated meaning but as the opinion held by the

greatest number of people. Collective representation, by contrast, is produced by members of society in (subconscious) collaboration with one another and thus exists as a substantive whole (Fields 1995; Perrin and McFarland 2011).

62 Wuthnow 1987.

63 In this vein, Jeffrey C. Alexander (2003) calls cultural sociology "a kind of social psychoanalysis" to convey that its project is to understand socially held subjective meanings.

64 Swidler 1995.

65 Swidler 1995.

66 Gamson 1998.

67 Shepard 2009; 2011.

68 Shepard 2011.

69 Boyd and Mitchell 2012; Shepard 2011.

70 Huizinga 1955.

71 McClish 2007.

72 Jordan 1998; Shepard 2011.

73 Furness 2007; Shepard 2011.

74 St. John 2008.

75 Durkheim [1912] 1995; Etzioni 2004; Santino 1994a.

76 Bellah 1967.

77 Etzioni 2004.

78 Santino 1994b.

79 Etzioni 2004.

80 Durkheim [1912] 1995.

81 Collins 2004. Conversely, *failed* rituals are those that intend to facilitate shared attention and mood but fall short—sapping emotional energy rather than producing it.

82 Hobsbawn 1959; Jasper 1998.

83 Gould 2001. This is not to equate "emotional" with "irrational" and thus discount emotional influences as somehow inferior to those based in cold calculation.

84 Jasper 1998; 2011.

85 Ehrenreich 2007.

86 The *Advocate* was founded in 1967 and by 1970 had the largest circulation of all gay periodicals. Unlike other gay periodicals of the time, it established a news focus rather than mixing news and fiction. While it was published in Los Angeles, the paper maintained a national focus, signaled by its name change—from the *Los Angeles Advocate* to simply the *Advocate*—in the spring of 1970 (Streitmatter 1993).

87 Paulsen 2009.

88 This is a bold claim, indeed, but I make it confidently. As social historians have shown, homosexuality as we define it in Western societies today—a feature of identity defined by exclusive sexual and romantic attraction to others of the same sex—did not exist in any societies before the Industrial Revolution (Adam 1995;

D'Emilio 1998). From the early 1800s to 1970, groups of gay men and lesbians gathered, mainly privately, but occasionally in public protests and never in the numbers of the first Pride marches. The only other large gathering in history is when gay men were imprisoned in Nazi camps during the Holocaust—in this case, the "homosexual" identification was imposed upon them and not always in accordance with their personal sexual identity.

CHAPTER 1. FROM "GAY IS GOOD" TO "UNAPOLOGETICALLY GAY"

1 All names in this chapter are real, not pseudonyms, used with the consent of interviewees. The only exception is Ruth Weiss, which is a pseudonym used for a participant who chose to remain anonymous.

2 Bisexual and transgender (the "B" and "T" in LGBT) were not regularly used identity labels until the 1990s (Adam 1995; Armstrong 2002). Thus, I use the term "gays and lesbians" rather than "LGBT" in chapters 1 and 2 when discussing this community in the 1970s.

3 Roughly 3,500 marched in New York City and 1,200 in Los Angeles, compared to 200 in Chicago. Crowd numbers come from *Advocate* estimates ("1,200 Parade in Hollywood" 1970).

4 Bernstein 2002; Carter 2004.

5 Carter 2004; Lahusen 1988.

6 Meeker 2006.

7 Adam 1995; D'Emilio 1998. Indeed, as Martin Meeker (2006) points out, leading homophile activists themselves were college-educated, middle class, and for the most part conformed to gender norms, thus were more personally interested in promoting an image of homosexuality as in line with heteronormative culture.

8 The Mattachine Society's founder, Harry Hay, began with radical aims, but more moderate activists took over the group within two years (Adam 1995). Even with a more modest strategy, however, homophiles' assertion—that homosexuality was an individual characteristic to be accepted rather than changed—was in itself quite a radical claim (Meeker 2006).

9 "Mattachine" referred to a French renaissance group of unmarried men that performed dances and rituals while wearing masks. Harry Hay, the founder of the Mattachine Society, felt that gays and lesbians were similarly masked in society because of the way that social repression forced them to keep their sexuality hidden (Katz 1976). "Bilitis" is the name of a fictional lesbian in the French poet's 1894 *The Songs of Bilitis*. The name Daughters of Bilitis refers to modern lesbians' kinship with this mythical character ("And Now We Are 3 . . ." 1958).

10 Adam 1995; D'Emilio 1998; Rimmerman 2008.

11 Adam 1995; D'Emilio 1998; Eisenbach 2006.

12 Eisenbach 2006.

13 Eskridge 2008.

14 Loftin 2012.

15 Meeker 2006.

16 Boyd 2003; Kennedy and Davis 1993.

17 Meeker 2006.

18 Adam 1995; Armstrong 2002; Fetner 2008; Valocchi 2001.

19 Armstrong 2002.

20 Shepard 2011.

21 Fetner 2008.

22 Armstrong and Crage 2006.

23 Kameny 2014, 160.

24 Kameny 2014.

25 Carter 2004; Ghaziani 2008; Herrell 1996.

26 This is not to say that homophile organizations were unsuccessful. The Mattachine Society, Daughters of Bilitis, and other groups created essential building blocks to post-Stonewall LGBT activism. These included collective identity and social networks among gays and lesbians (locally and nationally), periodicals for communication among individuals and groups, leadership and organizational development, and relationships with mainstream media, city officials, and medical professionals (Armstrong and Crage 2006; Bernstein 2002).

27 Carter 2004; Eskridge 2008.

28 Carter 2004; Duberman 1993.

29 Eskridge 2008. Cruising areas are places where gay men went to find (usually) anonymous sex.

30 Carter 2004; Leitsch 1969.

31 Carter 2004; Duberman 1993.

32 Leitsch 1969, 11.

33 Duberman 1993, 200.

34 Armstrong and Crage 2006.

35 Boyd 2003; Kennedy and Davis 1993; Meeker 2006.

36 Leitsch 1969, 11.

37 Carter 2004; Duberman 1993.

38 Jackson 1969, 11.

39 Leitsch 1969, 12.

40 Herek 2010; Herrell 1996.

41 The relationship of culture and the state here is that which Armstrong and Bernstein (2008) theorize with their multi-institutional politics approach. Cultural meanings are a constitutive part of state (and other institutional) power. As discussed later, gay and lesbian activists responded to Stonewall by targeting cultural meanings for change rather than solely focusing on state action.

42 Quoted in Lige and Jack 1969, 3.

43 Armstrong and Crage 2006; Meeker 2006.

44 Armstrong and Crage 2006; Eskridge 2008.

45 Jackson 1969; Wells 1969.

46 Carter 2004; Rimmerman 2008.

47 Armstrong 2002; Carter 2004; Rimmerman 2008.

48 Carter 2004; Kenney 2001.
49 Kenney 2001.
50 Quoted in Carter 2004, 225.
51 Carter 2004.
52 Carter 2004, 230.
53 Christopher Street West Association 2012; "Permit Hassle" 1970.
54 "Permit Hassle" 1970.
55 Quoted in "Permit Hassle" 1970, 1.
56 Mitch Berbrier (2002) showed that since the successes of the civil rights move-ment, a number of groups including gays and lesbians have attempted to gain legal rights and cultural esteem by defining themselves as a minority group rather than deficient individuals.
57 "Permit Hassle" 1970, 6.
58 D'Emilio 1998.
59 "N.Y. Gays Set Big Liberation Day March" 1970.
60 "Permit Hassle" 1970, 6.
61 "Permit Hassle" 1970, 1.
62 The fact that leaders like Rocco could mobilize such a vast network of gays and lesbians is evidence of the development of gay and lesbian community and orga-nization at the time, a credit to the work of homophile organizations (Armstrong and Crage 2006; Meeker 2006).
63 Armstrong and Crage 2006; Eskridge 2008.
64 Armstrong 2002.
65 Dansky accurately summarizes gays' cultural and legal inequality in 1970. In forty-nine states (all but Illinois), sex between homosexual couples was illegal and no laws protected gays and lesbians from being fired for their sexual orientation (Eskridge 1999; 2008). The American Psychological Association classified homo-sexuality as a mental illness in the first edition of its Diagnostic and Statistical Manual. This state and institutional inequality expressed cultural meanings in the world that understood gays and lesbians to be deviant and dangerous to society.
66 "Permit Hassle" 1970.
67 Tucker 1970, 5.
68 One could certainly interpret the first part of this statement as meaning that the police were the target of the march—and Martha Shelley herself was very con-cerned about ending police harassment—but I argue that the target was broader than that. Police harassment here is a symptom of the larger issue of cultural repression of gays and lesbians by codes defining them as "inferior, mentally disordered, [and] sinners." By marching in public as they did, participants defied these codes of meaning.
69 Shepard 2009; 2011.
70 Shepard 2011.
71 "1,200 Parade in Hollywood" 1970, 1.
72 "1,200 Parade in Hollywood" 1970, 6.

73 As at Stonewall, men's social dominance meant that gay men were better able to both take part in public action and to document it in the historical record. Those familiar with Pride parades today may wonder about the now-classic group Dykes on Bikes (leather-clad lesbians riding motorcycles). This tradition did not start until 1978 in San Francisco.

74 "1,200 Parade in Hollywood" 1970, 6.

75 The jar of Vaseline was a reference to the use of lubricant for anal sex.

76 Armstrong 2002; D'Emilio 1998.

77 Adam 1995; Valocchi 1999.

78 Duberman 1993.

79 "Readers Knock, Praise" 1970.

80 "Readers Knock, Praise" 1970; "N.Y. Figure: 5,000" 1970; "Remember, the 'Queens' Had the Balls!" 1970.

81 "Remember, the 'Queens' Had the Balls!" 1970, 18.

82 Shepard 2011.

CHAPTER 2. "UNITY IN DIVERSITY"

1 Armstrong 2002.

2 Adam 1995; Armstrong 2002; Valocchi 2001.

3 Adam 1995; Armstrong 2002; Bernstein 2002.

4 Armstrong 2002.

5 Armstrong 2002.

6 Gamson 1975; Ghaziani 2008; McAdam 1982.

7 Gamson 1975; McAdam 1982.

8 Ghaziani 2008.

9 Levitsky 2007.

10 Kepner 1971.

11 See Bruce 2013 for an example of how one community adapted the Pride form to fit their local context.

12 The words were a popular slogan of LGBT activism from the 1970s on, and a frequent chant at Pride.

13 This celebration itself is a cultural challenge to codes that treat homosexuality as a cause for shame.

14 "Great Day Coming!" 1971.

15 By 1971, the gay power group Gay Liberation Front (GLF), which played a large role in the 1970 events, was nearing its end. Meanwhile, gay pride activists, who split from GLF to form the Gay Activists Alliance (GAA) in late 1969, were seeing their influence grow.

16 Ardery 1971.

17 Ardery 1971.

18 "Hollywood" 1971, 1.

19 "Long, Well-Rounded Entry" 1971, 4.

20 Tackaberry and Fish 1971.

21 Stienecker 1970.
22 Tackaberry and Fish 1971.
23 Mitzel 1971.
24 Mitzel 1971.
25 Ardery 1971.
26 Ardery 1971.
27 Tackaberry and Fish 1971.
28 Mitzel 1971.
29 Like the Stonewall Inn in 1969, most gay bars in 1971 were dingy, poorly lit, and targets of police harassment (Carter 2004; Duberman 1993). Few allowed music and dancing. Pride Week offered community dances in well-lit, open spaces like the Daughters of Bilitis Center and the center of the Gay Activists Alliance in New York City (Ardery 1971).
30 "Infighting, Boycotts" 1972.
31 Ghaziani 2008.
32 "S.F. Parade May Be Most Spectacular" 1972.
33 Chauncey 1994; D'Emilio 1998; Valocchi 1999.
34 The butch/femme dynamic somewhat mirrors heterosexual norms, in that some women dressed and acted according to traditional masculine norms and others according to feminine norms and they formed relationships in masculine/feminine pairs (D'Emilio 1998; Gibson and Meem 2002; Kennedy and Davis 1993).
35 Adam 1995; D'Emilio 1998; Meeker 2006. As George Chauncey (1994) documents, New York gay men in the early twentieth century did have overlapping social networks and some understanding of themselves as unified by homosexuality. Homophile activists sought to grow these connections and make them publicly available.
36 The possible exception here might be the division along color lines. White gays and lesbians frequently discriminated against their non-white counterparts by denying them entry to bars and inclusion in social and activist groups and through more hostile acts of harassment (Armstrong 2002; Duberman 1993).
37 Even today, though, there are more mixed-gender gay social venues, like film festivals and co-ed sport leagues; gay bars tend to cater either to gay men or lesbians.
38 Moving to cities was not a universal experience for gay men, however. Many gay men of color and those living in the South, in particular, stayed rooted in their communities of origin, while carving out spaces in which to make connections with others (Howard 1999; Johnson 2011).
39 Adam 1995.
40 Adam 1995; D'Emilio 1998. Different priorities between gay men and lesbians reflect their structural locations in society. With greater autonomy, gay men were able to frequent bars and cruising areas, whereas lesbians were much more limited.
41 Adam 1995. Lesbians were by no means accepted within feminism movement activism. Activist Karla Jay (2000) documented how lesbians were frequently

treated as a "lavender menace"—a term attributed to National Organization for Women leader and author of *The Feminine Mystique* Betty Friedan—whose stigmatized sexuality would detract from the majority-straight women's demands for gender equality.

42 Young 1972.

43 "Infighting, Boycotts" 1972, 21.

44 In fact, "Unity in Diversity" was the theme of the 1971 CSW parade in Los Angeles ("CSW: 'Unity in Diversity'" 1971). Elizabeth Armstrong (2002) argues Pride parades were a visible demonstration of an emerging understanding of gay identity in which its essence was the free expression of one's true self.

45 Kepner 1971, 2.

46 We see this in Pride parades today. Most parades include at least one contingent that advocates specific legislative change.

47 This initial format was certainly not without dissenters. Many activists thought parade elements detracted from the event's serious purpose, while others advocated a full parade format (see also Armstrong 2002).

48 "Infighting, Boycotts" 1972. The debate over commercialism at Pride is another that continues and is perhaps even stronger today. In 1972, while gay liberationists saw gay bars as part of the oppressive power structure that include the state and religious institutions (among others), gay identity activists argued that bars were important cultural centers of gay life (Armstrong 2002). Meanwhile bar owners themselves, particularly in Los Angeles, advocated a homophile strategy of presenting gays and lesbians as respectable and nonthreatening to heteronormative culture ("'Image' Fight" 1972).

49 "Infighting, Boycotts" 1972.

50 Neither man identified as gay and thus did not participate as a member of the gay and lesbian community. Dr. Spock was active in many left-leaning causes and Mr. Pesce was a politician and ally of gays and lesbians (Pace 1998; Wicker 1972).

51 Owens 2005.

52 PFLAG 2013.

53 "'Image' Fight" 1972. Additionally, these displays may worsen already tense relations between the gay community and police. After 1971's parade, police referred the "cockapillar" entry to the city attorney for possible obscenity charges, though it appears these never materialized ("Long, Well-Rounded Entry" 1972).

54 "Infighting, Boycotts" 1972.

55 "Infighting, Boycotts" 1972, 21.

56 "'Image' Fight" 1972, 5.

57 "'Image' Fight" 1972.

58 "Smaller L.A. Parade" 1972; "Hollywood" 1971.

59 "Smaller L.A. Parade" 1972.

60 Ghaziani 2008.

61 Armstrong and Crage 2006.

62 "San Francisco" 1972.

63 "San Francisco" 1972, 3.

64 "San Francisco" 1972.

65 In Verta Taylor and Nella Van Dyke's (2004) framework, a social movement demonstration must have both contestation and intentionality. While CSW-SF may
still have contested cultural codes, the choice to avoid explicit contention points
to a lack of intentionality. This presents the question of whether, in this instance at
least, Pride could be considered a social movement demonstration. Without more
complete information about this specific event, I cannot answer the question, but
I do return to the question of intentionality in chapter 4.

66 "San Francisco" 1972.

67 "Infighting, Boycotts" 1972, 13.

68 "200 Brave Heavy Rains in New Jersey" 1972; "A First for Famed Peachtree Street"
1972; "Chicago Parade Draws Wide Support" 1972; "Proud Gays Prance Through
Dallas" 1972.

69 Camp is an over-the-top style that exaggerates mainstream norms, often those
related to gender, for humorous effect. It has long been a part of gay culture
(Bergman 1993).

70 A few sources list 1971 as the first year for the city's Pride march (Atlanta Pride
Committee 2016; Fleischmann and Hardman 2004). Aside from short mentions,
I have not been able to find more information about an event that year. It is clear
that there was a march in 1972 that drew many in the Atlanta gay and lesbian
community.

71 "A First for Famed Peachtree Street" 1972.

72 "A First for Famed Peachtree Street" 1972, 12.

73 "2,500 Gays March in Philly" 1972; Mitzel 1972.

74 "2,500 Gays March in Philly" 1972.

75 Bilow 2009.

76 Wicker 1973.

77 Dunfee 1973; Hansen 1973.

78 Hansen 1973, 24.

79 Fortune 1973, 3; "Pittsburgh Paraders" 1973, 3.

80 St. John 1973.

81 St. John 1973, 4.

82 St. John 1973.

83 Evans 1973.

84 Adam 1995; Bernstein 2002.

85 Adam 1995; Herek 2010.

86 "Pride is Busting Out All Over" 1974.

87 Kennedy 1974.

88 Kennedy 1974, 15.

89 "Frivolity Leads to Friction in S.F." 1974, 2.

90 "Frivolity Leads to Friction in S.F." 1974, 2.

91 "Frivolity Leads to Friction in S.F." 1974.

92 Brill 1975, 17.
93 Brill 1975.
94 Stone 1975, 22.
95 Stone 1975, 22.
96 Whitmore 1975.
97 "The Publisher's Opening Space" 1975, 3.
98 "Gay Pride" 1975.
99 This is not to say that there was no variation after 1974. Each community that staged a Pride event adapted the form to meet their needs. The point here is that by 1975 there *was* a form to adapt, and that form was a parade.
100 Sender 2004.
101 Kepner 1971, 2.

CHAPTER 3. "WE'RE HERE, WE'RE QUEER, GET USED TO IT!"

1 In a 2014 national survey, Utah was the fifth least-supportive state for same-sex marriage, with 58% of likely voters opposed to legalized same-sex marriage, 34% in support, and 10% unsure (Moore 2014).
2 Goodwill 2000; Gross and Byrnes 2005; Joseph, Law, and Hendy 2015.
3 Warner 1993.
4 Butler 1990; Warner 1993.
5 Butler 1990; Warner 1993.
6 Loftus 2001; Schafer and Shaw 2009; Schwadel and Garneau 2014; Treas 2002.
7 Andersen and Fetner 2008; Baunauch 2012; Bruce 2014; Sherkat et al. 2011. Academic understandings of opinion change are driven by the age-stability hypothesis, which posits that individuals form opinions on public issues like same-sex marriage early in adulthood and keep these opinions throughout their life. Thus, the aggregate change over time measured by public opinion polls is a function of younger cohorts with different opinions replacing their older counterparts (Alwin and Krosnick 1991; Davis 1992; Firebaugh and Davis 1988). With the case of same-sex marriage, however, scholars have found that as much as two-thirds of observed public opinion shift is driven by intracohort opinion change (Baunauch 2012; 2011).
8 Dean 2014; Ghaziani 2014b; McCormack 2012.
9 Dean 2014; Walters 2014. However, James Joseph Dean (2014) and Mark McCormack (2012) document a new pattern among some heterosexuals in which they accept LGBT friends without reservation, evincing at least a tentative weakening of the heteronormative cultural code.
10 Walters 2014; Sedgwick 1990; Warner 1993.
11 Bachrach 2011; Vaisey 2009.
12 One example is the frequent use of the word "gay" as a devaluing adjective.
13 Swidler 1995.
14 GLAAD 2014.
15 Gallup 2015.

16 Dean 2014.
17 Moscowitz 2014; Walters 2014.
18 Williams, Giuffre, and Dellinger 2009.
19 Dean 2014; Ghaziani 2014b; Seidman 2002.
20 Orne 2013.
21 Bernstein and Reimann 2001; Moore and Stambolis-Ruhstorfer 2013. To underscore this point, the U.S. Census is the most thorough and widely used source of demographic information on families—and yet it does not include same-sex couples with children in its definition of family. Researchers must therefore extrapolate data on the number of LGBT families in the U.S. using proxy measures (Gates 2011).
22 Gross 2001; Walters 2001.
23 Gross and Byrnes 2005; Joseph, Law, and Hendy 2015.
24 Gross and Byrnes 2005; Johns and Hanna 2011.
25 Canham 2012.
26 A huge win for LGBT families came in December 2013, when a federal judge overturned the state's constitutional ban on same-sex marriage. Gay and lesbian couples were seen throughout the state rushing to county clerk's offices to obtain marriage licenses. However, opponents of same-sex marriage have also been vocal in their disapproval of the court's ruling.
27 Corr 2012.
28 San Francisco Dykes on Bikes 2013.
29 These norms are problematic, as gay men find themselves subject to the often-unattainable standards of narrowly defined attractiveness that have long plagued women.
30 Visibility is by no means the only goal of LGBT activists or one that all pursue. Both historically and today, activists sometimes privilege community building, social services, and strategic work "behind the scenes" with politicians over deliberate cultural visibility (Gray 2009; Loftin 2012; Rimmerman 2008). As longtime LGBT activist Urvashi Vaid (1995) argued, increased cultural visibility can give the illusion of equality even as stark legal and cultural inequalities persist.
31 Bernstein 1997; Ghaziani 2008; Rupp and Taylor 2003. Like most classification schemes, these strategies are "ideal types." They are useful theoretical concepts but rarely occur in pure form (Weber 1949).
32 Bernstein 1997. As Bernstein (1997; 2002; 2003) demonstrates, activists often choose to present either sameness or difference in relation to the political opportunities to effect change. While committed organizers often make such strategic decisions, my analysis shows that casual Pride participants respond to local cultural challenges when they choose how to represent themselves.
33 Defiant and educational visibilities are comparable to Bernstein's (1997) identity for critique and identity for education, respectively. Though similar in substance, the concepts differ in the theoretical aims for which they are used. Bernstein uses the concepts to analyze the activists' strategic deployment of identity in their pri-

mary pursuit of state-focused legal change, while I use them to describe contestation to culture in the world and culture in the mind.

34 Interestingly, the few participants who judged sexual displays negatively objected not because they promoted a bad image of LGBT community, but because they worried these displays may signal to straight allies that they are not welcome at Pride events; see also chapter 5.

35 Chong and Druckman 2007.

36 Bernstein (1997) showed that activists strategically deployed identity for education (educational visibility) when they pursued narrow political goals and judged their chances for success as high. By contrast, they deployed identity for critique (defiant visibility) when they sought broader cultural change, often at the expense of achieving desired state action.

37 Many Pride parades today do set minimal rules on participant displays, but these rarely go further than what is legally allowed by indecent exposure laws. That is, men can go topless, but women cannot.

38 The irony, of course, is that while the stated goal may be educating the public about LGBT people, this education is usually not about LGBT people as the "really are," but as advocates want them to be perceived.

39 D'Emilio 1998; Herrell 1996.

40 Fetner 2008; McFarland 2011.

41 Pew Research Center 2013b.

42 Kinnamen and Lyons 2007.

43 D'Emilio 1998; Stein 2004.

44 Miceli 2005. I say "presumably" with quite a big asterisk here. Regardless of their sexual orientation or gender identity, students are routinely bullied when they are perceived to be LGBT (Patrick et al. 2013). Additionally, research finds that suicides are higher for both LGBT and straight youth in areas that are less gay-friendly (Hatzenbuehler 2011).

45 Joseph 2010.

46 Lauren J. Joseph (2010) describes how businesses confer symbolic capital, which brings honor and respect, through relationships with Pride organizations.

47 Chasin 2000.

48 Though similar in their view that corporate influence erodes Pride's protest edge, critiques have changed since the early years. In 1970, this critique was voiced most stridently by gay liberationists who argued that businesses—even those owned by and serving gays and lesbians—were part of the power structure that oppressed gays and lesbians ("Infighting, Boycotts" 1972). Contemporary critiques focus on how corporations' prominent role in Pride divides the LGBT community by privileging those with money to spend and an attractive, advertisement-ready image (Chasin 2000; Wilkey 2012).

49 Joseph 2010.

50 Kates and Belk 2001.

51 Even among those committed to LGBT equality, LGBT families are judged positively to the extent that they conform to heteronormative standards of monogamy and lifelong commitment between two parents (Peterson 2013). Heteronormative standards *define* family such that alternate forms, particularly those where one or more parents is LGBT, may not be included in representations of families (Bernstein and Reimann 2001; Landau 2009).

52 See Patterson 2005 for a review of studies on lesbian and gay parenting. Research on this issue is certainly much more nuanced than I mention here and does not lead to the conclusion that being LGBT makes one a better parent. My point here is that public debate holds heterosexuality as the gold standard, which I argue evinces a cultural code that interprets queerness as deviant and inferior.

53 Valenti 2009.

54 San Diego Military Advisory Council 2011.

55 Glenn 2003.

56 Hennen 2008.

57 Hennen 2008.

58 LGBT nightclubs in San Diego and elsewhere tend to be dominated by gay men. Though lesbians, bisexuals, and transgender people are not excluded, they are less a part of this scene.

59 Taylor and Van Dyke 2004; Taylor et al. 2009.

60 Cohen-Cruz 1998; Martin 2004.

61 Different normative responses point to variations in local cultural climate. Social norms in the more conservative Fargo, North Dakota or Salt Lake City, Utah may dictate condemnation, where in San Diego or Burlington they prescribe tolerance and support.

CHAPTER 4. "PRIDE COMES IN MANY COLORS"

1 Eugene's perception of the racial and ethnic diversity of New York compared to San Francisco was not quite accurate. Though both metropolitan areas have roughly the same percentage of Indian populations (2.8% of total population), San Francisco actually has a higher percentage of Asian populations (22.9%, compared to 9.7% in New York) (U.S. Census Bureau 2010a; 2010b).

2 Bruce 2013. In this previous project, I highlighted how advocates in a city I call Dixieville put on their city's first Pride parade. Like the U.S. military's now-defunct policy, in this community LGBT people were often met with hostility once they revealed their queer identity.

3 Dean 2014; Seidman 2002; Ghaziani 2014.

4 Readers familiar with social movement theories will notice that my approach to investigating factors that influence Pride variation corresponds with two dominant movement theories, political process and resource mobilization. Just as scholars working with political process theory examine how the external political and social system affects social movements (Meyer 2004), I look at how local cultural climates affect the communication of Pride messages. Likewise, I am concerned with how

community resources influence how groups communicate Pride messages in the same way that resource mobilization theorists focus on the role of internal resources like capable leaders, motivated activists, and money to fund movement activities (McCarthy and Zald 1977). While these are competing theories when one's goal is to determine the reason for the success or failure of a social movement, I treat them as useful perspectives on the types of factors that may influence the messages of Pride.

5 "Frivolity Leads to Friction" 1972, 2.

6 "1,200 Parade in Hollywood" 1970; "Long, Well-Rounded Entry" 1971. The jar of Vaseline referenced the use of lubricant for anal sex; the "cockapillar" was a costume worn by seven participants that resembled a penis.

7 Bernstein 1997; Ghaziani 2008; Rupp and Taylor 2003.

8 Bernstein 1997.

9 Ghaziani 2008.

10 The criticism of similarity came from gay liberationists who argued that marriage was an oppressive, heterosexual institution that gays and lesbians were well rid of. Those criticizing the wedding's portrayal of difference from heterosexuals argued that the event's inevitable campiness—a gay cultural style featuring the playful juxtaposition of heteronormative ritual and style on queer bodies—would only mock the institution and prove to the heterosexual mainstream that gays and lesbians should continue to be excluded from it (Ghaziani 2008).

11 Muñoz 1999.

12 I am referring here to those who are open about their transgender identity and do not attempt to "pass" as cisgender (those whose biological sex matches their gender identity).

13 Bernstein (1997), too, showed that organizations tended to be more exclusive when they deployed identity for education.

14 "Genderqueer" is a label used by many who either choose not to identify with one gender or who break norms of gender expression by, for instance, wearing skirts as a man.

15 Mayer et al. 2008.

16 Ryan et al. 2009; Ryan and Rivers 2003.

17 Many of these sponsors and community groups also participate in Pride.

18 Benford and Hunt 1992; Tilly 2008.

19 The inclusion of floats and music largely depends on community resources. Permits to allow these elements are more costly and thus require greater financial sponsorship.

20 Not to be confused with Southern Baptist, a staunchly anti-gay denomination.

21 The exception here is the Metropolitan Community Church, which was founded specifically to serve as a spiritual home for gays and lesbians who were frequently rejected from mainstream churches.

22 Chasin 2000; Sender 2004.

23 Badgett 2000; Badgett, Durso, and Schneebaum 2013; Capehart 2012. As Sender (2004) notes, early data on LGBT people's economic levels came from readership

surveys of gay periodicals. This is a non-representative sample that skews toward more affluent LGBT people.

24 Sender 2004.

25 Badgett, Durso, and Schneebaum 2013.

26 Sender 2004.

27 Sender 2004.

28 Sears and Badgett 2012.

29 Sears and Badgett 2012.

30 Kates and Belk 2001.

31 Barton 2010; Gray 2009.

32 Fleischmann and Hardman 2004.

33 Kruse 2005; Lloyd 2012. This is not to say that deep inequalities and persisting conflict are not present. Non-whites in Atlanta continue to suffer from high rates of poverty and residential segregation (Bayor 2000).

34 Lloyd 2012.

35 Fleischmann and Hardman 2004; Howard 1999. Though it is certainly part of LGBT history, the narrative that LGBT people leave repressive hometowns and migrate to cities in search of freedom and acceptance is exaggerated, particularly in the South. Many LGBT Southerners, both in the past and today, choose to stay in their communities of origin and seek alternative ways to express their sexuality while remaining connected to other facets of their identities (Gray 2009; Howard 1999).

36 See the "2010 U.S. Religion Census: Religious Congregations and Membership Study," published by the Association of Statisticians of American Religious Bodies and available at http://www.thearda.com/rcms2010/. I include as "LGBT-supportive" those denominations that do not consider queer sexuality a sin, ordain LGBT clergy, and perform same-sex weddings (though they may call them "commitment ceremonies" and refrain from calling the resulting unions "marriages").

37 As this woman's sign indicates, while it is the largest, the Southern Baptist Convention (SBC) is only one Baptist denomination. Others, including the Alliance of Baptists and American Baptists USA, have split with SBC over a range of issues, including its harsh condemnation of homosexuality.

38 St. Mark's congregation is quite welcoming to LGBT people, so much that it has frequently been voted "Best House of Worship" by GA Voice, an LGBT periodical. However, its denomination, the United Methodist Church takes the official position that while LGBT people should be welcomed into the church, homosexuality is incompatible with church teaching. The church does not ordain openly LGBT ministers, nor does it allow ministers to perform same-sex weddings (http://www.umc.org/what-we-believe/what-is-the-denominations-position-on-homosexuality). The Lutheran Church of the Redeemer follows its denominational position that LGBT people are welcome members and may be ordained. The denomination does not have an official position on same-sex mar-

riage (http://www.elca.org/Faith/Faith-and-Society/Social-Statements/Human-Sexuality).

39 Joseph 2010.

40 LGBT people in the military and those for whom a lack of marriage rights resulted in significant financial, health, or child custody issues certainly did experience the public debate in their daily lives.

41 Joseph 2010 found this attitude was common among Pride organizers.

42 Taylor and Van Dyke 2004; Taylor et al. 2009.

43 Cronin and Adair 2002. This is not to say that St. Patrick's Day parades cannot still be contentious. John Nagle (2005) argues that in London where the Irish are still marginalized, St. Patrick's Day still pushes for full Irish inclusion in British society. In a curious twist on the comparison between this event and LGBT Pride, in recent years, LGBT groups have fought for inclusion into St. Patrick's Day parades in Boston and New York, where organizers assert that queerness does not belong in their celebration of Irish identity (Assefa 2014; Marston 2002).

44 Jasper 1997.

45 Wright 2008.

46 Shepard 2011; 2009.

47 Jefferson 2009.

48 Cohen-Cruz 1998; Davis 1986; Martin 2004; Sobieraj 2011.

49 Petchesky 1987.

50 "Frivolity Leads to Friction in S.F." 1974.

51 Armstrong 2002; Boyd 2003.

52 Zind 2012.

53 U.S. Census Bureau 2015.

54 I interviewed Jason and other Pride participants roughly one month after the parade. See appendix A for details on research methods.

55 Ghaziani 2014b.

CHAPTER 5. "WE ARE FAMILY"

1 Taylor and Van Dyke 2004.

2 Ferdinand Tönnies ([1887] 1957) defined "community," or *Gemeinschaft*, as a group of people with mutual bonds and feelings of togetherness. According to Joseph R. Gusfield (1975), community often has two dimensions: relationships among people and geographic territory. In the case of the LGBT community, as I later describe, there is no geographic territory, so to "build community" means to build relationships and a feeling of mutual identification and togetherness. Social movement scholars often identify "collective identity"—the shared sense of self among activists—as the mechanism for building community (Polletta and Jasper 2001). With a greater focus on participants' emotional experience at one-day Pride parades, I treat collective effervescence as the mechanism for building community.

3 As evidenced by harsher treatment of and attitudes toward transgender individuals, gender transgression is culturally interpreted (at least in the West) as further

from the heteronormative standard than homosexuality. Though we often separate gender expression and sexuality conceptually, for many people, these two are
connected. Thus, for Shane, wearing skirts or performing in drag is an aspect of
queerness that is not yet fully accepted.

4 Evans and Boyte 1986; Polletta 1999; Polletta and Jasper 2001.

5 Morris 1984.

6 Taylor 1989.

7 Ghaziani 2014b.

8 Gates and Cooke 2014.

9 Gates and Newport 2012; Ghaziani 2014b; McFarland 2012. Zip code-level estimates come from my own analysis of 2005–2009 American Community Survey
five-year estimates. The Census measures same-sex couples but not individual
identification as LGBT, meaning that single gays and lesbians as well as bisexuals
and transgender people who are in opposite-sex relationships are not counted in
this tally.

10 Kates and Belk (2001) found a similar feeling of collective effervescence among
participants in Toronto's Pride parade.

11 Some sociologists theorize that growing cultural acceptance of LGBT people has
lead us into a "post-gay" era in which many consider their sexual orientation to
be only a small, but not defining, aspect of their identities (Ghaziani 2014b). I
did not tackle this question specifically in this study, but my evidence suggests
that the cultural dominance of heteronormativity still places queerness in the
foreground of many people's identities.

12 Gates and Newport 2012.

13 In her book *Dude, You're a Fag*, C.J. Pascoe (2007) explains that high school
boys use the "fag" epithet as a common way to insult one another's masculinity.
Though often not directly speaking to *sexuality*, it nonetheless communicates the
way queerness is considered a negative trait in American culture.

14 Scheff 1990; see also Smith-Lovin 1990.

15 With strict proscriptions on gender conformity, heteronormativity can produce
shame in heterosexuals as well. Though not stigmatized as a group, individual
straight people are socially sanctioned when they do not live up to the heteronormative ideal.

16 Britt and Heise 2000; Gould 2001.

17 Britt and Heise 2000; Davitz 1969; Scheff 1990.

18 Britt and Heise 2000.

19 Buechler 1990; Reger 2004.

20 Jasper 1998.

21 Reger 2004; Taylor 1995; 2000.

22 I leave educational visibility off the list here because its focus is on promoting a
(culturally determined) positive image of LGBT people, which can justify calls to
restrict more radical personal expressions.

23 Etzioni 2004.

24 Ehrenreich 2007.

25 "Genderqueer" is a term used by many to define a gender identity that is somewhere in between woman/feminine and man/masculine. Like transgender, it is separate from sexual orientation so that a person can be both genderqueer and gay. For Shane, being gay (attracted to other men) was connected to feeling in the middle of the gender spectrum. Other individuals may use the genderqueer label differently—for instance, to mark themselves as a third gender that is not man or woman—but this was not the case for Shane.

26 Dean 2014.

27 Whether the goal was to include straight allies or present a positive image of LGBT people to the world at large, as discussed in chapter 4, participants did not favor formal rules about personal expression.

28 Scheff 1990.

29 Durkheim [1912] 1995.

30 Collins 2004.

31 One straight ally described feeling a "contact high," an analogy to a sober person who feels mildly intoxicated simply from being near someone who is under the influence of drugs or alcohol.

32 Gates and Newport 2012.

33 Clark 2005.

34 Polletta and Jasper 2001; Taylor 1989; Taylor and Whittier 1992.

35 Ghaziani and Baldassarri 2011.

36 Braunstein, Fulton, and Wood 2014.

37 People with other identities that violate heteronormativity, such as intersex, are also frequently included under the queer umbrella. Many organizations, including Pride planning committees, add letters to the "LGBT" initialism to signal their inclusion, leading to an "alphabet soup" of ever-expanding letters. Other groups drop the initials altogether in favor of non-descript names like "Pride Alliance," a trend that may signal the eroding salience of queerness as a distinct identity (Ghaziani 2011).

38 A nationally representative sample of LGBT Americans found that 40% identified as bisexual, compared to 36% gay men, 19% lesbians, and 5% transgender (Pew Research Center 2013a).

39 Pew Research Center 2013a.

40 Beyond the stigmatization of homosexuality, bisexuals also experience biphobia—negative judgment and treatment based specifically on bisexuality (Ochs 1996).

41 McLean 2008; Ochs 1996.

42 Bisexuals do organize support and advocacy groups in many cities (see BiNet USA 2016 for a quite comprehensive directory) and I have seen them in Pride parades that I have attended outside this research project.

43 Alpert 2013; Ochs 1996.

44 As noted, groupings sometimes also include intersex (those with both male and female biological characteristics), queer (an umbrella term for those with non-

normative sexuality or gender), and ally (for straight supporters). I exclude them here since they have not yet approached universal inclusion in the LGBT (etc.) initialism.

45 In most states—even those that ban same-sex marriage—transgender individuals can legally change their gender. Those that wish to marry someone of the opposite gender (i.e., a trans-man who marries a woman) can then do so legally.

46 Currently, nineteen states prohibit employment discrimination based on both sexual orientation and gender identity and three states prohibit discrimination only based on sexual orientation (Human Rights Campaign 2015). The most prominent rift in this issue came in 2007, when the U.S. House of Representatives dropped gender identity from the federal Employment Non-Discrimination Act in the hopes that the bill would pass if it only protected lesbians, gays, and bisexuals, but not transgender individuals. LGBT activist organizations split on whether to support the bill. It ultimately failed (Tannehill 2013).

47 Butler 1990; Warner 1993.

48 Rupp and Taylor 2003.

49 Braunstein, Fulton, and Wood 2014.

50 Valocchi 1999.

51 This is the term preferred by Harlem Pride organizers.

52 OccupyWallSt 2012; Wilkey 2012.

53 Bunch 1972; Taylor and Rupp 1993.

54 Brown-Saracino and Ghaziani 2009.

CONCLUSION

1 As Elizabeth Armstrong and Suzanna M. Crage (2006, 740) put it, "a public gathering of homosexuals was perceived by authorities as confrontational and by homosexuals as a courageous display of political commitment." The specter of violent backlash was heightened in LA by the police department's initial demand for a $1.5 million bond against any property damage caused by citizens upset with the gay parade. See chapter 1 for the full story.

2 Swidler 1993.

3 Herek 2010.

4 Eskridge 2008. In 1970, many gay activists—gay liberationists, in particular— had no desire to legalize same-sex marriage. Marriage was seen as an essentially heterosexual and, to many, oppressive institution of which they wanted no part (Fetner 2008; Valocchi 2001). As Tina Fetner (2008) explains, same-sex marriage only became a gay rights priority when the Religious Right started to successfully pass state amendments defining marriage as between on man and on woman.

5 Bernstein 2005. Developing this shared sense of self, or collective identity, is no easy task. While forming a community within a group can be difficult, to be defined as an identity movement, a group must be defined by others according to a shared characteristic.

6 Butler 1990; Warner 1993.

7 Dean 2014; Ghaziani 2011; 2014b.

8 Walters 2014.

9 McAdam, Tarrow, and Tilly 2001; Tilly 1978; 2008.

10 Pichardo 1997.

11 Armstrong and Bernstein 2008; Rupp and Taylor 2003; Taylor and Van Dyke 2004; Taylor et al. 2009.

12 Rupp and Taylor's (2003) study on drag performances is an exception here, as it focuses on performers acting in the role of both organizer and participant. In the other studies cited, organizational leaders direct masses of participants toward specific strategic actions.

13 Armstrong and Crage 2006; see chapter 1 for further discussion.

14 Ghaziani 2008.

15 See appendix C for a description of Pride growth between 1975 and 2010.

16 Taylor et al. 2009.

17 Rupp and Taylor 2003.

18 Gamson 1995.

19 Ghaziani 2011; 2014b.

20 Ghaziani (2014b) documents this process already underway as LGBT people find safe spaces outside of gayborhoods and straight people feel comfortable living in them.

21 Ghaziani 2014a; 2014b.

22 Bachrach 2011; Vaisey 2009.

23 Bachrach 2011; Vaisey 2009.

24 Swidler 1995.

25 Swidler 1995.

26 With her comparable concept of identity for critique, Bernstein (1997) shows how activists may deploy their gay identities to challenge narrow gender and sexual norms, not to educate individuals about gay sexuality. Activists pursued identity for critique rather than identity for education when there was little opportunity to achieve their political goals.

27 Bernstein 1997; 2003.

28 I could not find survey data measuring public attitudes among Burlington residents specifically. The General Social Survey divides results by Census Division and reported that 75.1% of those in the U.S. Northeast believe that homosexuality is not wrong at all, the highest percentage among all divisions (Smith et al. 2011). Anecdotal evidence from Burlington participants supports the claim that residents have positive attitudes about LGBT people.

29 Joseph 2010.

30 InterPride 2009. Individual Pride events are not required to use the theme, but many choose to do so. In 2010, when I conducted my fieldwork, the theme was "One World, One Pride."

31 Oliver and Myers 2003; Soule 2004.

32 Participants and pundits also continue to debate on how best to represent LGBT people is a third long-running issue, but in my view, either a move toward dem-

onstrating greater sameness with or more difference from the mainstream would not threaten the viability of Pride as a contentious cultural protest.

33 I follow Taylor and colleagues' definition of a social movement tactic in which a tactic must have contestation, intentionality, and collective identity (Rupp and Taylor 2003; Taylor and Van Dyke 2004; Taylor et al. 2009). As discussed, Pride may lose the element of contestation if the dominant culture in the U.S. changes to accept queer sexuality and gender. In this section, I tackle ways that Pride may lose its intentionality. I do not think that Pride is in danger of losing the element of collective identity since LGBT identity is so central to its very definition.

34 Chasin 2000; Sender 2004.

35 Ghaziani 2008.

36 Halperin and Traub 2010.

37 "Frivolity Leads to Friction in S.F." 1974.

APPENDIX A

1 Paulsen 2009.

2 LGBT people commonly refer to one another as "family." My personal appearance includes markers of my lesbian identity.

3 Paulsen 2009, 509.

APPENDIX C

1 Armstrong 2002; Fetner 2008.

2 Adam 1995; Fetner 2008.

3 Armstrong 2002.

4 Gross 2001; Walters 2001.

5 McFarland 2011.

6 Information on parades includes only those in existence as of 2010. It does not track parades that were held for a time but were not staged in 2010, nor does it include those that have begun since 2010.

7 I could not find information on all 110 Pride parades in the U.S., so I do not know when 21 parades were first held.

8 Actually, I present data on the host Metropolitan Statistical Area. This is a Census region that includes the population of nearby suburbs as well as those who live within city limits. This is a more relevant measure for Pride parades because many people from these nearby suburbs travel into the city to attend.

9 Though Detroit hosted a Pride parade in the early 1970s, the parade stopped being held a few years later (exact dates are unclear). In 2011, one year after I conducted this research, the city once again started hosting a parade.

REFERENCES

"200 Brave Heavy Rains to Parade in New Jersey." 1972. *Advocate*, July 19. p. 26.

"1,200 Parade in Hollywood; Crowds Line Boulevard." 1970. *Advocate*, July 22–August 4. pp. 1, 6.

"2,500 Gays March in Philly." 1972. *Advocate*, July 5. p. 1.

Adam, Barry. 1995. *The Rise of a Gay and Lesbian Movement*. Rev. ed. New York: Twayne Publishers.

"A First for Famed Peachtree Street." 1972. *Advocate*, July 19. p. 12.

Alexander, Jeffrey C. 2003. *The Meanings of Social Life*. New York: Oxford University Press.

Alexander, Jeffrey C., and Philip Smith. 1993. "The Discourse of American Civil Society: A New Proposal for Cultural Studies." *Theory and Society* 22: 151–207.

Alpert, Emily. 2013. "Why Bisexuals Stay in the Closet." *Los Angeles Times*, July 14. Available at http://articles.latimes.com/2013/jul/14/local/la-me-bisexuality-20130715. Accessed September 26, 2013.

Alwin, Duane F., and Jon A. Krosnick. 1991. "Aging, Cohorts, and the Stability of Sociopolitical Orientations Over the Life Span." *American Journal of Sociology* 97: 169–195.

Andersen, Robert, and Tina Fetner. 2008. "Cohort Differences in Tolerance of Homosexuality: Attitudinal Change in Canada and the United States, 1981–2000." *Public Opinion Quarterly* 72: 311–30.

"And Now We Are 3 . . ." 1958. *Ladder*, October 3 (1): 4.

Ardery, Breck. 1971. "Village to Midtown: Cops Play it Cool, Gays Play it Big." *Advocate*, July 21. pp. 1, 3, 8.

Armstrong, Elizabeth A. 2002. *Forging Gay Identities*. Chicago, IL: University of Chicago Press.

Armstrong, Elizabeth A., and Mary Bernstein. 2008. "Culture, Power, and Institutions: A Multi-Institutional Politics Approach to Social Movements." *Sociological Theory* 26: 74–99.

Armstrong, Elizabeth A., and Suzanna M. Crage. 2006. "Movements and Memory: The Making of the Stonewall Myth." *American Sociological Review* 71: 724–751.

Assefa, Haimy. 2014. "New York, Boston Mayors Back LGBT Groups, Reject St. Patrick's Day Parades." *CNN*, March 17. Available at http://www.cnn.com/2014/03/17/us/mayors-st-patricks-day-parades/. Accessed August 2, 2014.

Atlanta Pride Committee. 2016. *History of Atlanta Pride*. Atlanta Pride Committee, Inc. Available at http://atlantapride.org. Accessed February 13, 2016.

Bachrach, Christine. 2011. "A Bio-Social Model of Culture for Demography." *J. Richard Udry Distinguished Lecture, Carolina Population Center*, March 23. Chapel Hill: University of North Carolina.

Badgett, M.V. Lee. 2000. "The Myth of Gay and Lesbian Affluence." *Gay and Lesbian Review* (Spring 2000): 22–25.

Badgett, M.V. Lee, Laura E. Durso, and Alyssa Schneebaum. 2013. *New Patterns of Poverty in the Lesbian, Gay, and Bisexual Community*. Los Angeles: Williams Institute. Available at http://williamsinstitute.law.ucla.edu/wp-content/uploads/LGB-Poverty-Update-Jun-2013.pdf. Accessed August 30, 2013.

Barton, Bernadette. 2010. "'Abomination'—Life as a Bible Belt Gay." *Journal of Homosexuality* 57: 465–484.

Baunach, Dawn Michelle. 2011. "Decomposing Trends in Attitudes Toward Gay Marriage, 1988–2006." *Social Science Quarterly* 92: 346–363.

———. 2012. "Changing Same-Sex Marriage Attitudes in America from 1988 through 2010." *Public Opinion Quarterly* 76: 364–378.

Bayor, Ronald H. 2000. *Race and the Shaping of Twentieth-Century Atlanta*. Chapel Hill: University of North Carolina Press.

Becker, Howard S. 1982. "Culture: A Sociological View." *Yale Review* 71: 513–527.

Bellah, Robert. 1967. "Civic Religion in America." *Daedalus* 96: 1–21.

Benford, Robert D., and Scott A. Hunt. 1992. "Dramaturgy and Social Movements: The Social Construction and Communication of Power." *Sociological Inquiry* 62: 36–55.

Benford, Robert D., and David A. Snow. 2000. "Framing Processes and Social Movements: An Overview and Assessment." *Annual Review of Sociology* 26: 611–639.

Berbrier, Mitch. 2002. "Making Minorities: Cultural Space, Stigma Transformation Frames, and the Categorical Status Claims of Deaf, Gay, and White Supremacist Activists in Late Twentieth-Century America." *Sociological Forum* 17: 553–591.

Bergman, David. 1993. "Introduction." In *Camp Grounds: Style and Homosexuality*, edited by David Bergman, 3–18. Amherst: University of Massachusetts Press.

Bernstein, Mary. 1997. "Celebration and Suppression: The Strategic Uses of Identity by the Lesbian and Gay Movement." *American Journal of Sociology* 103: 532–565.

———. 2002. "Identities and Politics: Toward a Historical Understanding of the Lesbian and Gay Movement." *Social Science History* 26: 531–581.

———. 2003. "Nothing Ventured, Nothing Gained? Conceptualizing Social Movement 'Success' in the Lesbian and Gay Movement." *Sociological Perspectives* 46: 353–379.

———. 2005. "Identity Politics." *Annual Review of Sociology* 31: 47–74.

Bernstein, Mary, and Renate Reimann. 2001. "Queer Families and the Politics of Visibility." In *Queer Families, Queer Politics*, edited by Mary Bernstein and Renate Reimann, 1–20. New York: Columbia University Press.

Bilow, John. 2009. "The Stonewall 40 Project." *Gay and Lesbian Times*, July 16. Available at http://www.gaylesbiantimes.com/?id=15143. Accessed July 2, 2013.

BiNet USA. 2016. "Bi Groups in the U.S." BiNet USA. Available at http://www.binetusa.org. Accessed February 26, 2016.

Boyd, Andrew, and Dave Oswald Mitchell. 2012. *Beautiful Trouble*. New York: OR Books.

Boyd, Nan Alamilla. 2003. *Wide Open Town: A History of Queer San Francisco to 1965*. Berkeley: University of California Press.

Braunstein, Ruth, Brad R. Fulton, and Richard L. Wood. 2014. "The Role of Bridging Cultural Practices in Racially and Socioeconomically Diverse Civic Organizations." *American Sociological Review* 79: 705–725.

Brickell, Chris. 2000. "Heroes and Invaders: Gay and Lesbian Pride Parades and the Public/Private Distinction in New Zealand Media Accounts." *Gender, Place, and Culture* 7: 163–178.

Brill, David. 1975. "Serious?" *Advocate*, July 30. pp 17, 22.

Britt, Lory, and David Heise. 2000. "From Shame to Pride in Identity Politics." In *Self, Identity, and Social Movements*, edited by Sheldon Stryker, Timothy J. Owens, and Robert W. White, 252–268. Minneapolis: University of Minnesota Press.

Brown-Saracino, Japonica, and Amin Ghaziani. 2009. "The Constraints of Culture: Evidence from the Chicago Dyke March." *Cultural Sociology* 3: 51–75.

Browne, Kath. 2007. "A Party With Politics? (Re)making LGBTQ Pride Spaces in Dublin and Brighton." *Social and Cultural Geography* 8: 63–87.

Bruce, Katherine McFarland. 2013. "LGBT Pride as a Cultural Protest Tactic in a Southern City." *Journal of Contemporary Ethnography* 42: 608–635.

———. 2014. "Opinion Change on Same-Sex Marriage." Annual Meeting of the American Sociological Association, San Francisco, CA, August 15–19.

Buechler, Steven M. 1990. *Women's Movements in the United States*. New Brunswick, NJ: Rutgers University Press.

Bunch, Charlotte. 1972. "Lesbians in Revolt: Male Supremacy Quakes and Quivers." *Furies: Lesbian/Feminist Monthly* 1: 8–9.

Butler, Judith. 1990. *Gender Trouble*. New York: Routledge.

Canham, Matt. 2012. "Census: Share of Utah's Mormon Residents Holds Steady." *Salt Lake Tribune*, April 17. Available at http://www.sltrib.com/sltrib/home3/53909710-200/population-lds-county-utah.html.csp. Accessed June 19, 2014.

Capehart, Jonathan. 2012. "Myth: 'Gays Make More Money Than Non-Gays.'" *Washington Post*, March 3 Available at http://www.washingtonpost.com/blogs/post-partisan/post/myth-gays-make-more-money-than-non-gays/2011/03/04/gIQA26CexQ_blog.html. Accessed August 30, 2013.

Carter, David. 2004. *Stonewall: The Riots that Sparked the Gay Revolution*. New York: St. Martin's Press.

Chasin, Alexandra. 2000. *Selling Out: The Gay and Lesbian Movement Goes to the Market*. New York: St. Martin's Press.

Chauncey, George. 1994. *Gay New York*. New York: Basic Books.

"Chicago Parade Draws Wide Support." 1972. *Advocate*, July 19. p. 19.

Chong, Dennis, and James N. Druckman. 2007. "Framing Theory." *Annual Review of Political Science* 10: 103–126.

Christopher Street West Association. 2012. *History of Christopher Street West/LA Pride*. Available at http://www.lapride.org/about/history.html. Accessed October 24, 2012.

Clark, Keith. 2005. "Are We Family? Pedagogy and the Race for Queerness." In *Black Queer Studies: A Critical Anthology*, edited by E. Patrick Johnson and Mae G. Henderson, 266–275. Durham, NC: Duke University Press.

Cohen-Cruz, Jan, ed. 1998. *Radical Street Performance: An International Anthology*. New York: Routledge.

Collins, Randall. 2004. *Interaction Ritual Chains*. Princeton, NJ: Princeton University Press.

Corr, Sarah. 2012. "A Brief History of the Rainbow Flag." *San Francisco Travel*. Available at http://www.sanfrancisco.travel/media/a-brief-history-of-the-rainbow-flag. html. Accessed August 30, 2012.

Cronin, Mike, and Daryl Adair. 2002. *The Wearing of the Green: A History of St. Patrick's Day*. London: Routledge.

"CSW: 'Unity in Diversity.'" 1971. *Advocate*, June 9. p. 2.

Davis, James C. 1992. "Changeable Weather in a Cooling Climate Atop the Liberal Plateau: Conversion and Replacement in Forty-Two General Social Survey Items, 1972–1989." *Public Opinion Quarterly* 56: 261–306.

Davis, Susan G. 1986. *Parades and Power: Street Theatre in Nineteenth-Century Philadelphia*. Philadelphia: Temple University Press.

Davitz, Joel R. 1969. *The Language of Emotion*. New York: Academic Press.

Dean, James Joseph. 2014. *Straights*. New York: New York University Press.

D'Emilio, John. 1998. *Sexual Politics, Sexual Communities*. 2nd ed. Chicago: University of Chicago Press.

Doan, Long, Annalise Loehr, and Lisa R. Miller. 2014. "Formal Rights and Informal Privileges for Same-Sex Couples: Evidence from a National Survey Experiment." *American Sociological Review* 79: 1172–1195.

Duberman, Martin. 1993. *Stonewall*. New York: Dutton.

Dunfee, Don. 1973. "3,000 Brave Heat for Chicago Pride Parade." *Advocate*, July 18. p. 5.

Durkheim, Emile. [1912] 1995. *The Elementary Forms of Religious Life*. Translated by Karen E. Fields. New York: Free Press.

Durso, Laura E., and Gary J. Gates. 2012. *Serving Our Youth: Findings from a National Survey of Service Providers Working with Lesbian, Gay, Bisexual, and Transgender Youth who are Homeless or At Risk of Becoming Homeless*. Los Angeles: Williams Institute with True Colors Fund and The Palette Fund.

Earl, Jennifer. 2004. "The Cultural Consequences of Social Movements." In *The Blackwell Companion to Social Movements*, edited by David A. Snow, Sarah A. Soule, and Hanspeter Kriesi, 508–530. Malden, MA: Blackwell.

Ehrenreich, Barbara. 2007. *Dancing in the Streets: A History of Collective Joy*. New York: Metropolitan Books.

Eisenbach, David. 2006. *Gay Power*. New York: Carroll and Graf.

Eliasoph, Nina, and Paul Lichterman. 2003. "Culture in Interaction." *American Journal of Sociology* 108: 4.

Eskridge, William N., Jr. 1999. *Gaylaw: Challenging the Apartheid of the Closet*. Cambridge, MA: Harvard University Press.

———. 2008. *Dishonorable Passions*. New York: Viking.

Etzioni, Amitai. 2004. "Holidays and Rituals: Neglected Seedbeds of Virtue." In *We Are What We Celebrate*, edited by Amitai Etzioni and Jared Bloom, 3–40. New York: New York University Press.

Evans, Arthur. 1973. "Gay Pride Affirms Will to Resist." *Advocate*, June 20. p. 37.

Evans, Sara, and Harry C. Boyte. 1986. *Free Spaces: The Sources of Democratic Change in America*. New York: Harper and Row.

Ferree, Myra Marx, and Beth B. Hess. 1985. *Controversy and Coalition: The New Feminist Movement*. Boston: Twayne Publishers.

Fetner, Tina. 2008. *How the Religious Right Shaped Lesbian and Gay Activism*. Minneapolis: University of Minnesota Press.

Fields, Karen E. 1995. "Translator's Introduction." In Durkheim, Emile. [1912] 1995. *The Elementary Forms of Religious Life*, xviii–xxiii. Translated by Karen E. Fields. New York: Free Press.

Firebaugh, Glenn, and Kenneth E. Davis. 1988. "Trends in Antiblack Prejudice, 1972–1984: Region and Cohort Effects." *American Journal of Sociology* 94: 251–272.

Fleischmann, Arnold, and Jason Hardman. 2004. "Hitting Below the Bible Belt: The Development of the Gay Rights Movement in Atlanta." *Journal of Urban Affairs* 26: 407–426.

Fortune, Richard. 1973. "Atlanta Pride Week Enthusiastic, Eventful." *Advocate*, July 18. p. 3.

Fraser, Nancy. 1995. "From Redistribution to Recognition: Dilemmas of Justice in a Post-Socialist Age." *New Left Review* 212: 68–93.

"Frivolity Leads to Friction in S.F." 1974. *Advocate*, July 24. p. 2.

Furness, Zack. 2007. "Critical Mass, Urban Space, and Velomobility." *Mobilities* 2: 299–319.

Gallup. 2015. "Gay and Lesbian Rights." *Gallup*. Available at http://www.gallup.com/poll/1651/gay-lesbian-rights.aspx. Accessed April 3, 2015.

Gamson, Joshua 1989. "Silence, Death, and the Invisible Enemy: AIDS Activism and Social Movement 'Newness'." *Social Problems* 36: 351–67.

———. 1995. "Must Identity Movements Self-Destruct? A Queer Dilemma." *Social Problems* 42: 390–407.

Gamson, William A. 1975. *The Strategy of Social Protest*. Belmont, CA: Wadsworth.

———. 1998. "Social Movements and Cultural Change." In *From Contention to Democracy*, edited by Marco G. Giugni, Doug McAdam, and Charles Tilly, 57–77. New York: Rowman and Littlefield Publishers.

Gates, Gary J. 2011. *United States Census Snapshot 2010*. Los Angeles: Williams Institute. Available at http://williamsinstitute.law.ucla.edu/research/census-lgbt-demographics-studies/us-census-snapshot-2010/. Accessed June 19, 2014.

Gates, Gary J., and Abigail M. Cooke. 2014. *Vermont Census Snapshot 2010*. Los Angeles: Williams Institute. Available at http://williamsinstitute.law.ucla.edu/census-snapshots/vermont/. Accessed August 12, 2014.

Gates, Gary J., and Frank Newport. 2012. *Gallup Special Report: The U.S. Adult LGBT Population*. Los Angeles: Williams Institute. Available at http://williamsinstitute.law.ucla.edu/research/census-lgbt-demographics-studies/gallup-special-report-18oct-2012/. Accessed September 18, 2014.

"Gay Pride." 1975. *Advocate*, July 30. p. 17.

Ghaziani, Amin. 2008. *Dividends of Dissent*. Chicago: University of Chicago Press.

———. 2011. "Post-Gay Collective Identity Construction." *Social Problems* 58: 99–125.

———. 2014a. "Measuring Urban Sexual Cultures." *Theory and Society* 43: 371–393.

———. 2014b. *There Goes the Gayborhood?* Princeton, NJ: Princeton University Press.

Ghaziani, Amin, and Delia Baldassarri. 2011. "Cultural Anchors and the Organization of Differences: A Multi-Method Analysis of LGBT Marches on Washington." *American Sociological Review* 76: 179–206.

Gibson, Michelle, and Deborah T. Meem. 2006. *Femme/Butch: New Considerations of the Way We Want to Go*. Binghamton, NY: Haworth Press.

GLAAD (Gay and Lesbian Alliance Against Defamation). 2014. *Where We Are On TV*. Los Angeles: GLAAD. Available at http://www.glaad.org/whereweareontv14. Accessed April 3, 2015.

Glenn, Cathy B. 2003. "Queering the (Sacred) Body Politic: Considering the Performative Cultural Politics of the Sisters of Perpetual Indulgence." *Theory and Event* 7 (1).

Goodwill, Kristopher Albert. 2000. "Religion and the Spiritual Needs of Gay Mormon Men." *Journal of Gay and Lesbian Social Services* 11: 23–37.

GoTopless. 2016. "Go Topless." Available at http://gotopless.org. Accessed February 4, 2016.

Gould, Deborah. 2001. "Rock the Boat, Don't Rock the Boat, Baby: Ambivalence and the Emergence of Militant AIDS Activism." In *Passionate Politics*, edited by Jeff Goodwin, James M. Jasper, and Francesca Polletta, 135–157. Chicago: University of Chicago Press.

Gray, Mary L. 2009. *Out in the Country*. New York: New York University Press.

"Great Day Coming!" 1971. *Advocate*, June 9. p. 24.

Gross, Emma R., and Edward Cahoon Byrnes. 2005. "A Study of Attitudes Toward Gays and Lesbians in the State of Utah, U.S.A." *Journal of GLBT Family Studies* 1: 53–84.

Gross, Larry P. 2001. *Up From Invisibility: Lesbians, Gay Men, and the Media in America*. New York: Columbia University Press.

Gusfield, Joseph R. 1975. *The Community: A Critical Response*. New York: Harper and Row.

Halperin, David M., and Valerie Traub. 2010. "Beyond Gay Pride." In *Gay Shame*, edited by David M. Halperin and Valerie Traub, 3–40. Chicago: University of Chicago Press.

Hansen, Gerald. 1973. "Color, Joy in San Francisco." *Advocate*, July 18. pp. 2, 24.

Hatzenbuehler, Mark L. 2011. "The Social Environment and Suicide Attempts in Lesbian, Gay, and Bisexual Youth." *Pediatrics* 127: 896–903.

Hennen, Peter. 2008. *Faeries, Bears, and Leathermen*. Chicago: University of Chicago Press.

Herek, Gregory M. 2010. "Sexual Orientation Differences as Deficits: Science and Stigma in the History of American Psychology." *Perspectives on Psychological Science* 6: 693–699.

Herrell, Richard K. 1996. "Sin, Sickness, and Crime: Queer Desire and the American State." *Identities: Global Studies in Culture and Power* 2: 273–300.

Hobsbawn, Eric J. 1959. *Primitive Rebels*. New York: W.W. Norton.

"Hollywood." 1971. *Advocate*, July 21. pp. 1, 4.

Howard, John. 1999. *Men Like That*. Chicago: University of Chicago Press.

Human Rights Campaign. 2015. *Statewide Employment Laws and Policies*. Washington, DC: Human Rights Campaign. Available at http://www.hrc.org/state_maps. Accessed July 23, 2015.

Huizinga, Johan. 1955. *Homo Ludens*. Boston: Beacon Press.

"'Image' Fight Dims L.A. Parade Outlook." 1972. *Advocate*. June 7. p. 5.

"Infighting, Boycotts Mar Pride Week Planning." 1972. *Advocate*, June 21. p. 21.

Ingraham, Chrys. 2003. "Ritualizing Heterosexuality: Weddings as Performance." In *Sexual Lives: A Reader on the Theories and Realities of Human Sexualities*, edited by R. Heasley and B. Crane, 235–245. New York: McGraw Hill.

InterPride. 2009. *InterPride.org*. http://www.interpride.org. Accessed March 28, 2010.

Jackson, Don. 1969. "Reflections on the N.Y. Riots." *Advocate*, October. p. 11.

Jasper, James M. 1997. *The Art of Moral Protest*. Chicago: University of Chicago Press.

———. 1998. "The Emotions of Protest: Affective and Reactive Emotions in and Around Social Movements." *Sociological Forum* 13: 397–424.

———. 2011. "Emotions and Social Movements: Twenty Years of Theory and Research." *Annual Review of Sociology* 37: 285–303.

Jay, Karla. 2000. *Tales of the Lavender Menace: A Memoir of Liberation*. New York: Basic Books.

Jefferson, Cord. 2009. "Where's the Pride in Pride Parades?" *The Root*, June 15. Available at http://www.theroot.com/views/where-s-pride-pride-parades. Accessed September 2, 2013.

Johns, R. David, and Fred J. Hanna. 2011. "Peculiar and Queer: Spiritual and Emotional Salvation for the LGBTQ Mormon." *Journal of LGBT Issues in Counseling* 5: 197–219.

Johnson, E. Patrick. 2011. *Sweet Tea: Black Gay Men of the South*. Rev. ed. Chapel Hill: University of North Carolina Press.

Johnston, Lynda. 2005. *Queering Tourism: Paradoxical Performances of Gay Pride Parades*. New York: Routledge.

Johnston-Hanks, Jennifer A., Christine A. Bachrach, S. Philip Morgan, and Hans-Peter Kohler. 2011. *Understanding Family Change and Variation: Toward a Theory of Conjunctural Action*. New York: Springer.

Jordan, John. 1998. "The Art of Necessity: the Subversive Imagination of Anti-Road Protest and Reclaim the Street." In *Party and Protest in Nineties Britain*, edited by George McKay, 129–151. London: Verso.

Joseph, Lauren J. 2010. "The Production of Pride: Institutionalism and LGBT Pride Organizations." PhD diss., Stony Brook University.

Joseph, Lauren J., Charles L. Law, and Helen M. Hendy. 2015. "Resolving 'True Blue' and Gay: Lesbian, Gay, and Bisexual Mormons and Ex-Mormons on Church, Family, and Social Change." Working paper. *Archives of Sexual Behavior.*

Kameny, Frank. 2014. *Gay Is Good.* Edited by Michael G. Long. Syracuse, NY: Syracuse University Press.

Kann, Laura, Emily O'Malley Olsen, Tim McManus, Steve Kinchen, David Cyen, William A. Harris, and Howell Wechsler. 2011. "Sexual Identity, Sex of Sexual Contacts, and Health-Risk Behaviors among students in Grades 9–12—Youth Risk Behavior Surveillance, Selected Sites, United States, 2001–2009." *Morbidity and Mortality Weekly Report* 60 (June 2011): 1–133.

Kates, Steven M., and Russell W. Belk. 2001. "The Meanings of Lesbian and Gay Pride Day." *Journal of Contemporary Ethnography* 30: 392–429.

Katz, Jonathan Ned. 1976. *Gay American History.* New York: Crowell.

Kennedy, Elizabeth Lapovsky, and Madeline Davis. 1993. *Boots of Leather, Slippers of Gold: The History of a Lesbian Community.* New York: Routledge.

Kennedy, Joe. 1974. "Biggest N.Y. Parade: 43,000." *Advocate,* July 24. p. 3.

Kenney, Moira Rachel. 2001. *Mapping Gay L.A.* Philadelphia: Temple University Press.

Kepner, Jim. 1971. "Armageddon or Building?" *Advocate,* September 1. p. 2.

Kinnamen, David, and Gabe Lyons. 2007. *UnChristian.* Grand Rapids, MI: Baker Books.

Kruse, Kevin M. 2005. *White Flight: Atlanta and the Making of Modern Conservatism.* Princeton, NJ: Princeton University Press.

Lahusen, Kay Tobin. 1988. "Second and Third Annual Reminder Day Pickets at Independence Hall, Philadelphia, PA, July 4, 1966 and 1967." Barbara Gittings and Kay Tobin Lahusen Gay History Papers and Photographs, New York Public Library Digital Collections.

Landau, Jamie. 2009. "Straightening Out (the Politics of) Same-Sex Parenting: Representing Gay Families in U.S. Print News Stories and Photographs." *Critical Studies in Media Communication* 26: 80–100.

Leitsch, Dick. 1969. "Police Raid on N.Y. Club Sets Off First Gay Riot." *Advocate,* September. pp. 3, 11–12.

Levitsky, Sandra R. 2007. "Niche Activism: Constructing a Unified Movement Identity in a Heterogeneous Organizational Field." *Mobilization* 12: 271–86.

Lige and Jack. 1969. "N.Y. Gays: Will the Spark Die?" *Advocate,* September. pp. 3, 12.

Lloyd, Richard. 2012. "Urbanization and the Southern United States." *Annual Review of Sociology* 38: 483–506.

Loftin, Craig M. 2012. *Masked Voices: Gay Men and Lesbians in Cold War America.* Albany: State University of New York Press.

Loftus, Jeni. 2001. "America's Liberalization in Attitudes Toward Homosexuality, 1973 to 1998." *American Sociological Review* 66: 762–782.

"Long, Well-Rounded Entry Clouds Parade Aftermath." 1971. *Advocate,* July 21. pp. 4, 11.

Marston, Sallie A. 2002. "Making a Difference: Conflict Over Irish Identity in the New York City St. Patrick's Day Parade." *Political Geography* 21: 373–392.

Martin, Bradford D. 2004. *The Theater is in the Street*. Amherst: University of Massachusetts Press.

Mayer, Kenneth H., Judith B. Bradford, Harvey J. Makadon, Ron Stall, Hilary Goldhammer, and Stewart Landers. 2008. "Sexual and Gender Minority Health: What We Know and What Needs to Be Done." *American Journal of Public Health* 98: 989–995.

Mazzulo, Yvonne P. 2012. "Organization Petitions Obama for the Right for Women to Go Topless." *Examiner.com*, August 16. Available at http://www.examiner.com/article/organization-petitions-obama-to-uphold-the-right-for-women-to-go-topless. Accessed June 3, 2013.

McAdam, Doug. 1982. *Political Process and the Development of Black Insurgency*. Chicago: University of Chicago Press.

McAdam, Doug, Sidney Tarrow, and Charles Tilly. 2001. *Dynamics of Contention*. New York: Cambridge University Press.

McCarthy, John D., and Mayer N. Zald. 1977. "Resource Mobilization and Social Movements: A Partial Theory." *American Journal of Sociology* 82: 1212–1241.

McClish, Carmen L. 2007. "Social Protest, Freedom, and Play as Rebellion." PhD diss., University of Massachusetts, Amherst.

McCormack, Mark. 2012. *The Declining Significance of Homophobia*. New York: Oxford University Press.

McFarland, Katherine. 2011. "Media Influence and Frame Diversity in the Debate Over Same-Sex Marriage." *Communication Review* 14: 255–278.

———. 2012. "Cultural Contestation and Community Building at LGBT Pride Parades." PhD diss., University of North Carolina, Chapel Hill.

McLean, Kirsten. 2008. "Inside, Outside, and Nowhere: Bisexual Men and Women in the Gay and Lesbian Community." *Journal of Bisexuality* 8: 63–80.

McPhail, Clark, and Ronald T. Wohlstein. 1986. "Collective Locomotion as Collective Behavior." *American Sociological Review* 15: 447–463.

Meeker, Martin. 2006. *Contacts Desired: Gay and Lesbian Communications and Community, 1940s–1970s*. Chicago: University of Chicago Press.

Melucci, Alberto. 1985. "The Symbolic Challenge of Contemporary Movements." *Social Research* 52: 790–816.

Meyer, David S. 2004. "Protest and Political Opportunities." *Annual Review of Sociology* 30: 125–145.

Miceli, Melinda. 2005. *Standing Out, Standing Together*. New York: Routledge.

Mitzel, John. 1971. "Boston." *Advocate*, July 21. pp. 1, 6.

———. 1972. "Boston's Week Includes March to Jail, Capitol." *Advocate*, July 19. p. 14.

Moore, Mignon R., and Michael Stambolis-Ruhstorfer. 2013. "LGBT Sexuality and Families at the Start of the Twenty-First Century." *Annual Review of Sociology* 39: 491–507.

Moore, Peter. 2014. "Voters in 31 States Favor Same-Sex Marriage." *CBS News/YouGov. com*, June 10. Available at https://today.yougov.com/news/2014/10/06/voters-31-states-favor-same-sex-marriage/. Accessed February 19.

Morris, Aldon D. 1984. *The Origins of the Civil Rights Movement: Black Communities Organizing for Change*. New York: Free Press.

Morris, Aldon D., and Suzanne Staggenborg. 2004. "Leadership in Social Movements." In *The Blackwell Companion to Social Movements*, edited by David A. Snow, Sarah A. Soule, and Hanspeter Kriesi, 171–196. Malden, MA: Blackwell.

Moscowitz, Leigh. 2014. *The Battle Over Marriage: Gay Rights Activism through the Media*. Champaign: University of Illinois Press.

Muñoz, José Esteban. 1999. *Disindentifications*. Minneapolis: University of Minnesota Press.

Nagle, John. 2005. "'Everybody is Irish on St. Paddy's': Ambivalence and Alterity at London's St. Patrick's Day." *Identities: Global Studies in Culture and Power* 12: 562–583.

Newport, Frank, and Igor Himelfarb. 2013. "In U.S., Record-High Say Gay, Lesbian Relations Morally OK." *Gallup*. Available at http://www.gallup.com/poll/162689/record-high-say-gay-lesbian-relations-morally.aspx. Accessed February 3, 2015.

"N.Y. Figure: 5,000." 1970. *Advocate*, August 19. p. 18.

"N.Y. Gays Set Big Liberation Day March." 1970. *Advocate*, June 24. p. 1.

Ochs, Robyn. 1996. "Biphobia: It Goes More Than Two Ways." In *Bisexuality: The Psychology and Politics of an Invisible Minority*, edited by Beth A. Firestein, 217–239. New York: Sage Publications.

OccupyWallSt. 2012. "Call To Action: Reclaim Pride from the 1% #OccuPride." *Occupy-WallSt.org*. Available at http://occupywallst.org/article/pride-season-occupy-wall-street-calls-trans-and-qu/. Accessed September 27, 2013.

Oliver, Pamela E., and Daniel J. Myers. 2003. "Networks, Diffusion, and Cycles of Collective Action." In *Social Movements and Networks*, edited by Mario Diani and Doug McAdam, 173–203. New York: Oxford University Press.

Orne, Jason. 2013. "Queers in the Line of Fire: Goffman's Stigma Revisited." *Sociological Quarterly* 54: 229–253.

Owens, Tom. 2005. "One Mother's Voice: PFLAG Cofounder Recalls Group's Beginnings." *Tolerance.org*. Available at http://community.pflag.org/page.aspx?pid=267. Accessed August 30, 2012.

Pace, Eric. 1998. "Benjamin Spock, World's Pediatrician, Dies at 94." *New York Times*, March 17. Available at http://www.nytimes.com/learning/general/onthisday/bday/0502.html. Accessed August 25, 2013.

Parsons, Talcott. 1937. *The Structure of Social Action*. New York: Free Press.

Pascoe, C.J. 2007. *Dude, You're a Fag*. Berkeley: University of California Press.

Patrick, Donald L., Janice F. Bell, Jon Y. Huang, Nicholas C. Lazarakis, and Todd C. Edwards. 2013. "Bullying and Quality of Life in Youths Perceived as Gay, Lesbian, or Bisexual in Washington State, 2010." *American Journal of Public Health* 103: 1255–1261.

Patterson, Charlotte J. 2005. *Lesbian and Gay Parenting*. Washington, DC: American Psychological Association. Available at http://www.apa.org/pi/lgbt/resources/parenting-full.pdf. Accessed August 1, 2013.

Paulsen, Krista E. 2009. "Ethnography of the Ephemeral: Studying Temporary Scenes Through Individual and Collective Approaches." *Social Identities* 15: 509–524.

"Permit Hassle Fails to Kill Celebration of Gay Pride." 1970. *Advocate*, July 8–21. pp. 1, 6.

Perrin, Andrew J., and Katherine McFarland. 2011. "Social Theory and Public Opinion." *Annual Review of Sociology* 37: 87–107.

Petchesky, Rosalind Pollack. 1987. "Fetal Images: The Power of Visual Culture in the Politics of Reproduction." *Feminist Studies* 13: 263–292.

Peterson, Cassie. 2013. "The Lies That Bind: Heteronormative Constructions of 'Family' in Social Work Discourse." *Journal of Gay and Lesbian Social Services* 25: 486–508.

Pew Research Center. 2013a. *A Survey of LGBT Americans*. Washington, DC: Pew Research Center.

———. 2013b. *In Gay Marriage Debate, Both Supporters and Opponents See Legal Recognition as Inevitable*. Washington, DC: Pew Research Center for the People and the Press. Available at http://www.people-press.org/2013/06/06/in-gay-marriage-debate-both-supporters-and-opponents-see-legal-recognition-as-inevitable/. Accessed June 20, 2014.

PFLAG (Parents and Friends of Lesbians and Gays). 2013. "About PFLAG." *PFLAG.org*. Available at http://community.pflag.org/page.aspx?pid=191. Accessed August 25, 2013.

Pichardo, Nelson A. 1997. "New Social Movements: A Critical Review." *Annual Review of Sociology* 23: 411–30.

"Pittsburgh Paraders Fling Rusty Closet Doors Open." 1973. *Advocate*, July 18. p. 3.

Piven, Frances Fox, and Richard A. Cloward. 1977. *Poor People's Movements*. New York: Vintage Books.

Polletta, Francesca. 1999. "'Free Spaces' in Collective Action." *Theory and Society* 28: 1–38.

Polletta, Francesca, and James M. Jasper. 2001. "Collective Identity and Social Movements." *Annual Review of Sociology* 27: 283–305.

Poushter, Jacob. 2014. *What's Morally Acceptable? It Depends on Where in the World You Live*. Washington, DC: Pew Research Center. Available at http://www.pewresearch.org/fact-tank/2014/04/15/whats-morally-acceptable-it-depends-on-where-in-the-world-you-live/. Accessed February 3, 2015.

"Pride is Busting Out All Over." 1974. *Advocate*, July 3. p. A8.

"Proud Gays Prance Through Dallas." 1972. *Advocate*, July 19. p. 15.

"The Publisher's Opening Space." 1975. *Advocate*, July 30. p. 3.

"Readers Knock, Praise the Big Parade." 1970. *Advocate*, August 5. p. 18.

Reger, Jo. 2004. "Organizational 'Emotion Work' Through Consciousness-Raising: An Analysis of a Feminist Organization." *Qualitative Sociology* 27: 205–222.

"Remember, the 'Queens' Had the Balls!" 1970. *Advocate*, September 2. p. 18.

Rimmerman, Craig A. 2008. *The Lesbian and Gay Movements*. Philadelphia, PA: Westview Press.

Rupp, Leila J., and Verta Taylor. 2003. *Drag Queens at the 801 Cabaret*. Chicago: University of Chicago Press.

Ryan, Caitlin, David Huebner, Rafael Diaz, and Jorge Sanchez. 2009. "Family Rejection as a Predictor of Negative Health Outcomes in White and Latino Lesbian, Gay, and Bisexual Adults." *Pediatrics* 123: 346–352.

Ryan, Caitlin, and Ian Rivers. 2003. "Lesbian, Gay, Bisexual, and Transgender Youth: Victimization and Its Correlates in the U.S.A. and U.K." *Culture, Health, and Sexuality* 5: 103–119.

San Diego Military Advisory Council. 2011. *San Diego Military Economic Impact Study*. Available at http://www.public.navy.mil/spawar/Press/Documents/Publications/2011_SDMAC.pdf. Accessed June 18, 2014.

"San Francisco." 1972. *Advocate*, July 19. p. 3.

San Francisco Dykes on Bikes. 2013. "A Short History of Dykes on Bikes." *DykesonBikes.org*. Available at http://www.dykesonbikes.org/index.php/about-dykes-on-bikes/history/a-short-history. Accessed September 10, 2014.

Santino, Jack. 1994a. *All Around the Year: Holidays and Celebrations in American Life*. Urbana: University of Illinois Press.

———, ed. 1994b. *Halloween and Other Festivals of Death and Life*. Knoxville: University of Tennessee Press.

Schafer, Chelsea E., and Greg M. Shaw. 2009. "Trends—Tolerance in the United States." *Public Opinion Quarterly* 73: 404–431.

Scheff, Thomas J. 1990. "Socialization of Emotions: Pride and Shame as Causal Agents." In *Research Agendas in the Sociology of Emotions*, edited by Theodore D. Kemper. Albany: State University of New York Press.

Schwadel, Philip, and Christopher R.H. Garneau. 2014. "An Age-Period-Cohort Analysis of Political Tolerance in the United States." *Sociological Quarterly* 55: 421–452.

Sears, Brad, and M.V. Lee Badgett. 2012. "Beyond Stereotypes: Poverty in the LGBT Community." *Momentum Magazine*. San Francisco: TIDES. Available at http://williamsinstitute.law.ucla.edu/headlines/beyond-stereotypes-poverty-in-the-lgbt-community/. Accessed July 21, 2014.

Sedgwick, Eve Kosofsky. 1990. *Epistemology of the Closet*. Berkeley: University of California Press.

Seidman, Steven. 2002. *Beyond the Closet*. New York: Routledge.

Sender, Katherine. 2004. *Business, Not Politics*. New York: Columbia University Press.

"S.F. Parade May Be Most Spectacular." 1972. *Advocate*, July 5. p. 2.

Shepard, Benjamin. 2009. *Queer Political Performance and Protest*. New York: Routledge.

———. 2011. *Play, Creativity, and Social Movements*. New York: Routledge.

Sherkat, Darren E., Melissa Powell-Williams, Gregory Maddox, and Kylan Mattias de Vries. 2011. "Religion, Politics, and Support for Same-Sex Marriage in the United States, 1988–2008." *Social Science Research* 40: 167–180.

"Smaller L.A. Parade Has Its Problems With 'Jesus Freaks.'" 1972. *Advocate*, July 19. p. 5.

Smith, Tom W., Peter V. Marsden, Michael Hout, and Jibum Kim. 2011. *General Social Surveys, 1972–2010*. Chicago: National Opinion Research Center; Storrs, CT: Roper Center for Public Opinion Research, University of Connecticut.

Smith-Lovin, Lynn. 1990. "Emotion as the Confirmation and Disconfirmation of Identity: An Affect Control Model." In *Research Agendas in the Sociology of Emotions*, edited by T.D. Kemper, 238–270. Albany: State University of New York Press.

Sobieraj, Sarah. 2011. *Soundbitten: The Perils of Media-Centered Political Activism*. New York: New York University Press.

Soule, Sarah A. 2004. "Diffusion Processes within and across Movements." In *The Blackwell Companion to Social Movements*, edited by David A. Snow, Sarah A. Soule, and Hanspeter Kriesi, 294–310. Malden, MA: Blackwell.

Stein, Marc. 2004. *City of Sisterly and Brotherly Loves*. Philadelphia: Temple University Press.

Stienecker, David. 1970. "Several Hundred Gays March in Chicago Pride Celebration." *Advocate*, July 22. p. 2.

St. John, Graham. 2008. "Protestival: Global Days of Action and Carnivalized Politics in the Present." *Social Movement Studies* 7: 167–190.

St. John, Martin. 1973. "No Gay Parade in Los Angeles." *Advocate*, July 4. pp. 4, 21.

Stone, Christopher. 1975. "Circus?" *Advocate*, July 30. pp. 17, 22.

Streitmatter, Rodger. 1993. "The Advocate: Setting the Standard for the Gay Liberation Press." *Journalism History* 19: 93–102.

Swidler, Ann. 1986. "Culture in Action: Symbols and Strategies." *American Sociological Review*. 51: 273–286.

———. 1995. "Cultural Power and Social Movements." In *Social Movements and Culture*, edited by Hank Johnston and Bert Klandermans, 25–40. Minneapolis: University of Minnesota Press.

Swidler, Arlene, ed. 1993. *Homosexuality and World Religions*. Valley Forge, PA: Trinity Press International.

Tackaberry, John, and Bob Fish. 1971. "Chicago Gays Show Strength." *Advocate*, July 21. pp. 1–2.

Tannehill, Brynn. 2013. "Why ENDA Matters to the Trans Community." *Huffington Post*, May 12. Available at http://www.huffingtonpost.com/brynn-tannehill/why-enda-matters-to-the-trans-community_b_3223419.html. Accessed September 27, 2013.

Taylor, Verta. 1989. "Social Movement Continuity: The Women's Movement in Abeyance." *American Sociological Review* 54: 761–775.

———. 1995. "Watching for Vibes: Bringing Emotions in the Study of Feminist Organizations." In *Feminist Organizations: Harvest of the New Women's Movement*, edited by Myra Marx Ferree and Patricia Yance Martin, 223–233. Philadelphia: Temple University Press.

———. 2000. "Emotions and Identity in Women's Self-Help Movements." In *Self, Identity, and Social Movements*, edited by Sheldon Stryker, Timothy Joseph Owens, and Robert W. White, 271–299. Minneapolis: University of Minnesota Press.

———. 2010. "Culture, Identity, and Emotions: Studying Social Movements as if People Really Matter." *Mobilization* 15: 113–134.

Taylor, Verta, Katrina Kimport, Nella Van Dyke, and Ellen Ann Anderson. 2009. "Culture and Mobilization: Tactical Repertoires, Same-Sex Weddings, and the Impact on Gay Activism." *American Sociological Review* 74: 865–890.

Taylor, Verta, and Leila J. Rupp. 1993. "Women's Culture and Lesbian Feminist Activism: A Reconsideration of Cultural Feminism." *Signs* 19: 32–61.

Taylor, Verta, and Nella Van Dyke. 2004. "'Get Up, Stand Up': Tactical Repertoires of Social Movements." In *The Blackwell Companion to Social Movements*, edited by David A. Snow, Sarah A. Soule, and Hanspeter Kriesi, 262–293. Malden, MA: Blackwell.

Taylor, Verta, and Nancy E. Whittier. 1992. "Collective Identity in Social Movement Communities: Lesbian Feminist Mobilization." In *Frontiers in Social Movement Theory*, edited by Aldon D. Morris and Carol McClurg Mueller, 104–129. New Haven, CT: Yale University Press.

Tilly, Charles, ed. 1975. *The Formation of National States in Western Europe*. Princeton, NJ: Princeton University Press.

Tilly, Charles. 1978. *From Mobilization to Revolution*. Reading, MA: Addison-Wesley.

———. 2008. *Contentious Performances*. New York: Cambridge University Press.

Tönnies, Ferdinand. [1887] 1957. *Community and Society (Geimenschaft und Gessellschaft)*. Translated and edited by Charles P. Loomis. East Lansing: Michigan State University Press.

Treas, Judith. 2002. "How Cohorts, Education, and Ideology Shaped a New Sexual Revolution on American Attitudes toward Nonmarital Sex, 1972–1998." *Sociological Perspectives* 45: 267–283.

Tucker, Nancy. 1970. "New York City Has Largest Turnout, Longest Gay March." *Advocate*, July 22. pp. 1, 5.

U.S. Census Bureau. 2010a. *American Community Survey 5-Year Estimates, Table B02006*. Generated by Author using American FactFinder. http://factfinder2.census.gov. Accessed November 5, 2012.

———. 2010b. *American Community Survey 5-Year Estimates, Table B03002*. Generated by Author using American FactFinder. http://factfinder2.census.gov. Accessed November 5, 2012.

———. 2015. *State and County QuickFacts*. Available at http://quickfacts.census.gov/qfd/states/50/5010675.html. Accessed August 26, 2014.

Vaid, Urvashi. 1995. *Virtual Equality*. New York: Anchor Books.

Vaisey, Stephen. 2008. "Socrates, Skinner, and Aristotle: Three Ways of Thinking About Culture in Action." *Sociological Forum* 23: 603–13.

———. 2009. "Motivation and Justification: A Dual-Process Model of Culture in Action." *American Journal of Sociology* 114: 1675–1715.

Valenti, Jessica. 2009. *The Purity Myth*. Berkeley, CA: Seal Press.

Valocchi, Steve. 1999. "The Class-Inflected Nature of Gay Identity." *Social Problems* 46: 207–224.

———. 2001. "Individual Identities, Collective Identities, and Organizational Structure: The Relationship of the Political Left and Gay Liberation in the United States." *Sociological Perspectives* 44 (4): 445–467.

———. 2010. *Social Movements and Activism in the U.S.A.* New York: Routledge.

Walters, Suzanna Danuta. 2001. *All The Rage: The Story of Gay Visibility in America.* Chicago: University of Chicago Press.

———. 2014. *The Tolerance Trap: How God, Genes, and Good Intentions Are Sabatoging Gay Equality.* New York: New York University Press.

Warner, Michael. 1993. "Introduction." In *Fear of a Queer Planet*, edited by Michael Warner, vii–xxxi. Minneapolis: University of Minnesota Press.

Weber, Max. 1949. *The Methodology of the Social Sciences.* Translated and edited by Edward Shils and Henry A. Finch. Glencoe, IL: Free Press.

———. 1978. *Economy and Society.* Translated and edited by Guenther Roth and Claus Wittich. Berkeley: University of California Press.

Wells, Shannon. 1969. "On Gay Militancy: Are You Ready?" *Advocate*, December. p. 12.

Whitmore, George. 1975. "The Movement–Where Has It Gone." *Advocate*, July 30. p. 11.

Whittier, Nancy. 1995. *Feminist Generations.* Philadelphia: Temple University Press.

Wicker, Randy. 1972. "Thousands Parade Under Sunny Skies in Damp New York." *Advocate*, July 19. p. 2.

———. 1973. "Gays Pour Through New York." *Advocate*, July 18. pp. 2, 5, 19.

Wilkey, Robin. 2012. "OccuPride at San Francisco Pride: Radical Group to Protest Commercialization of Event." *Huffington Post*, June 19. Available at http://www.huffingtonpost.com/2012/06/19/occupride-at-san-francisco-pride_n_1610784.html. Accessed May 21, 2013.

Williams, Christine, Patti A. Giuffre, and Kirsten Dellinger. 2009. "The Gay-Friendly Closet." *Sexuality Research and Social Policy* 6: 29–45.

Willis, Ellen. 1984. "Radical Feminism and Feminist Radicalism." *Social Text* 9/10: 91–118.

Wright, Amy Nathan. 2008. "Labour, Leisure, Poverty, and Protest: The 1968 Poor People's Campaign as a Case Study." *Leisure Studies* 27: 443–458.

Wuthnow, Robert. 1987. *Meaning and Moral Order.* Berkeley: University of California Press.

Wuthnow, Robert, and Marsha Witten. 1988. "New Directions in the Study of Culture." *Annual Review of Sociology* 14: 49–67.

Young, Allen. 1972. "Letter to the Editor." *Advocate*, July 5. p. 29.

Zind, Steve. 2012. "VT Officials Reach Out to LGBT Visitors." *Vermont Public Radio*, September 18. Available at http://www.vpr.net/news_detail/95942/vt-tourism-officials-reach-out-to-lgbt-visitors/. Accessed August 4, 2014.

INDEX

accommodationist strategy, 35–36, 111. *See also* homophile activism; gay liberation

Advocate (periodical), 41, 43, 54, 65, 91, 253n86

AIDS Coalition to Unleash Power (ACT UP), 13, 18, 251n44

American Psychological Association, 89, 256n65

Annual Reminder, 33–34, 44–45, 57, 107, 163

Atlanta Pride. *See* Pride parades by city: Atlanta

Atlanta Pride Band, 1–2, 15, 20

Baptist. *See* churches and religious groups: Baptist

bears (LGBT subgroup), 125

Bernstein, Mary, 137, 220–221, 262n32, 262n33, 263n36, 271n26

Bible Belt, 133, 150–151. *See also* culture: local climates

bisexuals, 110, 195–196, 254n2, 269n40

Black Cat Tavern (Los Angeles), 43

Black Gay Pride, 7, 194, 203

Burlington, Vermont Pride. *See* Pride parades by city: Burlington, VT

business involvement. *See* commercial sector, involvement in Pride; gay bars

"camp," 40, 84, 90, 260n69, 265n10

Catholic Church. *See* churches and religious groups: Catholic

celebration: as activism, 4, 20, 90–91, 127–128, 155, 163; controversy over, 58–60, 87–88, 90–91, 127, 134–135, 160–164, 169, 226–227; Pride as, 4, 48, 56, 83–84, 160, 188, 210–211. *See also* fun: at Pride; and social movements; Pride messages: celebration

Christianity: anti-gay, 1, 4, 42, 90, 115, 117–118, 120–121, 150–151, 243; pro-gay, 1, 72, 117–118, 121, 152–153, 156. *See also* churches and religious groups; counter-protesters at Pride

Christopher Street Liberation Day (CSLD) (New York City), 31–33, 45, 47–53, 57–60, 67–69, 78–79, 87, 214–215. *See also* Pride parades by city: New York

Christopher Street West (CSW) (Los Angeles), 32–33, 45–50, 53–60, 67–70, 81–82, 88–89, 214–215. *See also* Pride parades by city: Los Angeles

churches and religious groups: Baptist, 150, 152–153, 266n37; Catholic, 90; Episcopal, 117–118, 121, 153, 166; Jewish; 153, Latter-Day Saints (Mormon), 98, 102; Lutheran, 153, 266n38; participation in Pride, 120–121, 133–134, 147, 152–153, 155–156, 158, 166, 223; Society of Friends (Quaker), 155; Unitarian-Universalist, 117; United Church of Christ, 123; United Methodist, 153, 266n38. *See also* Christianity: anti-gay; pro-gay; counter-protesters at Pride

civil rights movement, 162, 176; influence of, 36–38, 44, 64, 249n13, 256n56

closet, the (publicly hiding one's sexuality), 36, 51–52, 71, 101. *See also* coming out (term)

ABOUT THE AUTHOR

Katherine McFarland Bruce is Assistant Professor of Sociology at Salem College in North Carolina. She went to her first Pride parade in 1998 during a summer college study program in Chicago, and has been fascinated ever since. She researches social movements, sexuality, and political participation.